SCIENCE FACTS!

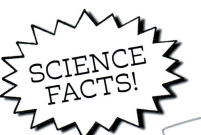

How to Make a DIAMOND

And Other Incredible Ideas About Chemistry

William Potter

Richard Watson

ARCTURUS

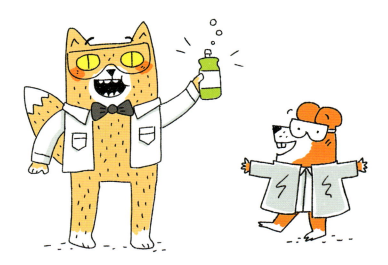

This edition published in 2025 by Arcturus Publishing Limited
26/27 Bickels Yard, 151-153 Bermondsey Street,
London SE1 3HA

Copyright © Arcturus Holdings Limited

All rights reserved. No part of this publication may be reproduced, stored in a retrieval system, or transmitted, in any form or by any means, electronic, mechanical, photocopying, recording or otherwise, without prior written permission in accordance with the provisions of the Copyright Act 1956 (as amended). Any person or persons who do any unauthorised act in relation to this publication may be liable to criminal prosecution and civil claims for damages.

Author: William Potter
Illustrator: Richard Watson
Consultant: Robert Snedden
Editor: Lydia Halliday
Designers: Noel and Sarah Fountain
Design Manager: Rosie Bellwood-Moyler
Managing Editor: Joe Harris

ISBN: 978-1-3988-4966-2
CH011644US
Supplier 29, Date 1024, Print run 00008292

Printed in China

Contents

Clever Chemistry	4
What Is Chemistry For?	6
Chapter 1: It's Elementary	7
How to Be an Atom	8
How to Be in Your Element	10
The Periodic Table	12
How to Mix Water	14
How to Measure with a Mole	16
How to Count Atoms	18
How to Lose an Electron	20
How to Season	22
How to Share	24
How to Make a Diamond	26
How to Date a Dinosaur	28
The Alloy Age	30
How to Make Money	32
How to Avoid Slipping	34
Chapter 2: What's the Matter?	35
How to Be Different	36
How to Be Scratchy	38
In a State	40
How to See Your Name in Lights	42
How to Be Supercool	44
How to Let Off Steam	46
How to Get in a Mix-Up	48
How to Be Smelly	50
How to Concentrate	52
How to Be Sweeter	54
How to Split Up	56
How to Be Purer	58
How to Lift Off	60
Chapter 3: Getting a Reaction	61
How to Stink Like an Egg	62
How to Be Unstable	64
All Change!	66
How to React Faster	68
How to Power a Rocket	70
How to Put on a Fireworks Display	72
How to Heat a Compost Heap	74
How to Chill Out	76
How to Build a Battery	78
How to Recycle Your Pee	80
How to Walk on Water	82
How to Spring a Leak	84
How to Become a Fossil	86
How to Stay Afloat	88
Chapter 4: The Acid Test	89
How to Top a Pancake	90
How to Make Your Cake Rise	92
How to Clean Up	94
Taking the Measure	96
How to Make Hard Water	98
How to Build a Shell	100
How to Stop Being Rusty	102
How to Get Galvanized	104
How to Turn Objects into Gold	106
Chapter 5: Chemical World	107
How to Breathe Easy	108
How to Fry an Egg	110
Fossil Fuels	112
How to Be a By-Product	114
How to Weather Away	116
How to Feed Your Plants	118
How to Reduce Your Carbon Footprint	120
How to Heat Up a Planet	122
How to Recycle	124
How to Make the Future	126
Index	128

Professor Albert Katzenstein's Compendium of Clever Chemistry

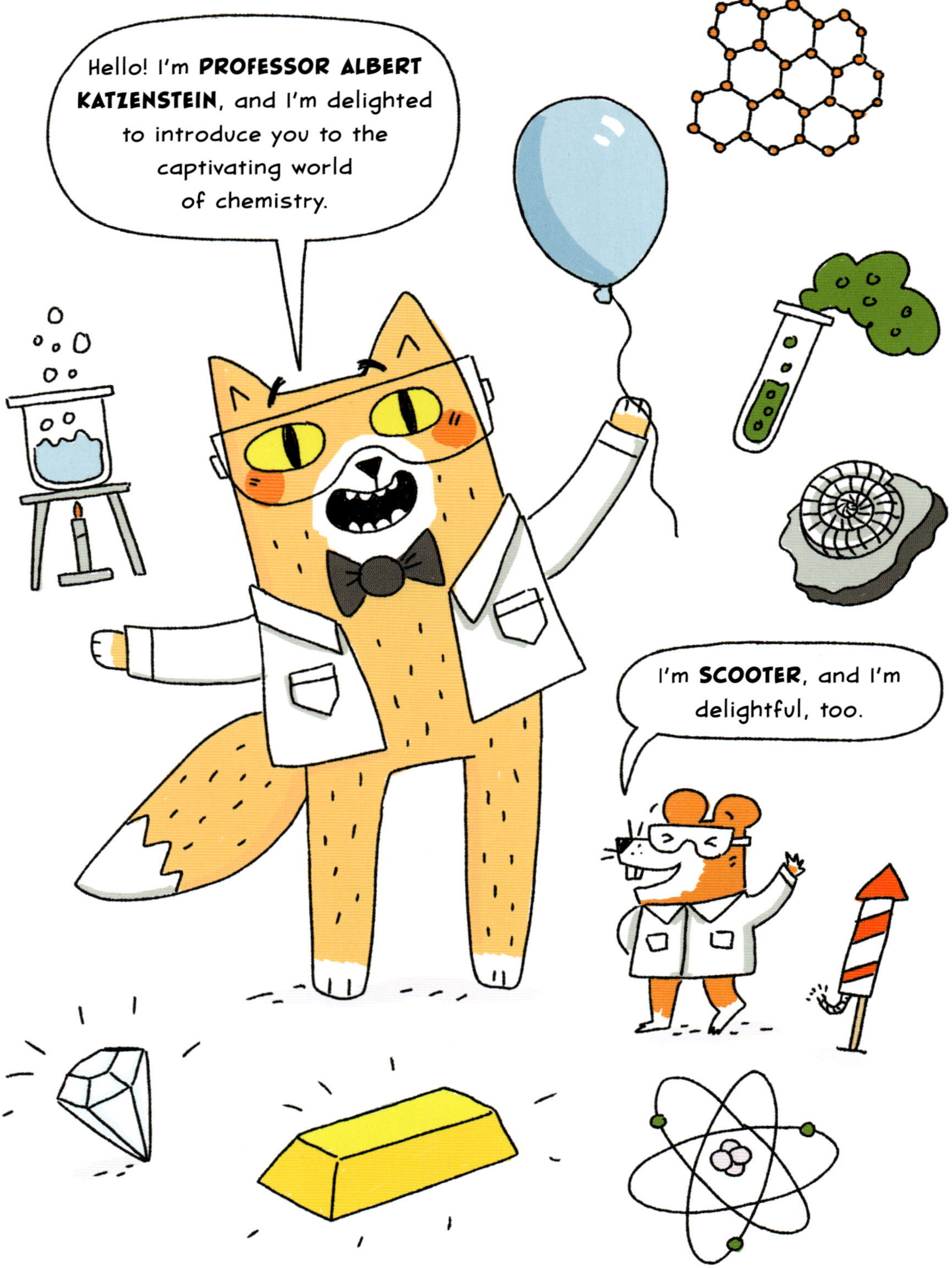
Hello! I'm **PROFESSOR ALBERT KATZENSTEIN**, and I'm delighted to introduce you to the captivating world of chemistry.
I'm **SCOOTER**, and I'm delightful, too.

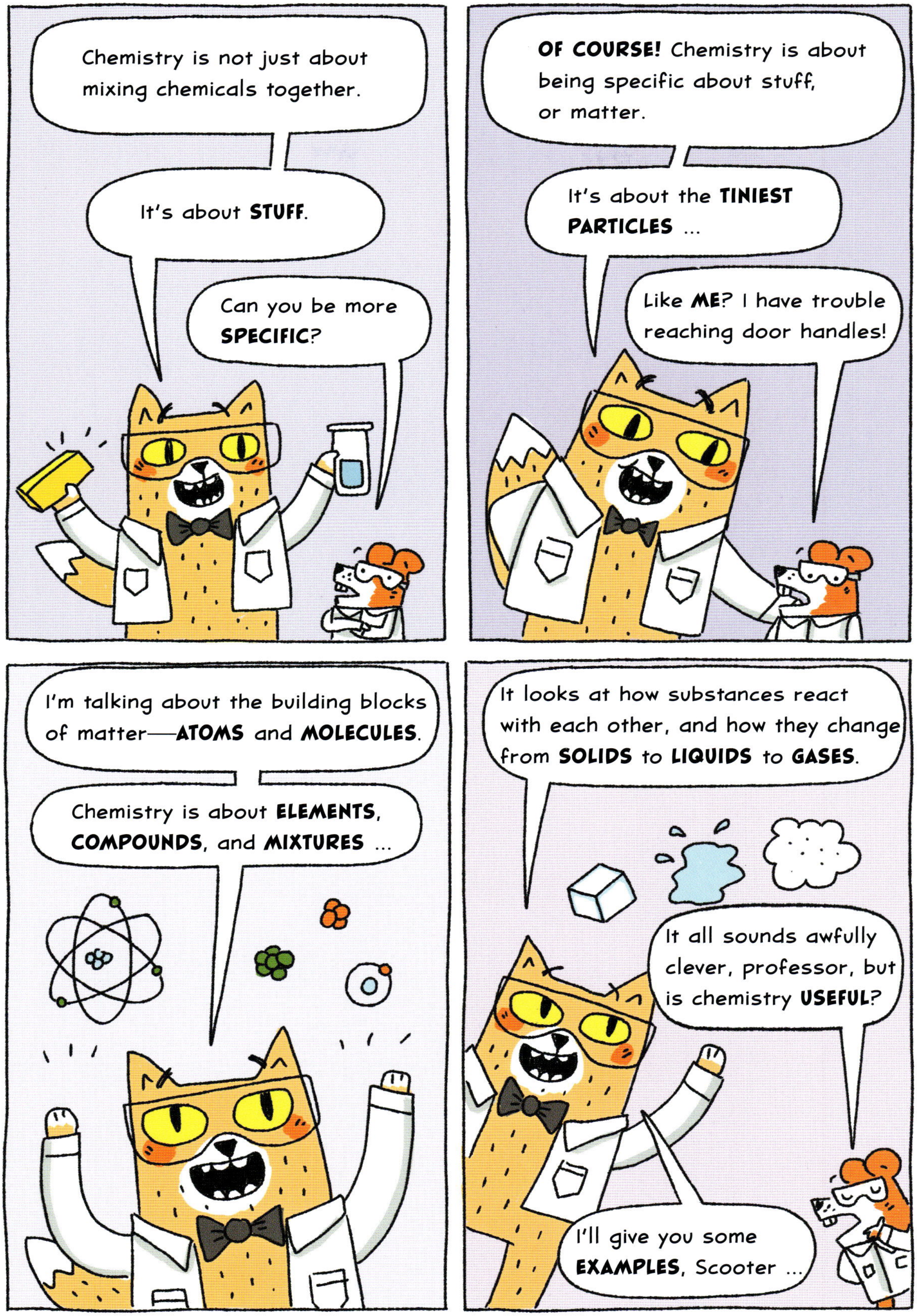

Chemistry is not just about mixing chemicals together.
It's about STUFF.
Can you be more SPECIFIC?
OF COURSE! Chemistry is about being specific about stuff, or matter.
It's about the TINIEST PARTICLES ...
Like ME? I have trouble reaching door handles!
I'm talking about the building blocks of matter—ATOMS and MOLECULES.
Chemistry is about ELEMENTS, COMPOUNDS, and MIXTURES ...
It looks at how substances react with each other, and how they change from SOLIDS to LIQUIDS to GASES.
It all sounds awfully clever, professor, but is chemistry USEFUL?
I'll give you some EXAMPLES, Scooter ...

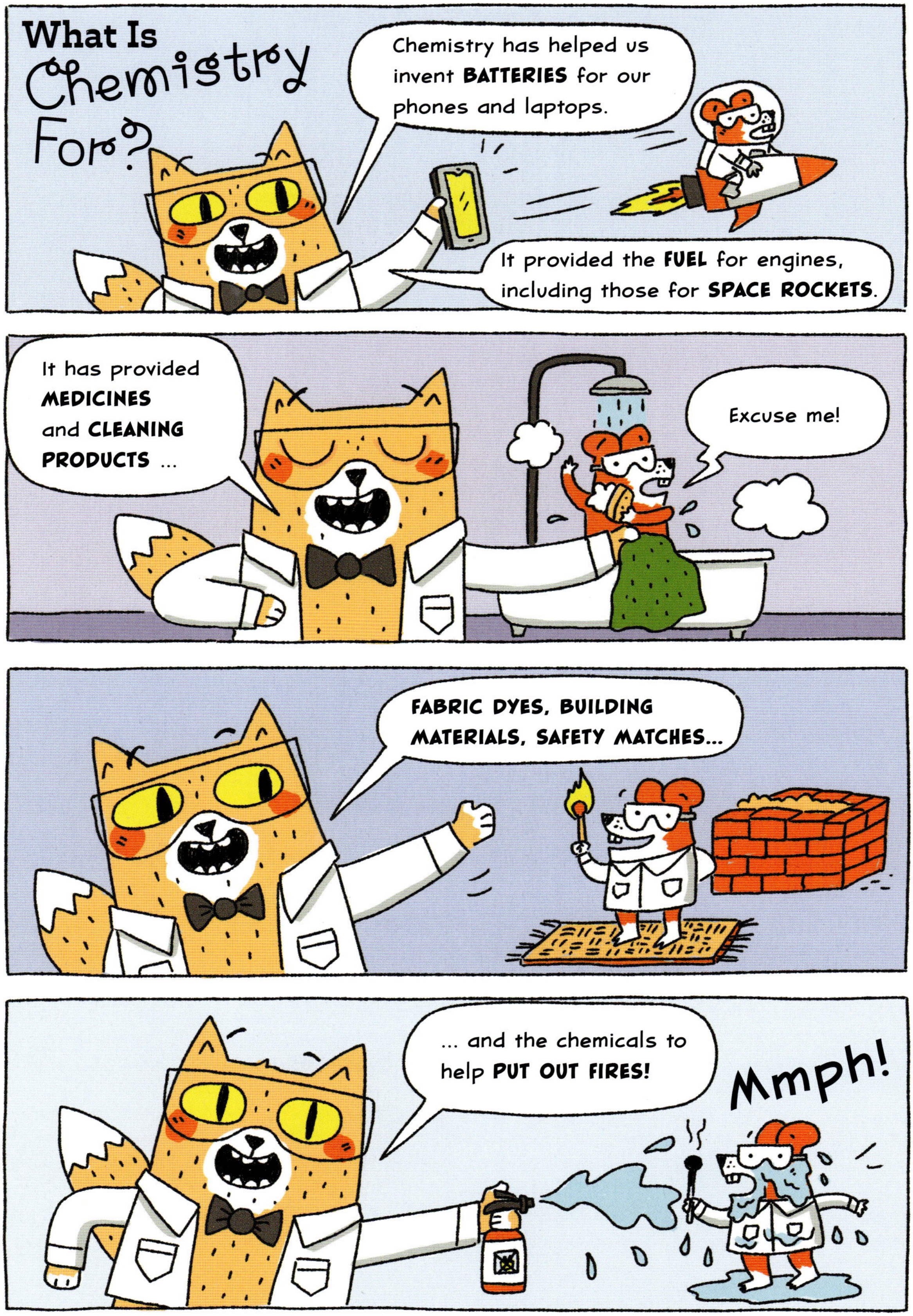
What Is Chemistry For?
Chemistry has helped us invent BATTERIES for our phones and laptops.
It provided the FUEL for engines, including those for SPACE ROCKETS.
It has provided MEDICINES and CLEANING PRODUCTS ...
Excuse me!
FABRIC DYES, BUILDING MATERIALS, SAFETY MATCHES...
... and the chemicals to help PUT OUT FIRES!
Mmph!

It's Elementary

(Properties of Matter, Solids, Liquids, Gases, Transforming Matter)

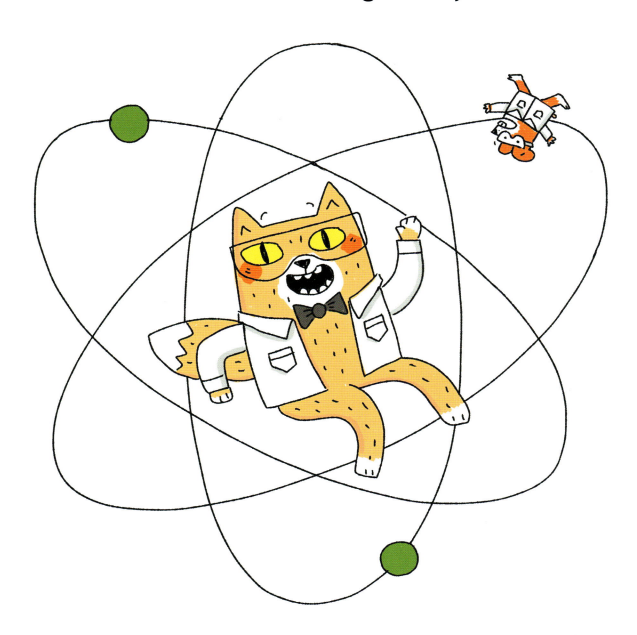

How to Be an Atom
Well, what do you think?
Um ... I can't see anything. Have you invented an invisible thingy?
Not INVISIBLE ... it's a MICROSCOPIC SHIP!
We're going on a voyage into an ATOM!
In a ship that we're TOO BIG to fit in?!
Easily fixed!
FZZT!
Now we're MICROSCOPIC SIZE!
Where's the ship?
It's over there.
THREE HOURS LATER...
Maybe you should have shrunk us closer to the ship.
PUFF! PANT!
Exercise is good for you, Scooter. Hop in!
We're now the size of ATOMS, Scooter.
How small is that?
About a million times smaller than the width of a whisker.

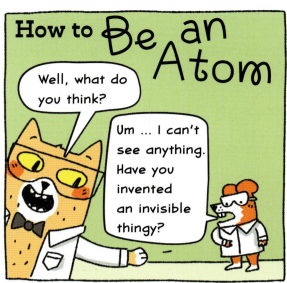

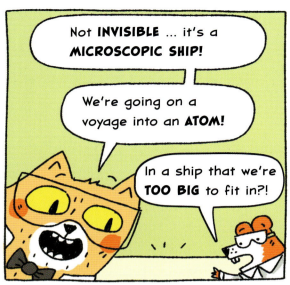

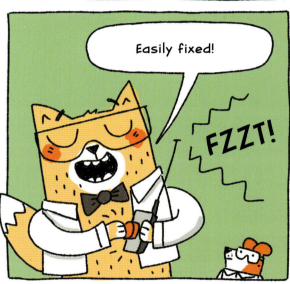

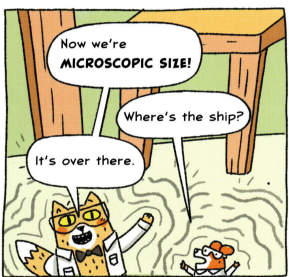

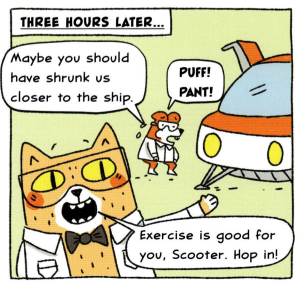

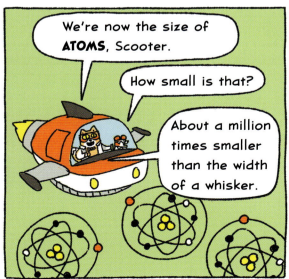

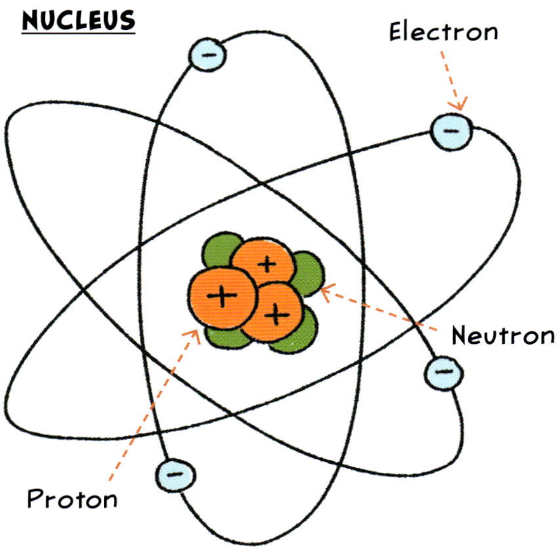
NUCLEUS
Electron
Neutron
Proton

Atoms are the tiny particles that everything is made from.

They have a **nucleus** in the middle made up of **positively charged protons**, and **neutrons** with no charge. The nucleus makes up almost all of the atom's mass. Surrounding the nucleus are **negatively charged electrons**.

If a substance is made up of one type of atom, it's called an **element**. Different elements have atoms with different numbers of protons, neutrons, and electrons.

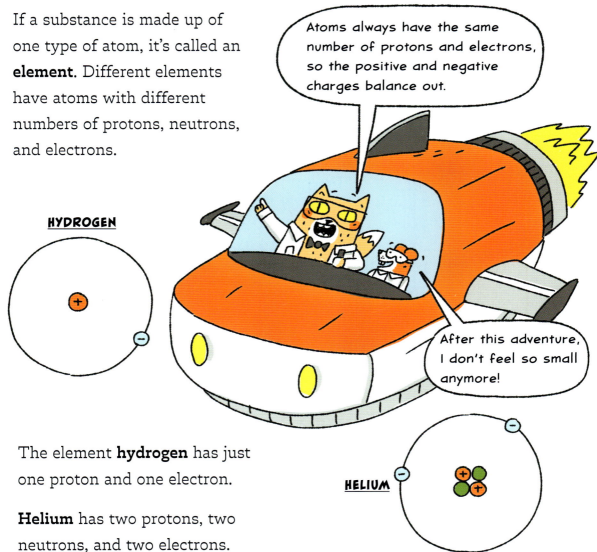

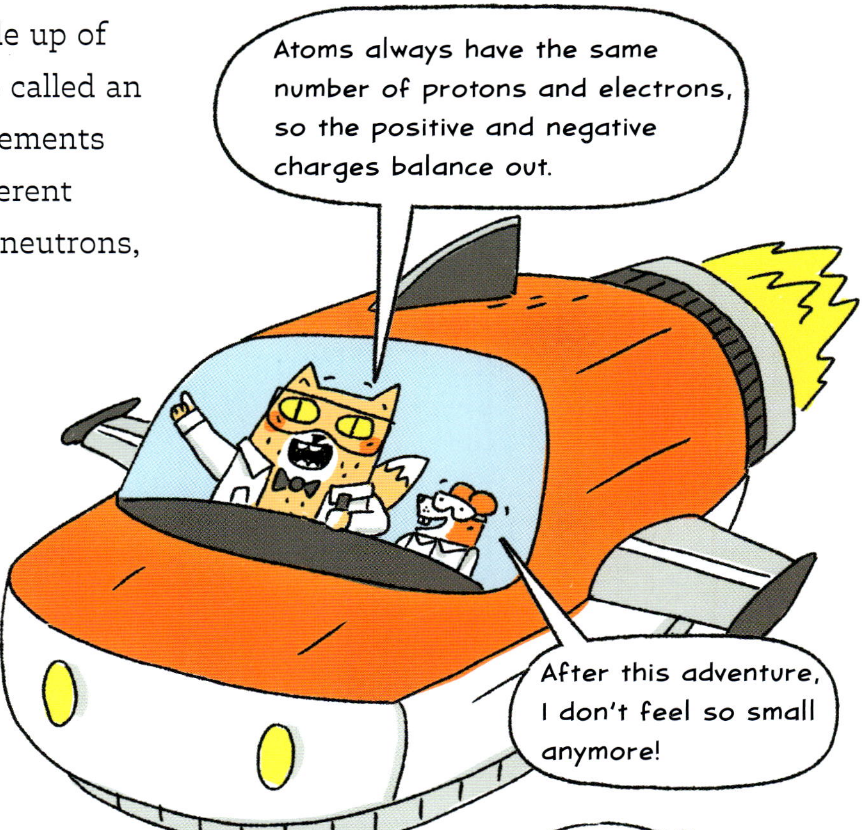
Atoms always have the same number of protons and electrons, so the positive and negative charges balance out.
After this adventure, I don't feel so small anymore!

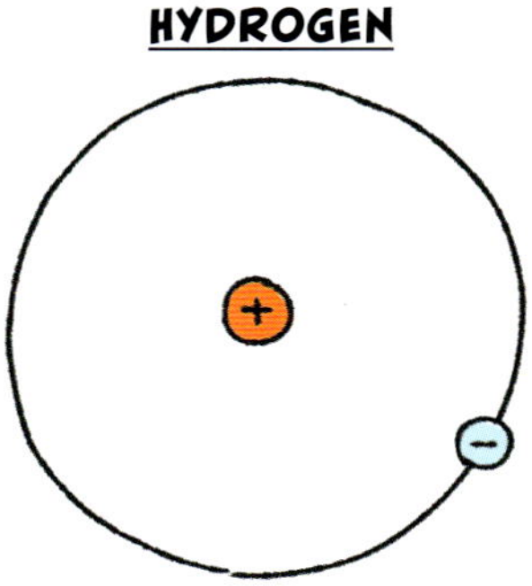
HYDROGEN

The element **hydrogen** has just one proton and one electron.

Helium has two protons, two neutrons, and two electrons.

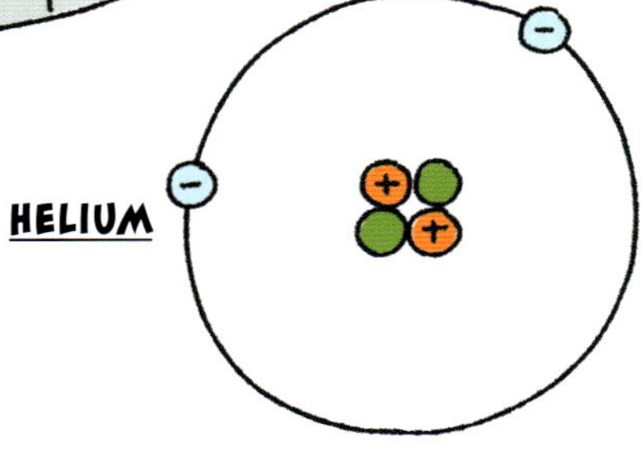
HELIUM

How to Be in Your Element
I have the results of your annual health check, Scooter.
Break it to me gently, Doctor.
SNIFF! The doctor says I'm lacking calcium and potassium.
You just need to eat more cheese and bananas.
I LOVE cheesy bananas!
But what are CALCIUM and POTASSIUM?
They're ELEMENTS.
EVERYTHING is made of substances called elements.
Even ME?
I said everything, so EVEN you!
What am I made of mostly?
I would say cheesy bananas.

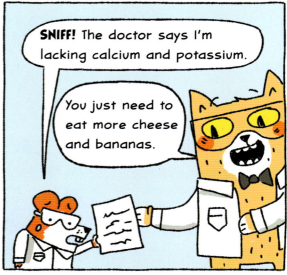

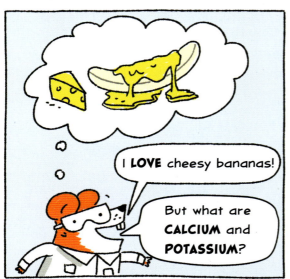

Everything in the Universe is made of different **elements**. There are more than 100 of these substances. They cannot be broken down into simpler ingredients, but they can be joined and mixed together to form other gases, liquids, and solids.

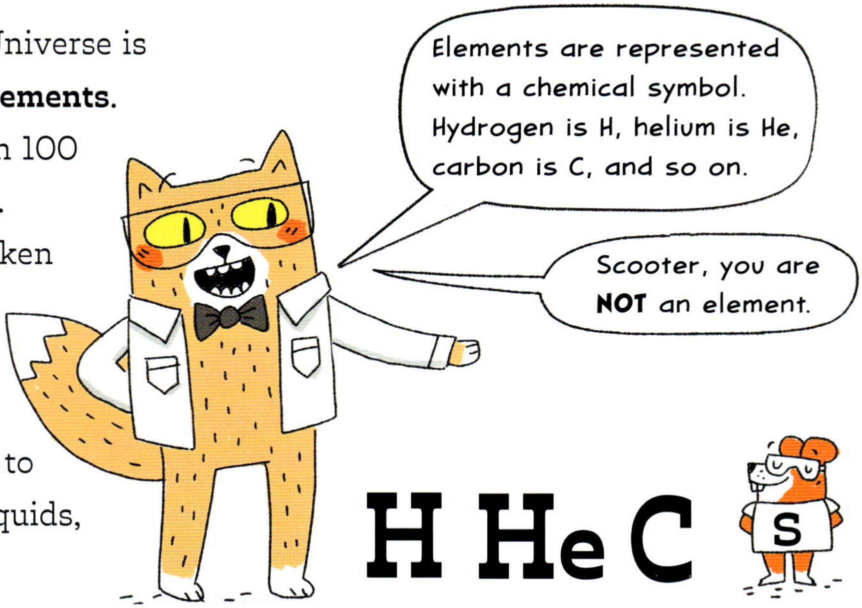
Elements are represented with a chemical symbol. Hydrogen is H, helium is He, carbon is C, and so on.
Scooter, you are **NOT** an element.
H He C
S

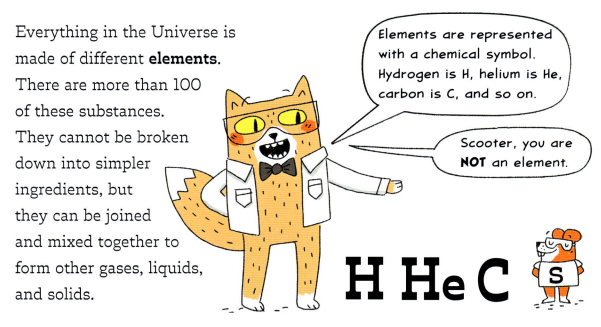

The atoms of each element are formed from protons, neutrons, and electrons. Each element has a unique number of protons.

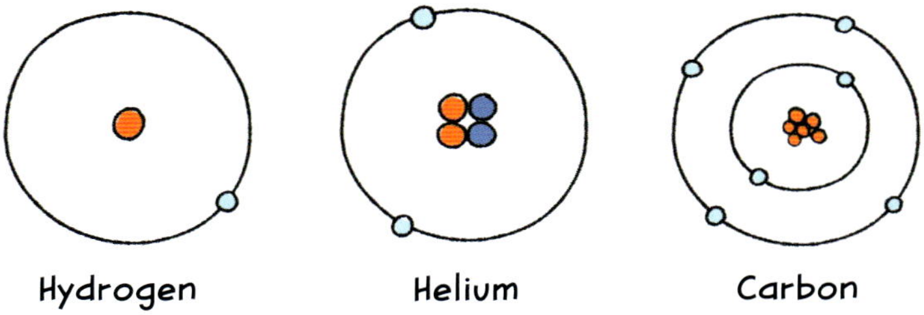
Hydrogen
Helium
Carbon

Hydrogen atoms have one proton, helium atoms have two, carbon atoms have six.

You may see an element shown as a chemical symbol with two numbers.

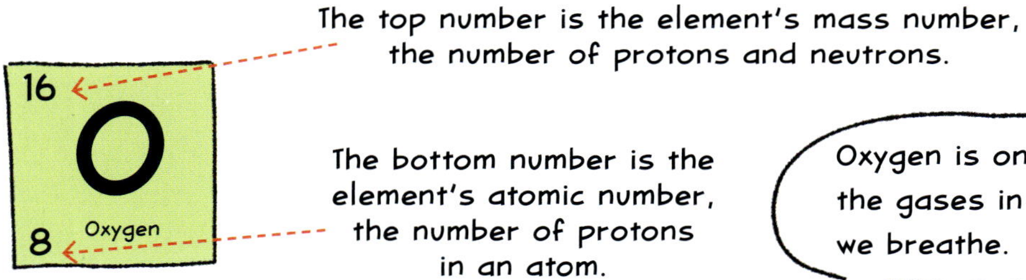
16
O
8
Oxygen
The top number is the element's mass number, the number of protons and neutrons.
The bottom number is the element's atomic number, the number of protons in an atom.

Oxygen has eight protons and eight neutrons, so it has an atomic number of eight and a mass number of 16.

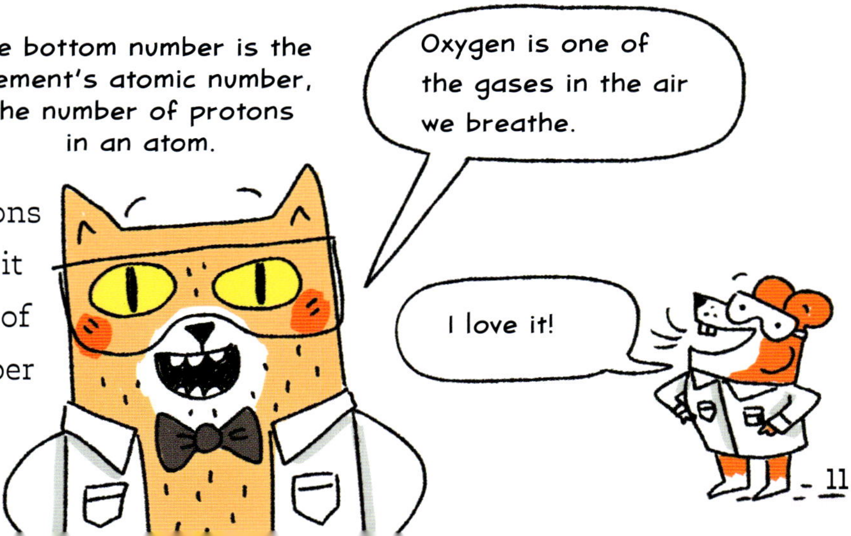
Oxygen is one of the gases in the air we breathe.
I love it!

The Periodic Table

If only there were some handy chart to help me remember all the different elements ...
There is! It's called the Periodic Table.

The first row of elements (Hydrogen and Helium) only have one energy shell.

The second row have two energy shells, and so on.

The Periodic Table arranges all 118 elements in columns and rows depending on their atomic number.

- Alkali metal
- Alkaline earth metal
- Metal
- Transition metal
- Lanthanides

Where each element appears in the table reveals something about its properties and activity. The key groups elements with similar properties.

H Hydrogen								
Li Lithium	Be Beryllium							
Na Sodium	Mg Magnesium							
K Potassium	Ca Calcium	Sc Scandium	Ti Titanium	V Vanadium	Cr Chromium	Mn Manganese	Fe Iron	Co Cobalt
Rb Rubidium	Sr Strontium	Y Yttrium	Zr Zirconium	Nb Niobium	Mo Molybdenum	Tc Technecium	Ru Ruthenium	Rh Rhodium
Cs Cesium	Ba Barium	La Lanthanum	Hf Hafnium	Ta Tantalum	W Tungsten	Re Rhenium	Os Osmium	Ir Iridium
Fr Francium	Ra Radium	Ac Actinium	f Rutherfordium	Db Dubnium	Sg Seaborgium	Bh Bohrium	Hs Hassium	Mt Meitnerium

Ce Cerium	Pr Praseodymium	Nd Neodymium	Pm Promethium	Sm Samarium	Eu Europium	Gd Gadolinium
Th Thorium	Pa Protactinium	U Uranium	Np Neptunium	Pu Plutonium	Am Americium	Cm Curium

Most of the elements on the bottom row are radioactive.

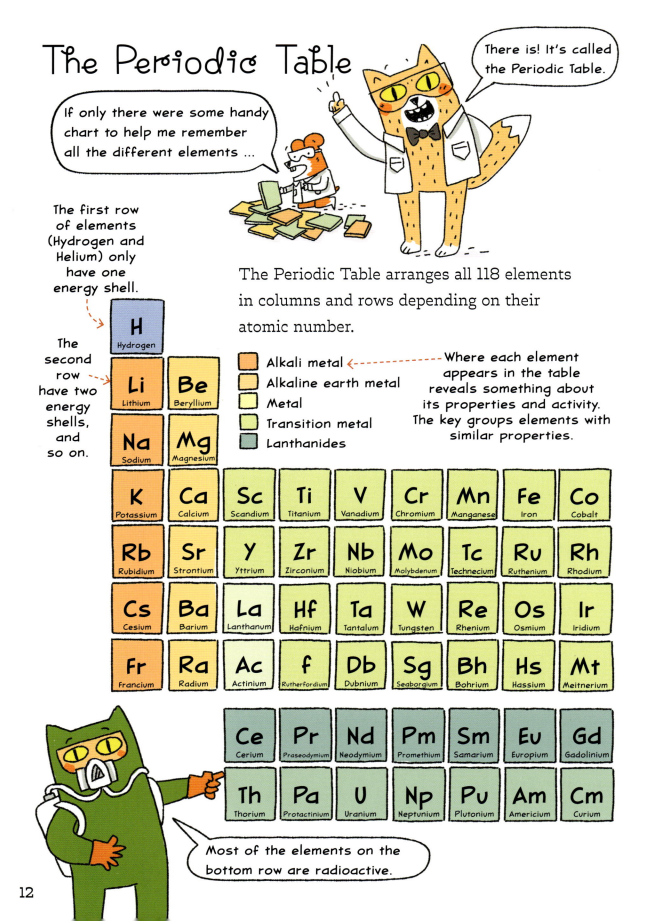

Atoms have different numbers of electrons orbiting their nucleus. These form energy shells.

The elements in each column have the same number of electrons in their outer shell.

Atoms like to have a full set of electrons in their outer shell.
Na
They will take or give away an electron to end up with a complete shell.
Gimme!
Cl

- Metalloid
- Nonmetal
- Halogen
- Noble gas
- Actinide

								He Helium
			B Boron	C Carbon	N Nitrogen	O Oxygen	F Fluorine	Ne Neon
			Al Aluminum	Si Silicon	P Phosphorus	S Sulfur	Cl Chlorine	Ar Argon
Ni Nickel	Cu Copper	Zn Zinc	Ga Gallium	Ge Germanium	As Arsenic	Se Selenium	Br Bromine	Kr Krypton
Pd Palladium	Ag Silver	Cd Cadmium	In Indium	Sn Tin	Sb Antimony	Te Tellurium	I Iodine	Xe Xenon
Pt Platinum	Au Gold	Hg Mercury	Tl Thallium	Pb Lead	Bi Bismuth	Po Polonium	At Astatine	Rn Radon
Ds Darmstadtium	Rg Roentgenium	Cn Copernicium	Nh Nihonium	Fl Flerovium	Mc Moscovium	Lv Livermorium	Ts Tennessine	Og Oganesson

Tb Terbium	Dy Dysprosium	Ho Holmium	Er Erbium	Tm Thulium	Yb Ytterbium	Lu Lutetium
Bk Berkelium	Cf Californium	Es Einsteinium	Fm Fermium	Md Mendelevium	No Nobelium	Lr Lawrencium

These elements don't fit in their row in the table. How awkward!

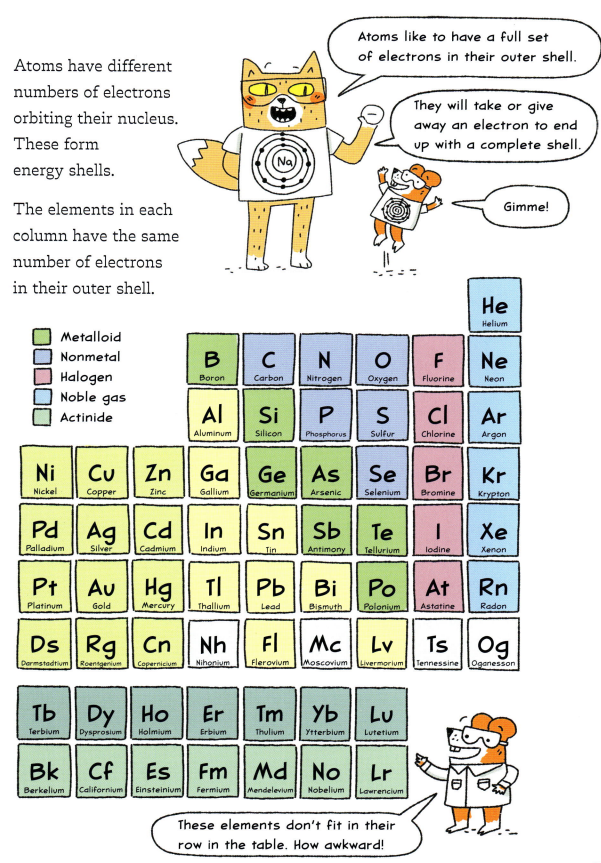

How to Mix Water
What's wrong with your water, Scooter?
It tastes TOO watery.
I'll dilute it. That will help.
You can't make water less watery by adding MORE water!
How can I make it less so?
Water is a COMPOUND made of the elements hydrogen and oxygen.
They are chemically bonded, so you get the same proportions throughout.
Hydrogen and oxygen, you say ...
That's what it is! The water tastes too HYDROGENY!

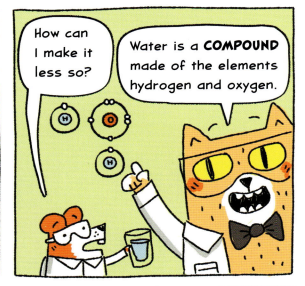

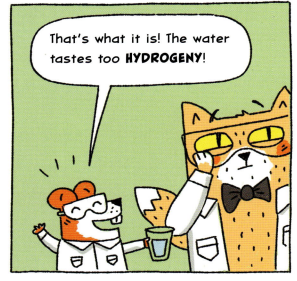

Compounds are two or more elements that are chemically combined. Compounds may take on different properties to their individual elements.

Fe + Scooter = Iron Scooter

Compounds are made up of **molecules**, which are atoms connected by chemical bonds. Water is a compound made up of **hydrogen** and **oxygen** atoms.

In water, two hydrogen (H) atoms bond with one oxygen (O) atom to make a water molecule.

A water molecule can be shown like this and written as **H₂O**.

Most materials around you are compounds. Examples are:

Table salt (NaCl) which is made from the elements **sodium** (Na) and **chlorine** (Cl).

Carbon dioxide (CO_2), the gas in the air taken in by plants, which is made from **carbon** (C) and **oxygen** (O).

Silica (SiO_2), a compound of **silicon** (Si) and **oxygen** (O), which makes up most of the sand on the beach.

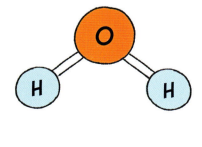

15

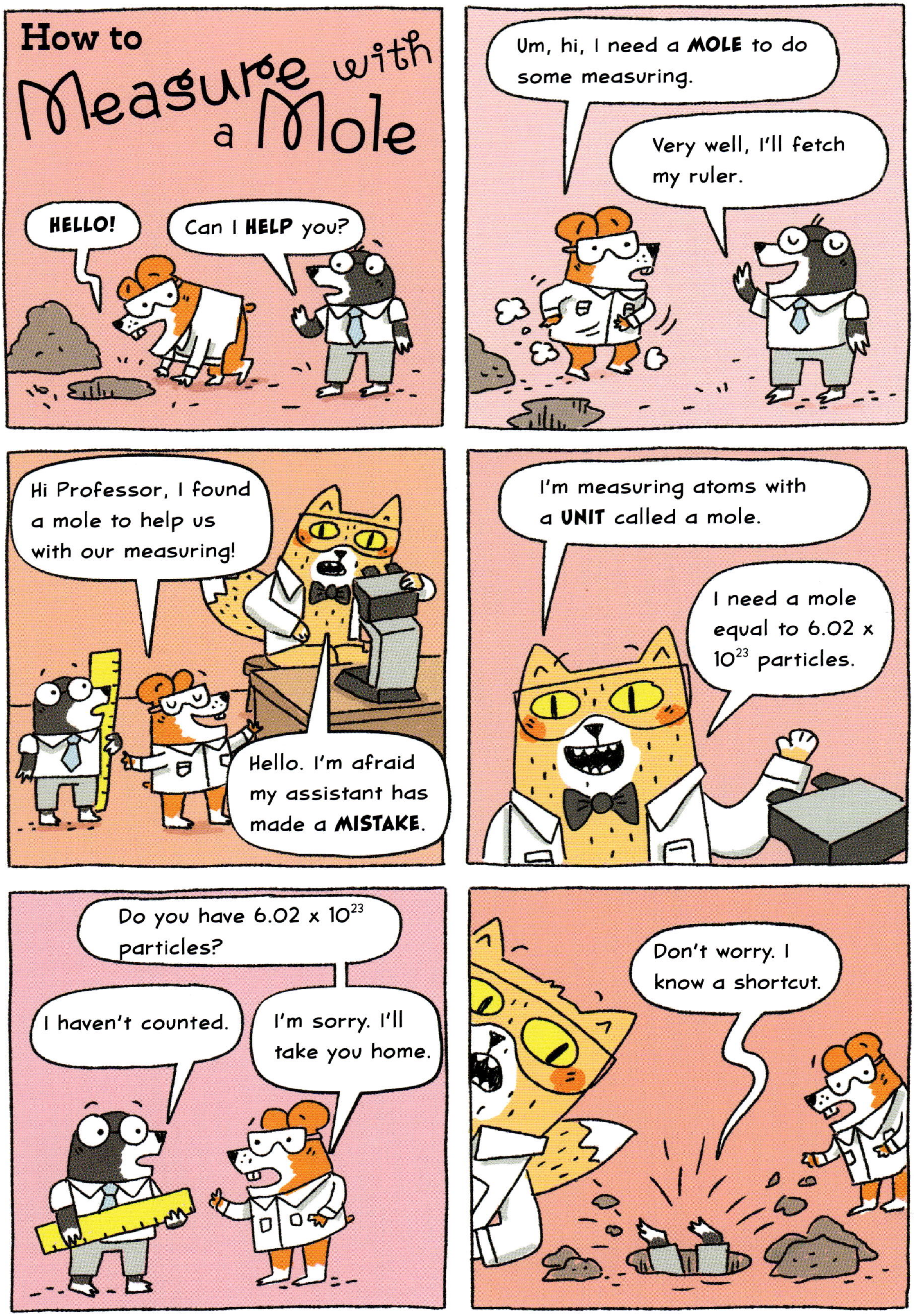
How to Measure with a Mole
HELLO!
Can I HELP you?
Um, hi, I need a MOLE to do some measuring.
Very well, I'll fetch my ruler.
Hi Professor, I found a mole to help us with our measuring!
Hello. I'm afraid my assistant has made a MISTAKE.
I'm measuring atoms with a UNIT called a mole.
I need a mole equal to 6.02 x 10²³ particles.
Do you have 6.02 x 10²³ particles?
I haven't counted.
I'm sorry. I'll take you home.
Don't worry. I know a shortcut.

Moles are units used to measure amounts.

They are based on a number called the **Avogadro constant.**

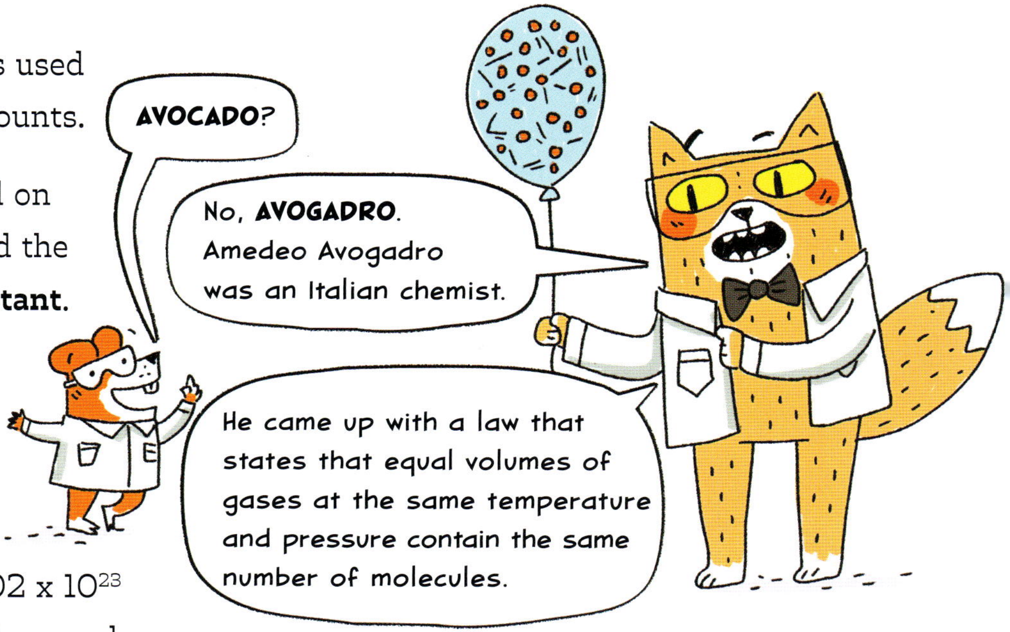
AVOCADO?
No, AVOGADRO. Amedeo Avogadro was an Italian chemist.
He came up with a law that states that equal volumes of gases at the same temperature and pressure contain the same number of molecules.

The Avogadro constant is the number 6.02×10^{23} which is 602 thousand billion billion.

While this seems a crazy big number to be dealing with, it actually makes calculating the mass of elements really simple.

One mole of an element equals its atomic mass in grams.

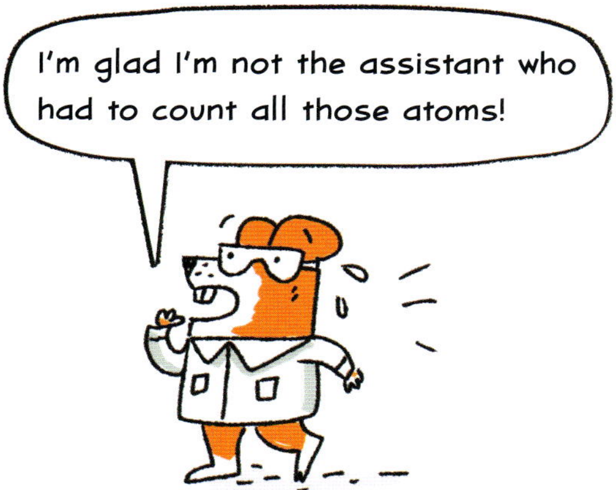
I'm glad I'm not the assistant who had to count all those atoms!

For example, Helium has an atomic mass of 4. So, 6.02×10^{23} atoms, or one mole of helium, has a mass of 4 grams (4g).

Carbon has an atomic mass of 12. One mole of carbon has a mass of 12 grams (12g).

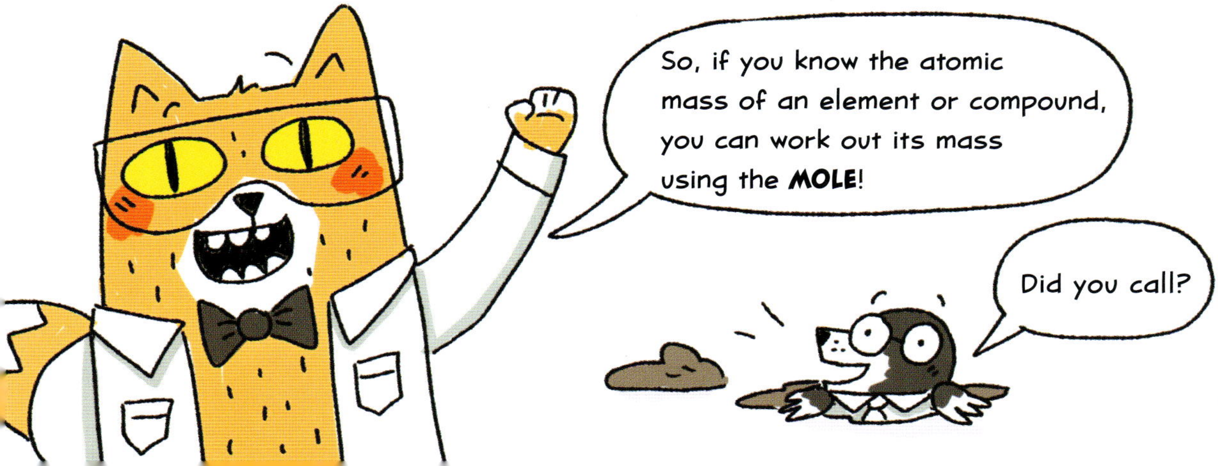
So, if you know the atomic mass of an element or compound, you can work out its mass using the MOLE!
Did you call?

How to Count Atoms
576,762, 576,763, 576,764 ...
What are you counting, Scooter?
SHUSH!
576,765, 576,766...
Those are BIG numbers...
576,767, 576,768 ...
Atoms.
576,769, 576,770 ...
ATOMS?! You'll be counting for MONTHS!
There is a much better way.
576,7... WAUGH! I lost my place! I have to start all over again!
No need, Scooter. You can weigh the gas and use MOLES to calculate the number of atoms.
It's hard enough counting on my fingers, never mind on MOLES!

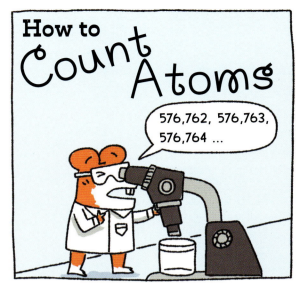

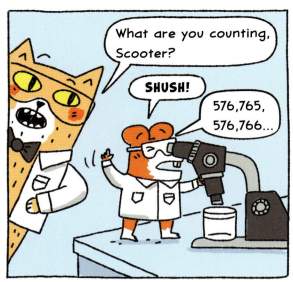

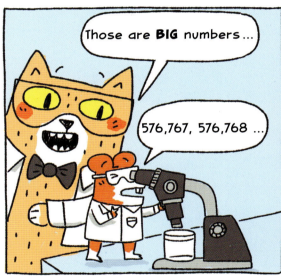

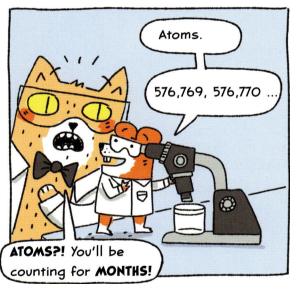

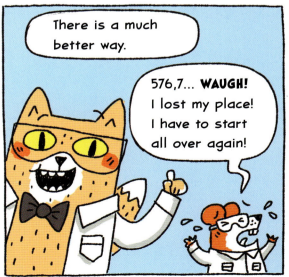

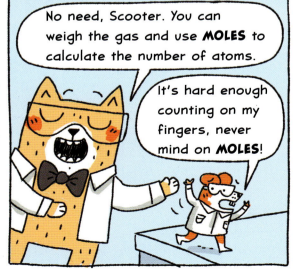

If you know the atomic mass of all the elements, you can figure out how many moles there are in an amount of a substance.

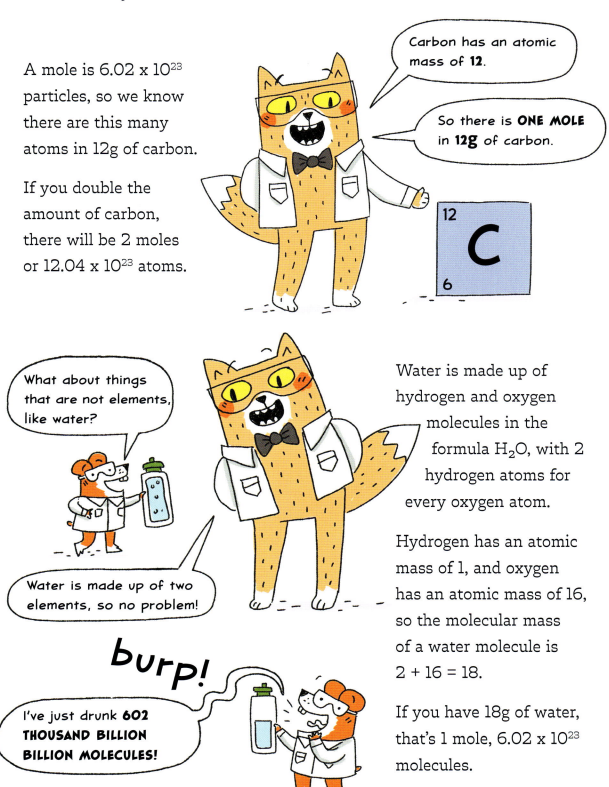

A mole is 6.02×10^{23} particles, so we know there are this many atoms in 12g of carbon.

If you double the amount of carbon, there will be 2 moles or 12.04×10^{23} atoms.

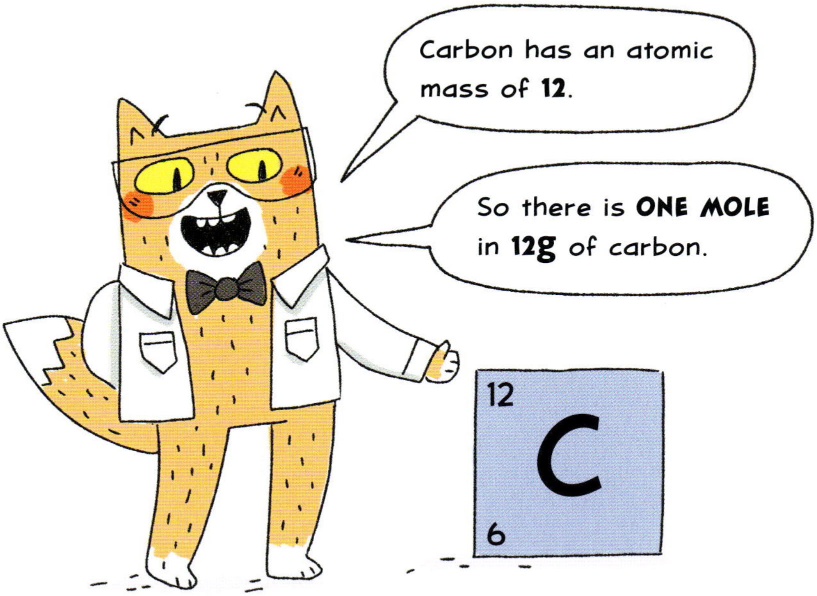
Carbon has an atomic mass of **12**.
So there is **ONE MOLE** in **12g** of carbon.
12
C
6

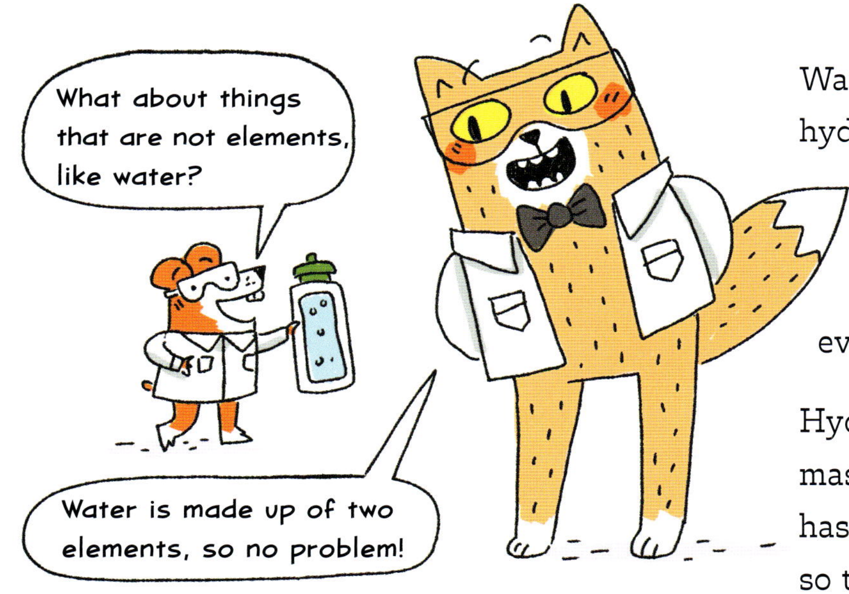
What about things that are not elements, like water?
Water is made up of two elements, so no problem!

Water is made up of hydrogen and oxygen molecules in the formula H_2O, with 2 hydrogen atoms for every oxygen atom.

Hydrogen has an atomic mass of 1, and oxygen has an atomic mass of 16, so the molecular mass of a water molecule is $2 + 16 = 18$.

If you have 18g of water, that's 1 mole, 6.02×10^{23} molecules.

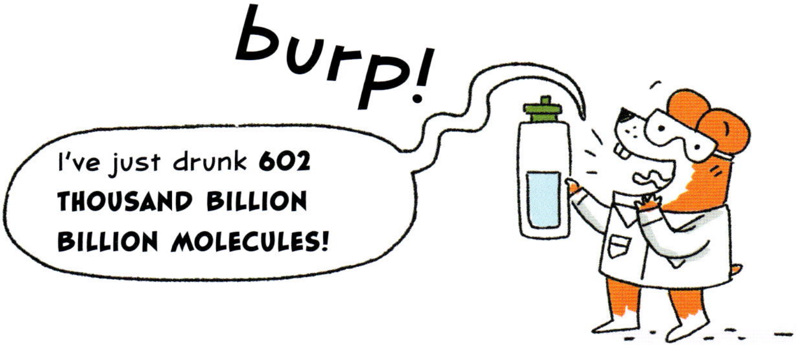
burp!
I've just drunk **602 THOUSAND BILLION BILLION MOLECULES!**

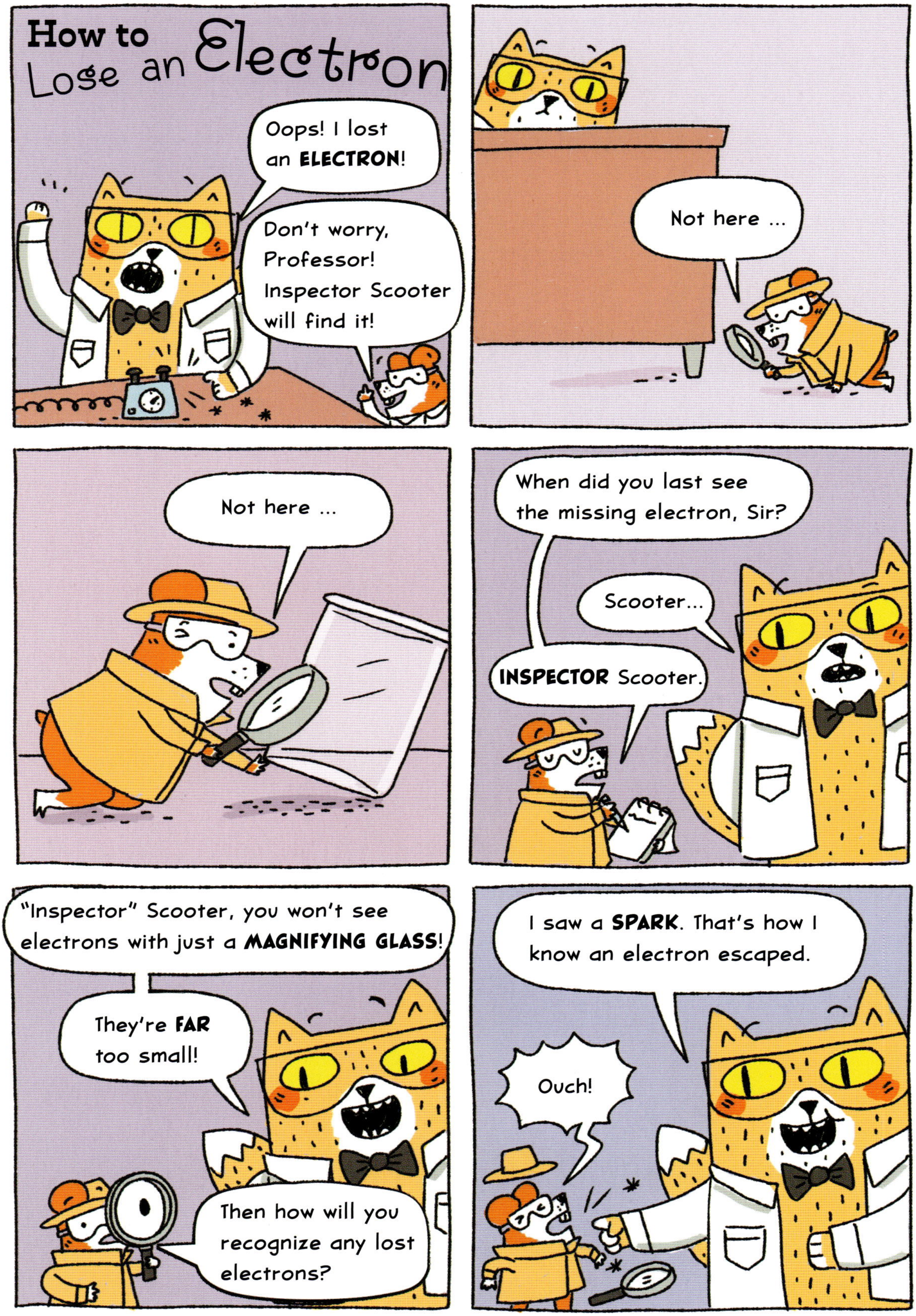
How to Lose an Electron
Oops! I lost an ELECTRON!
Don't worry, Professor! Inspector Scooter will find it!
Not here ...
Not here ...
When did you last see the missing electron, Sir?
Scooter...
INSPECTOR Scooter.
"Inspector" Scooter, you won't see electrons with just a MAGNIFYING GLASS!
They're FAR too small!
Then how will you recognize any lost electrons?
I saw a SPARK. That's how I know an electron escaped.
Ouch!

Atoms have a balance of positively charged protons, negatively charged electrons, and neutrons that have no charge.

But sometimes atoms lose or gain an electron and become an **ion**.

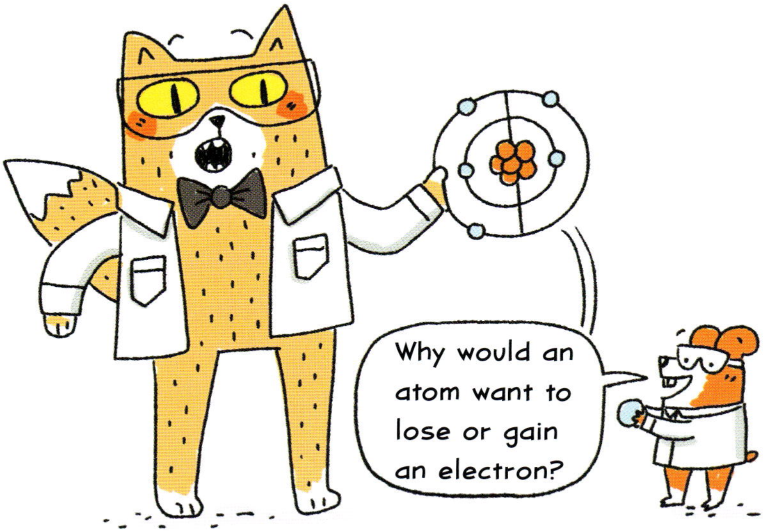

Why would an atom want to lose or gain an electron?

When two or more elements meet they may chemically react and swap electrons.

When electrons move from one material to another, this creates an **electrical charge**.

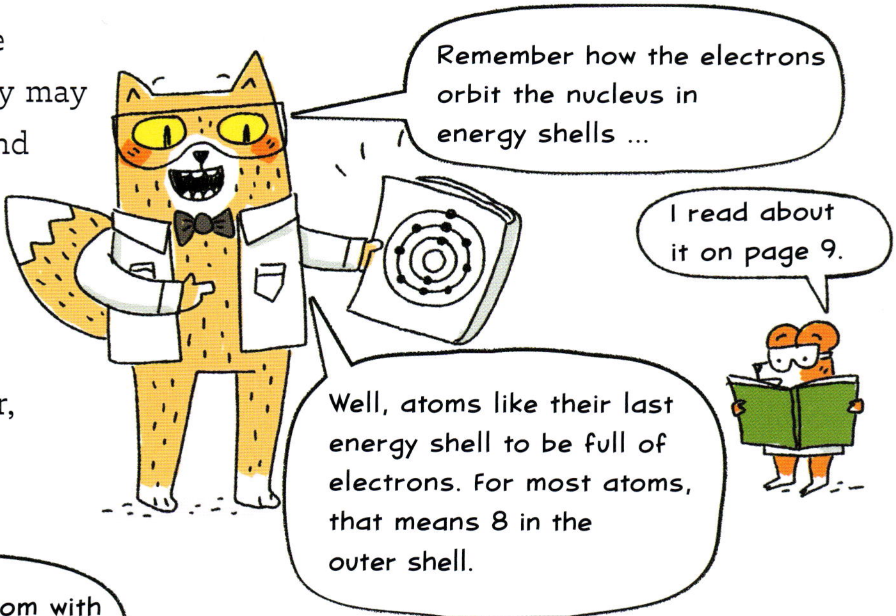

Remember how the electrons orbit the nucleus in energy shells ...
I read about it on page 9.
Well, atoms like their last energy shell to be full of electrons. For most atoms, that means 8 in the outer shell.

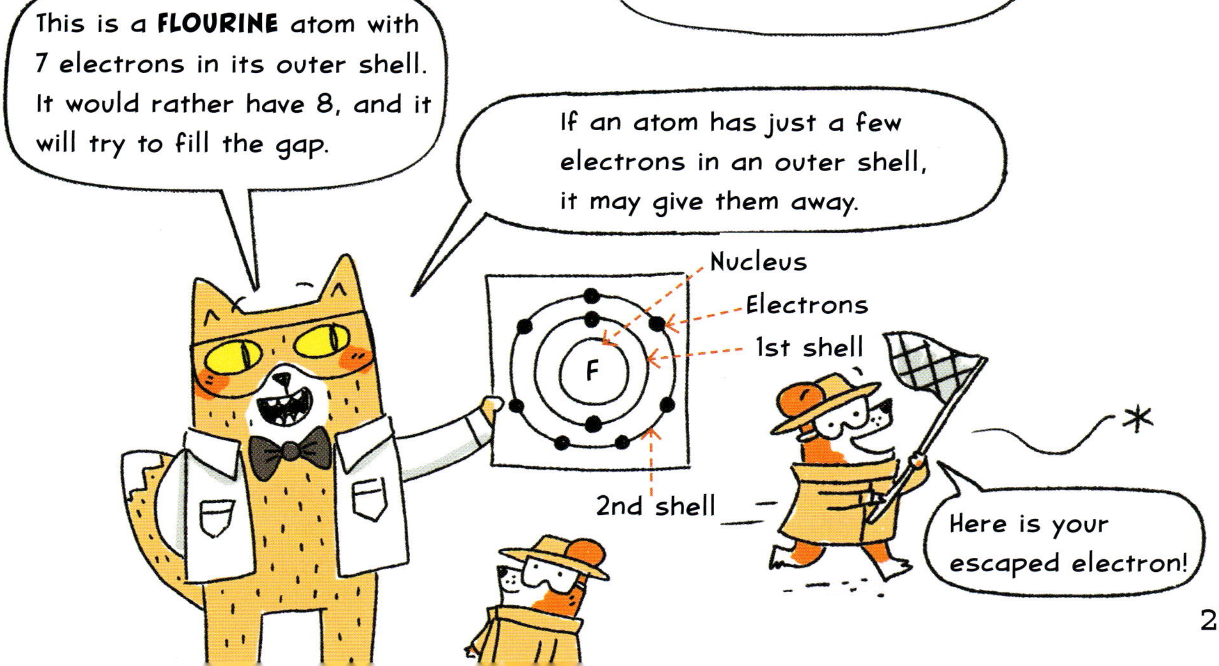

This is a **FLOURINE** atom with 7 electrons in its outer shell. It would rather have 8, and it will try to fill the gap.
If an atom has just a few electrons in an outer shell, it may give them away.
Nucleus
Electrons
1st shell
F
2nd shell
Here is your escaped electron!

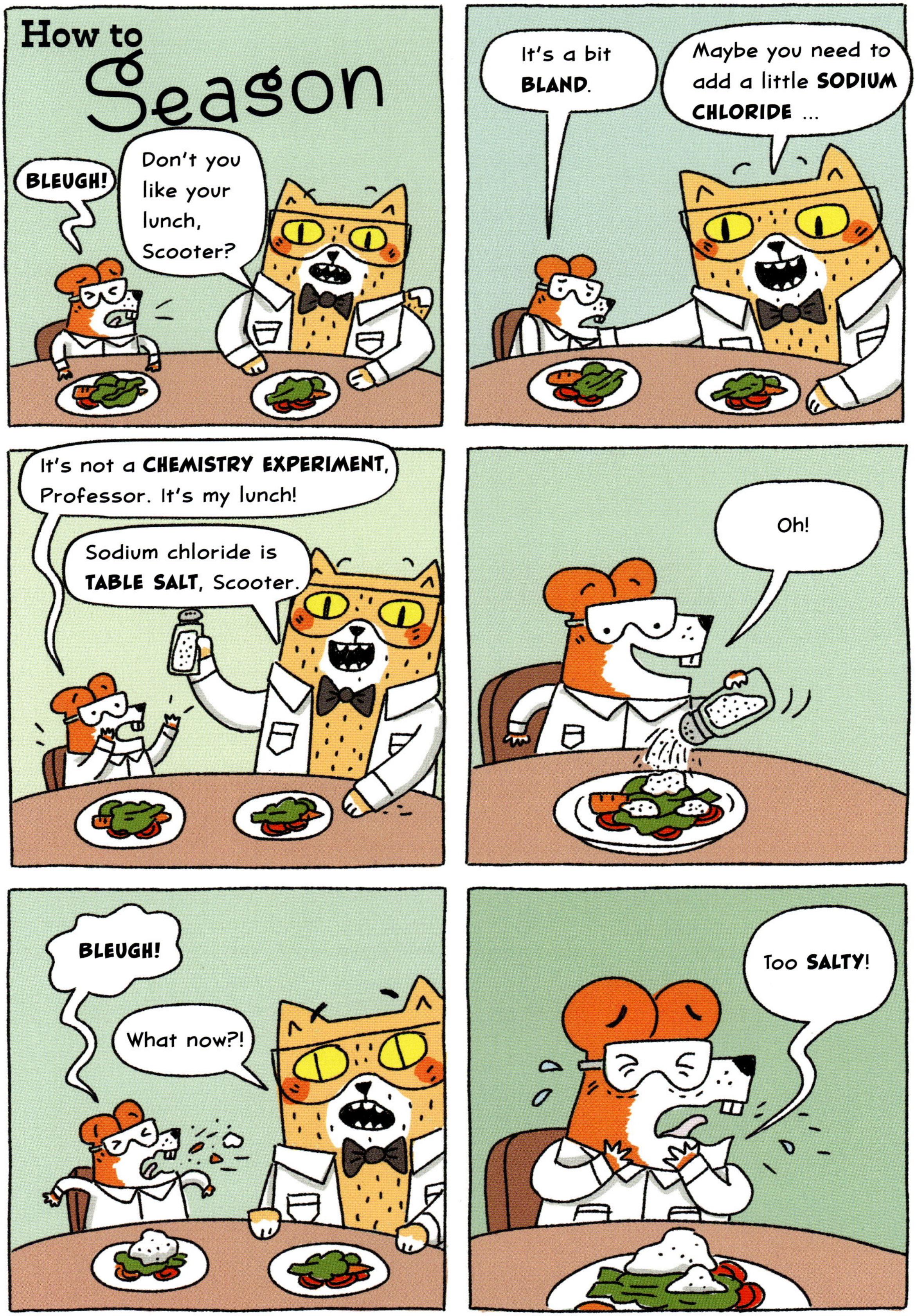
How to Season
BLEUGH!
Don't you like your lunch, Scooter?
It's a bit BLAND.
Maybe you need to add a little SODIUM CHLORIDE ...
It's not a CHEMISTRY EXPERIMENT, Professor. It's my lunch!
Sodium chloride is TABLE SALT, Scooter.
Oh!
BLEUGH!
What now?!
Too SALTY!

Salt, or sodium chloride, is a **compound** made of two elements, **sodium** (Na) and **chlorine** (Cl).

Sodium has 11 electrons with a single electron in its outer shell. Chlorine has 17 electrons with 7 in its outer shell. It needs an electron to fill the gap.

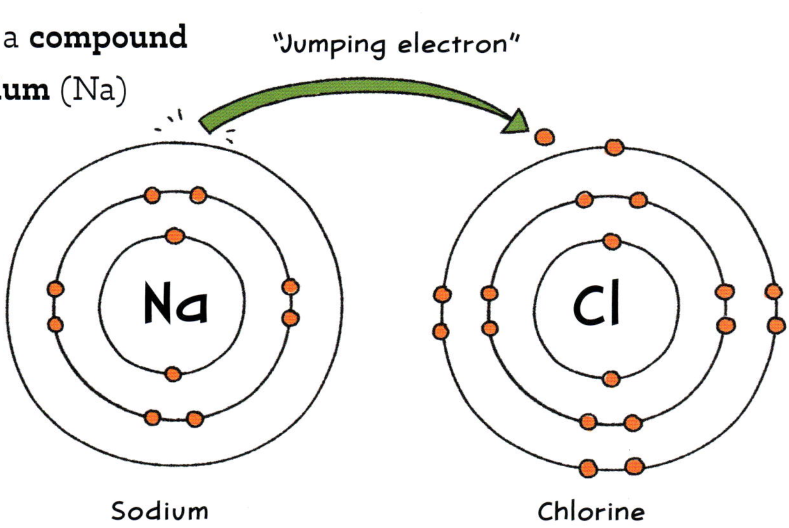

"Jumping electron"

Sodium   Chlorine

When sodium reacts with chlorine, it gives its outer electron away, so that both elements end up with a full outer shell of electrons. The sodium now has an overall positive charge. It is written as Na+. The chlorine (now called chloride) has an overall negative charge. It is written as Cl-.

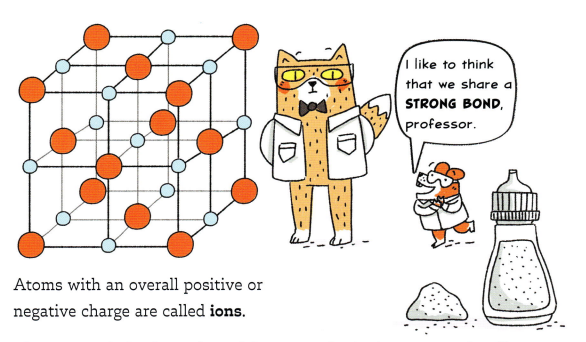

I like to think that we share a **STRONG BOND**, professor.

Atoms with an overall positive or negative charge are called **ions**.

These oppositely charged particles attract each other with strong **ionic bonds**.

The ionic compound sodium chloride (NaCl) is better known as table salt.

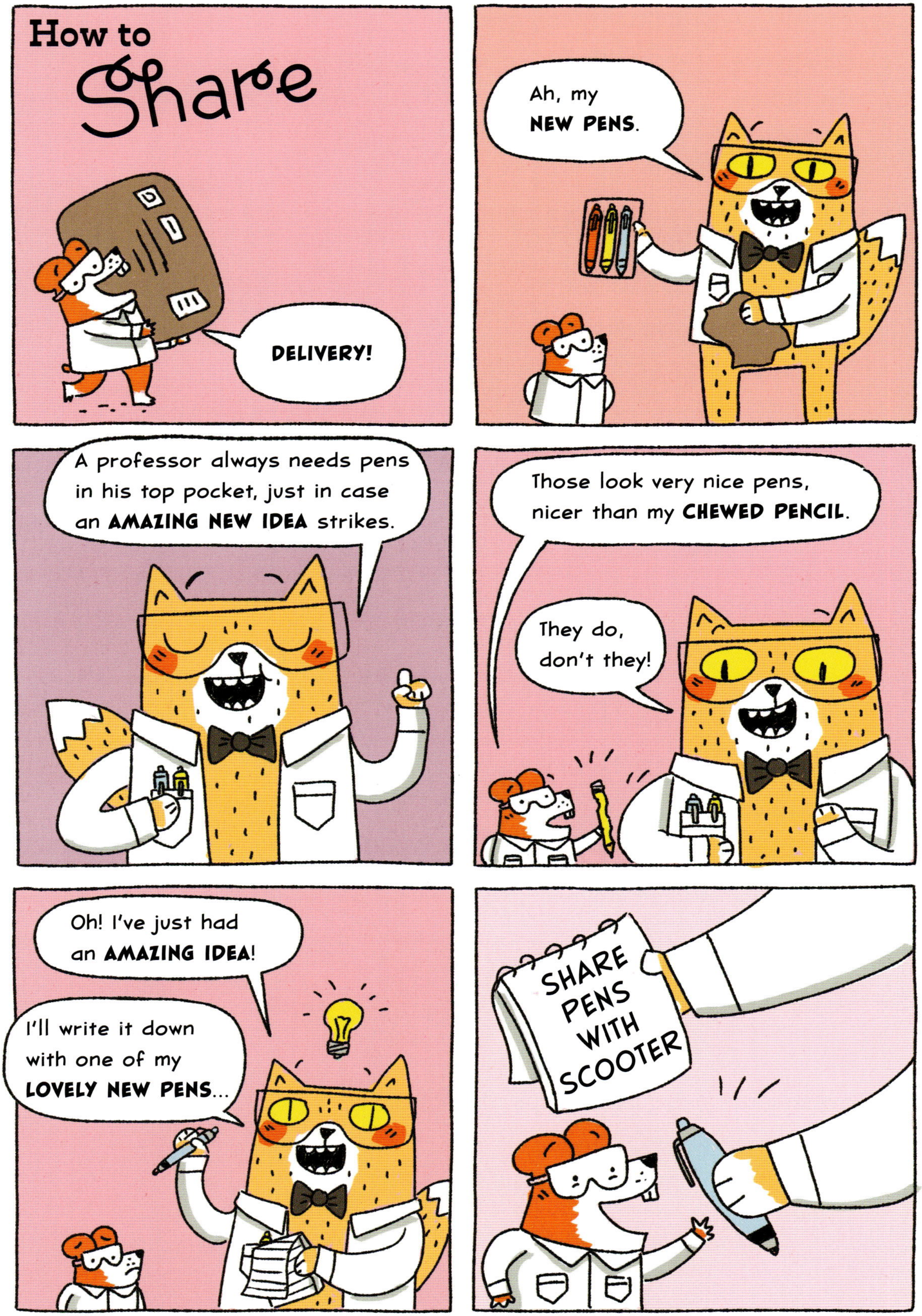
How to Share
DELIVERY!
Ah, my NEW PENS.
A professor always needs pens in his top pocket, just in case an AMAZING NEW IDEA strikes.
Those look very nice pens, nicer than my CHEWED PENCIL.
They do, don't they!
Oh! I've just had an AMAZING IDEA!
I'll write it down with one of my LOVELY NEW PENS...
SHARE PENS WITH SCOOTER

When atoms bond together, they form **molecules.** They can bond in two different ways—by swapping or sharing electrons. A bond formed by swapping electrons is called an **ionic bond.** One formed by sharing electrons is called a **covalent bond.**

One electron
H
+
H
Hydrogen atoms—no bond

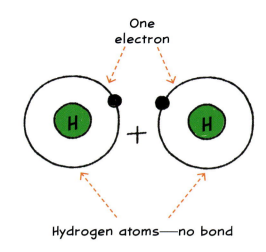

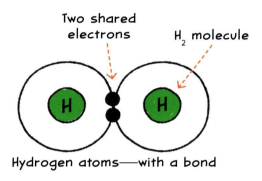

Covalent bonding is a neat way for two atoms of the same element to have the maximum number of electrons in their outer energy shell and become stable.

Compounds of more than one element may also have covalent bonds.

The gas **ammonia** is made up of **nitrogen** and **hydrogen.**

Two shared electrons
H₂ molecule
H
H
Hydrogen atoms—with a bond

Nitrogen has space for three electrons in its outer shell, and hydrogen has space for one.

By bonding with three hydrogen atoms, a nitrogen atom gains a full outer electron shell.

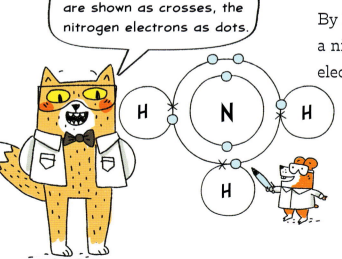

The hydrogen electrons are shown as crosses, the nitrogen electrons as dots.
H
N
H
H

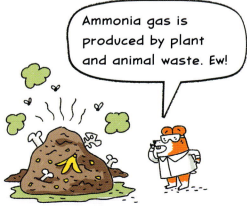

Ammonia gas is produced by plant and animal waste. Ew!

How to Make a Diamond
What are you drawing, Scooter?
I'm drawing a GIANT DIAMOND.
Interesting.
Do you know that the GRAPHITE in your pencil and DIAMOND are made of the SAME ELEMENT?
REALLY?!
Yes. Both are made of CARBON.
But they look so DIFFERENT.
That's because of the way that their carbons atoms are bonded together.
So, my drawing and expensive diamonds are almost the SAME.
I guess so.
Do you want to buy my drawing for $1,000?
$1,000

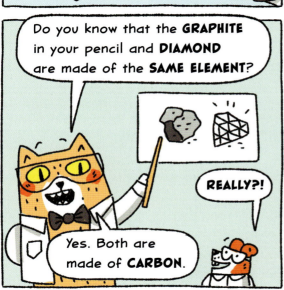

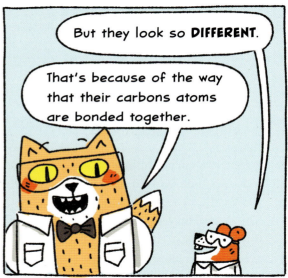

Like the gases hydrogen and oxygen, the element **carbon** can form **covalent bonds**.

But although gases can spread out and fill a room, carbon can form bonds to create one of the hardest materials on Earth—**diamond**.

To make diamond, a carbon atom joins with **four** other carbon atoms, building a **crystal lattice**. The bonds in a lattice are very strong, giving diamond its very hard form and a high melting point.

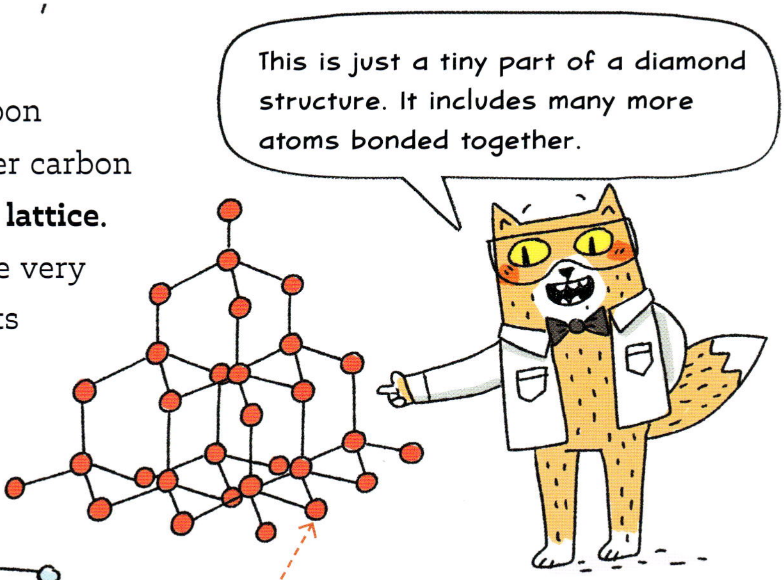

Gasp!

This is just a tiny part of a diamond structure. It includes many more atoms bonded together.

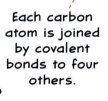

Each carbon atom is joined by covalent bonds to four others.

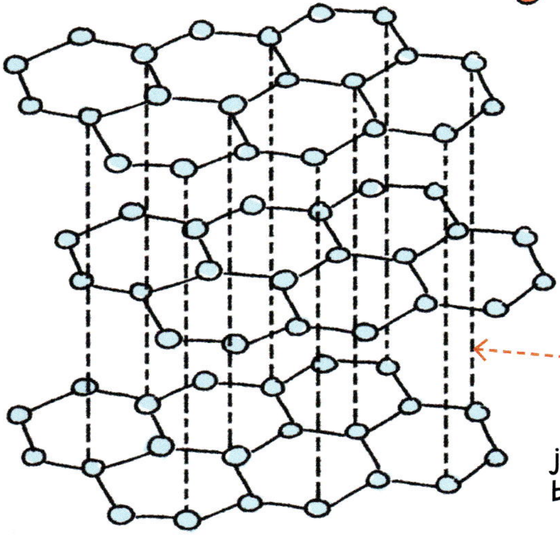

The layers of atoms in graphite are joined together by weak forces.

Another form of carbon with covalent bonds is **graphite**, the "lead" in a pencil. Graphite is formed from sheets of carbon atoms with each atom joined to two others. It has fewer bonds than diamond, so it is much softer.

And I can **DRAW** with it!

27

How to Date a Dinosaur
Today, I'm DATING A DINOSAUR.
Shouldn't you find someone more your age?
I'm not going ON A DATE. I'm figuring out the AGE of a dinosaur bone.
How can you find out?
We'll use ISOTOPES!
Dr. Rosie Ringtail, our nature expert, will explain.
You know atoms have PROTONS and NEUTRONS, right, Scooter?
Uhuh.
Well, an isotope is a variant of the element with a different number of NEUTRONS.
What's THAT got to do with dinosaurs?
Well, many isotopes are radioactive. Over thousands of years they release radiation in a process called DECAY.
We can measure the decay and work out how much time has passed.
The bone is 67 MILLION YEARS OLD!
Happy birthday, dinosaur!

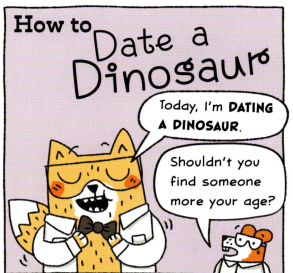

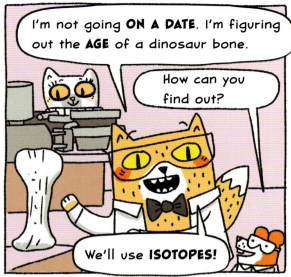

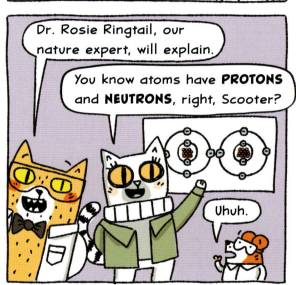

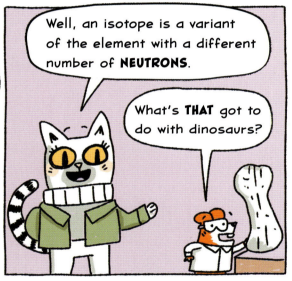

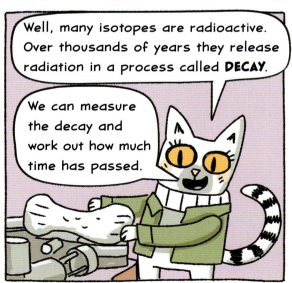

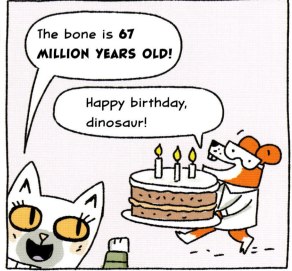

An **isotope** is a form of an **element** with the same number of protons but a different number of **neutrons** in its nucleus.

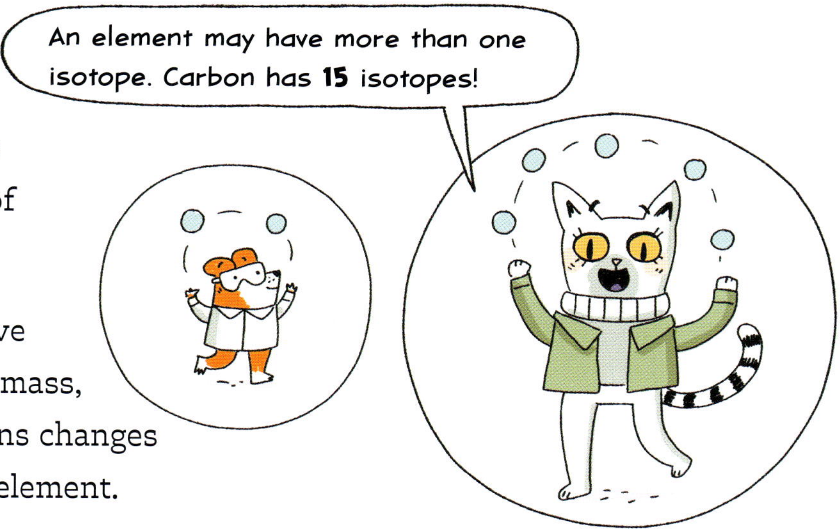
An element may have more than one isotope. Carbon has **15** isotopes!

While neutrons don't have a charge, they do have a mass, so a difference in neutrons changes the mass number of the element.

Though regular carbon has a mass number of 12, its isotopes have a higher mass and are named for their mass numbers—carbon 13, carbon 14, and so on. Over time, the isotopes in bones change from one type to another.

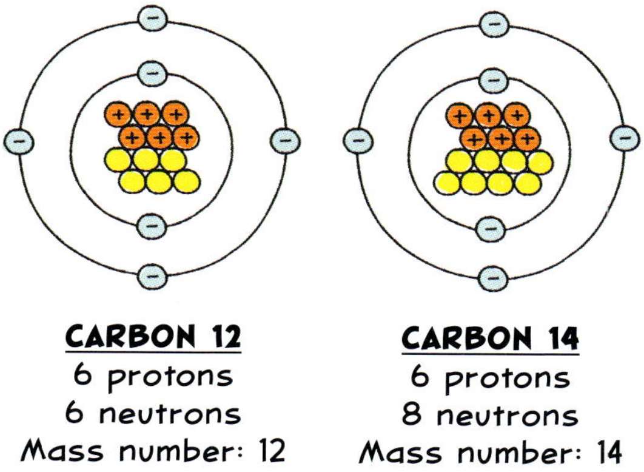
CARBON 12
6 protons
6 neutrons
Mass number: 12
CARBON 14
6 protons
8 neutrons
Mass number: 14

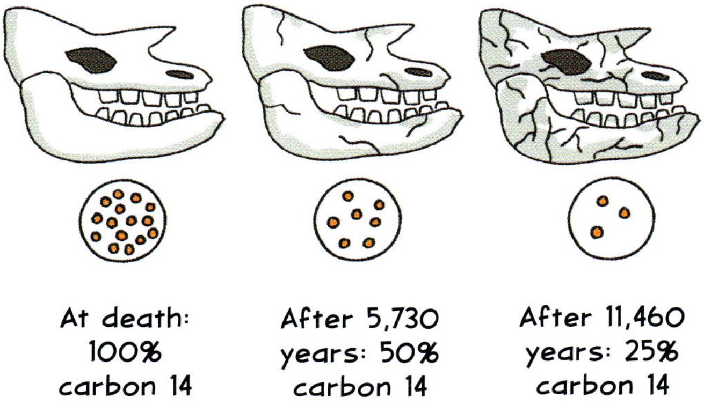
At death: 100% carbon 14
After 5,730 years: 50% carbon 14
After 11,460 years: 25% carbon 14

For scientists wanting to date materials, including fossils, isotopes are really handy.

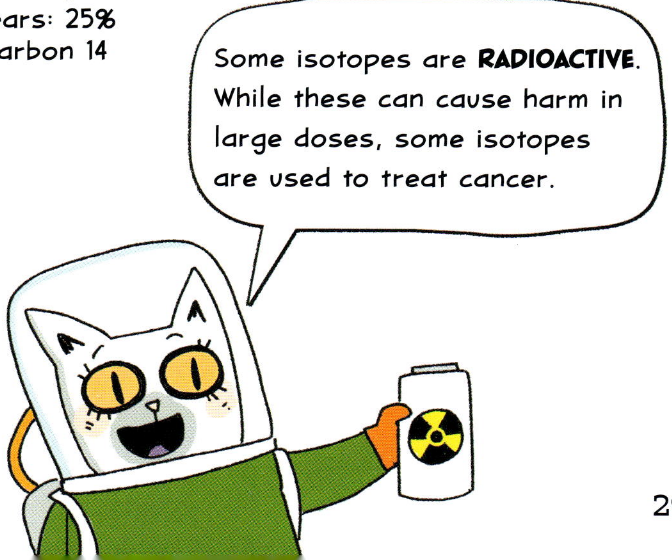
Some isotopes are **RADIOACTIVE**. While these can cause harm in large doses, some isotopes are used to treat cancer.

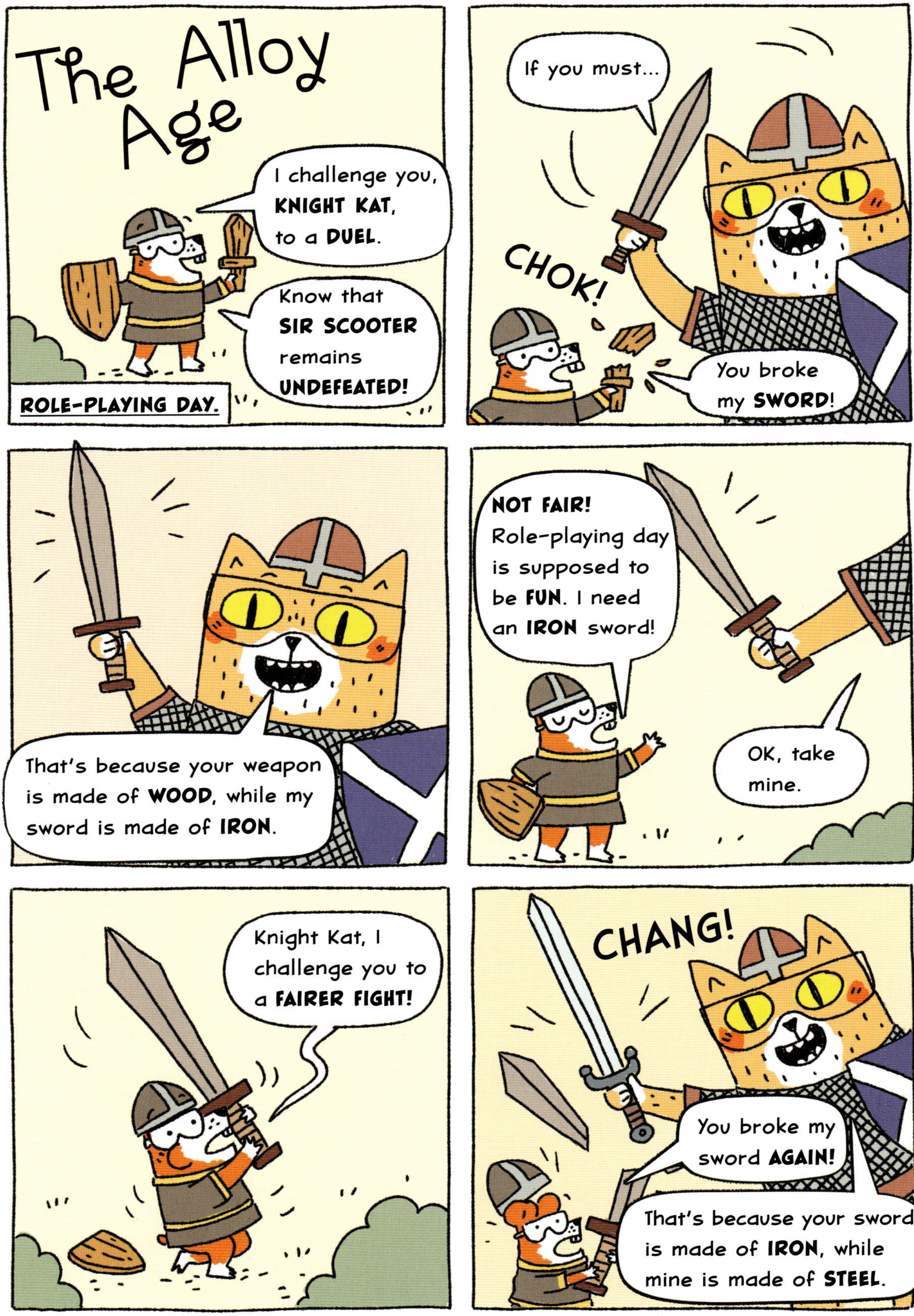
The Alloy Age
I challenge you, KNIGHT KAT, to a DUEL.
Know that SIR SCOOTER remains UNDEFEATED!
ROLE-PLAYING DAY.
If you must...
CHOK!
You broke my SWORD!
That's because your weapon is made of WOOD, while my sword is made of IRON.
NOT FAIR! Role-playing day is supposed to be FUN. I need an IRON sword!
OK, take mine.
Knight Kat, I challenge you to a FAIRER FIGHT!
CHANG!
You broke my sword AGAIN!
That's because your sword is made of IRON, while mine is made of STEEL.

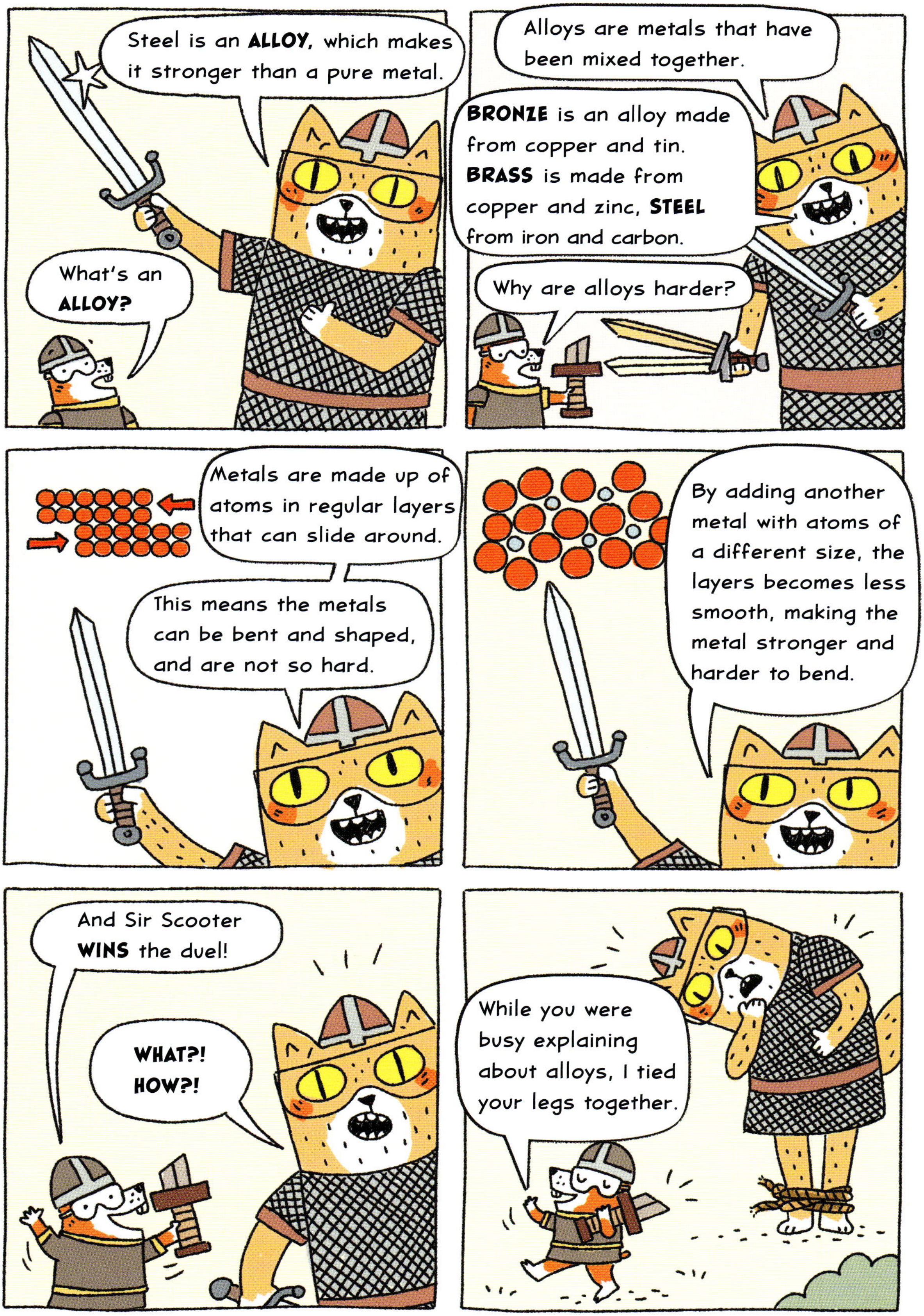

Steel is an **ALLOY,** which makes it stronger than a pure metal.
What's an **ALLOY?**
Alloys are metals that have been mixed together.
BRONZE is an alloy made from copper and tin. **BRASS** is made from copper and zinc, **STEEL** from iron and carbon.
Why are alloys harder?
Metals are made up of atoms in regular layers that can slide around.
This means the metals can be bent and shaped, and are not so hard.
By adding another metal with atoms of a different size, the layers becomes less smooth, making the metal stronger and harder to bend.
And Sir Scooter **WINS** the duel!
WHAT?! HOW?!
While you were busy explaining about alloys, I tied your legs together.

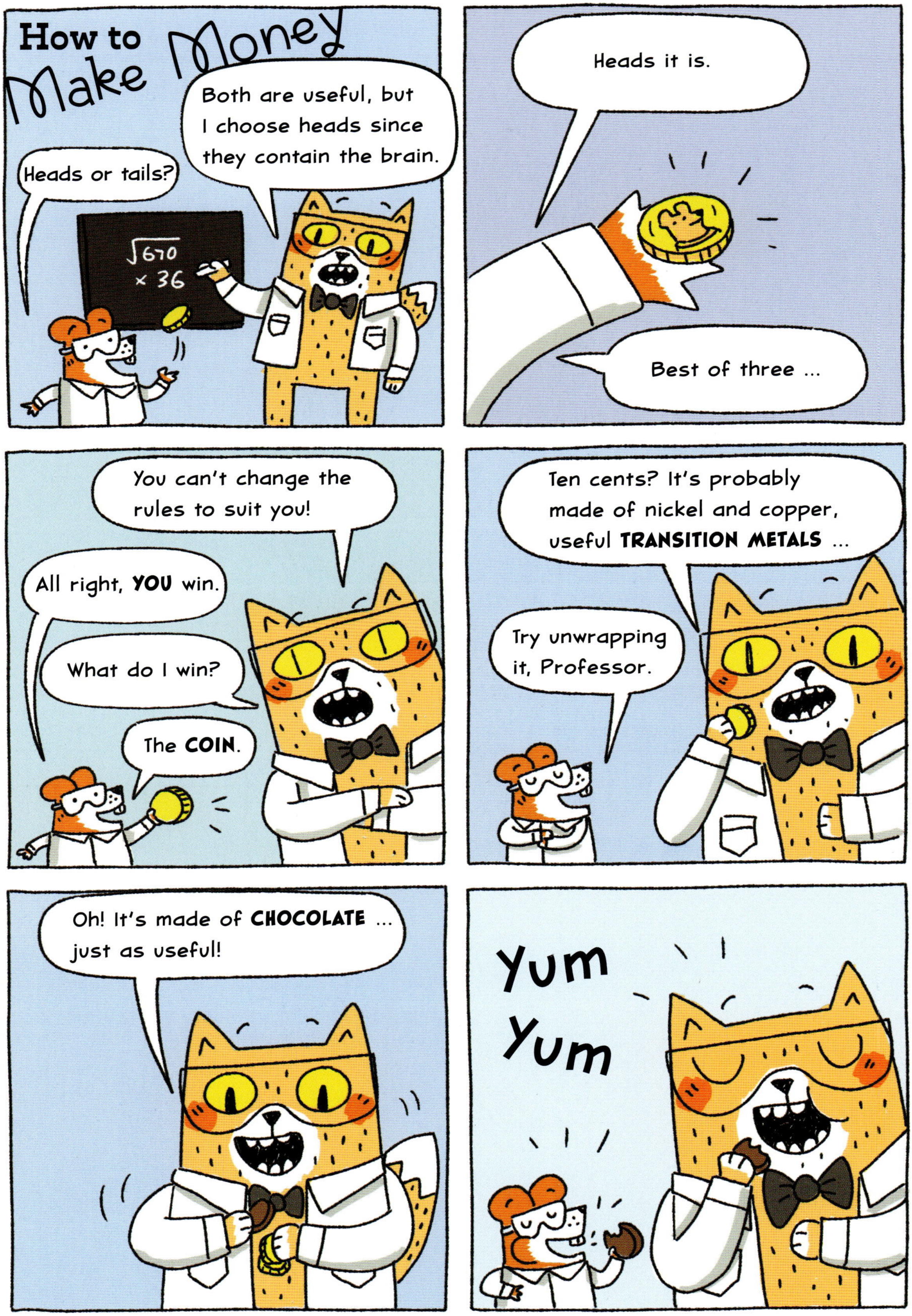
How to Make Money
Heads or tails?
Both are useful, but I choose heads since they contain the brain.
√670 × 36
Heads it is.
Best of three ...
You can't change the rules to suit you!
All right, YOU win.
What do I win?
The COIN.
Ten cents? It's probably made of nickel and copper, useful TRANSITION METALS ...
Try unwrapping it, Professor.
Oh! It's made of CHOCOLATE ... just as useful!
Yum Yum

If you look at the Periodic Table, you'll see that most metals are transition metals.

Sc Scandium
Ti Titanium
V Vanadium
Cr Chromium
Mn Manganese
Fe Iron
Co Cobalt
Ni Nickel
Cu Copper
Zn Zinc
Y Yttrium
Zr Zirconium
Nb Niobium
Mo Molybdenum
Tc Tecnecium
Ru Ruthenium
Rh Rhodium
Pd Palladium
Ag Silver
Cd Cadmium
Hf Hafnium
Ta Tantalum
W Tungsten
Re Rhenium
Os Osmium
Ir Iridium
Pt Platinum
Au Gold
Hg Mercury
Rf Rutherfordium
Db Dubenium
Sg Seaborgium
Bh Bohrium
Hs Hassium
Mt Meiterium
Ds Darmstadtium
Rg Roentgenium
Cn Copernicium

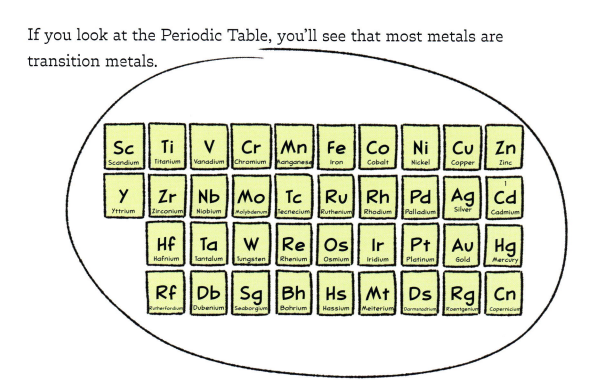

Transition metals include iron, nickel, copper, silver, and gold. These metals usually have high melting points and densities, and they are good at conducting heat and electricity. Many also form alloys when combined.

These metals have many uses. Usually coins are made of one metal coated—or plated—by another. Transition metals are chosen because they are hard-wearing, with the outer metal chosen for its appearance.

Valuable metals like silver and gold are used in jewelry.
Nickel, copper, and zinc are used to make coins.
Coins need to be hard-wearing since they get passed around so much!

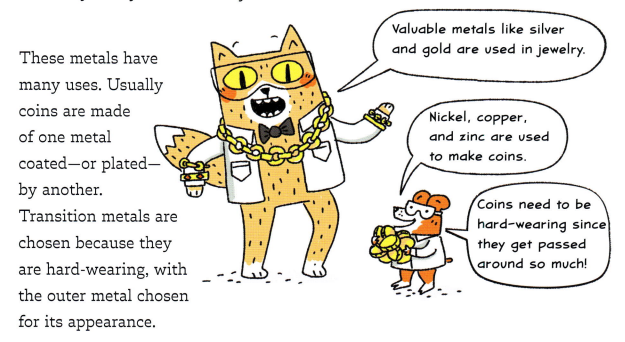

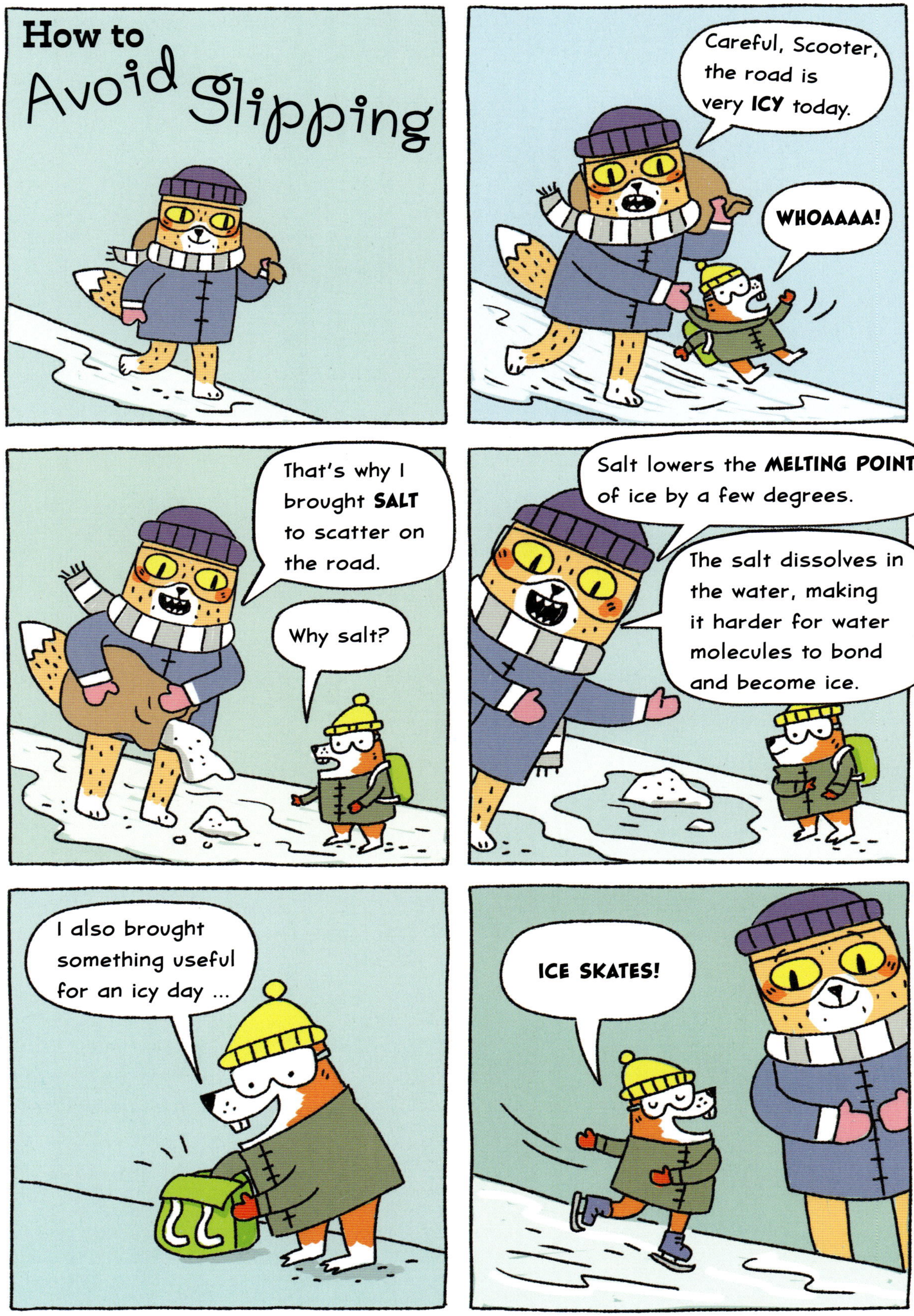
How to Avoid Slipping
Careful, Scooter, the road is very ICY today.
WHOAAAA!
That's why I brought SALT to scatter on the road.
Why salt?
Salt lowers the MELTING POINT of ice by a few degrees.
The salt dissolves in the water, making it harder for water molecules to bond and become ice.
I also brought something useful for an icy day ...
ICE SKATES!

What's the Matter?

(Properties of Matter, Solids, Liquids, Gases, Transforming Matter)

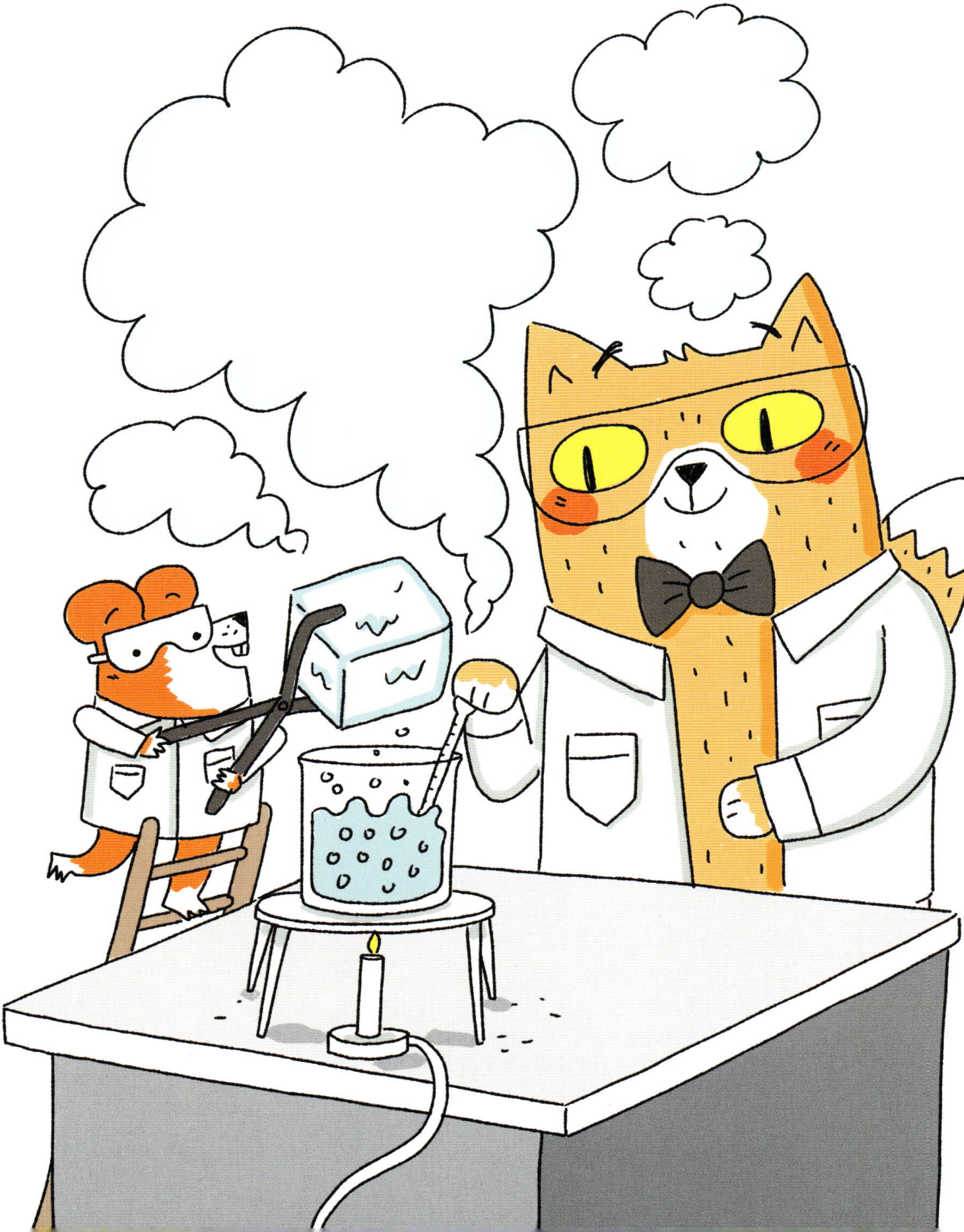

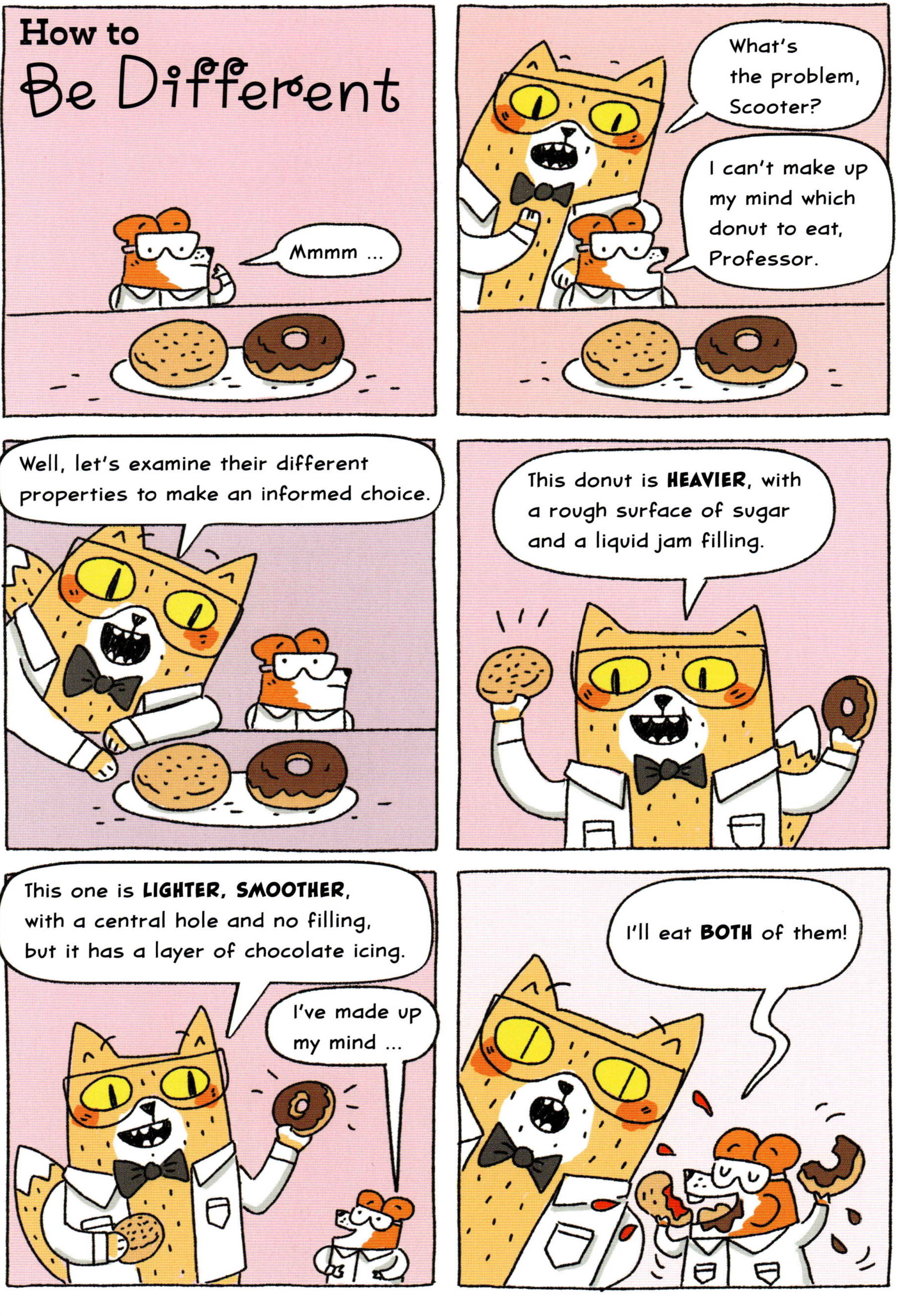
How to
Be Different
Mmmm ...
What's the problem, Scooter?
I can't make up my mind which donut to eat, Professor.
Well, let's examine their different properties to make an informed choice.
This donut is **HEAVIER**, with a rough surface of sugar and a liquid jam filling.
This one is **LIGHTER, SMOOTHER**, with a central hole and no filling, but it has a layer of chocolate icing.
I've made up my mind ...
I'll eat **BOTH** of them!

Chemistry involves looking at the different properties of substances and trying to work out why they appear and behave in a certain way.

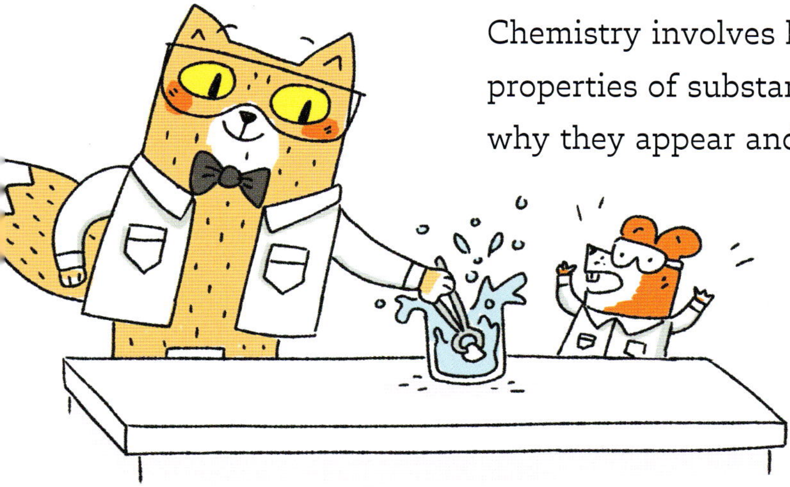

Properties include **mass, density, buoyancy, texture, hardness,** and **conductivity**.

Mass is a measure of how much matter is in an object. The more mass an object has, the heavier it feels.

Density is a measure of how tightly packed matter is within an object. A ball of iron is more dense than a ball of rubber.

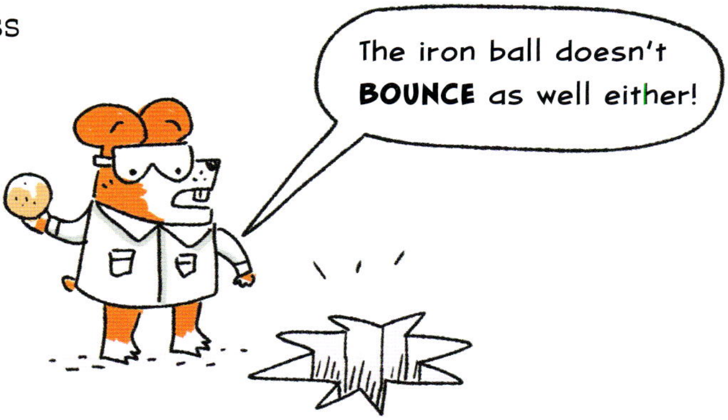
The iron ball doesn't BOUNCE as well either!

Density affects how **buoyant** an object is. If an object is less dense than water, it will float.

Other properties to check are an object's color, transparency, shine, and smoothness.

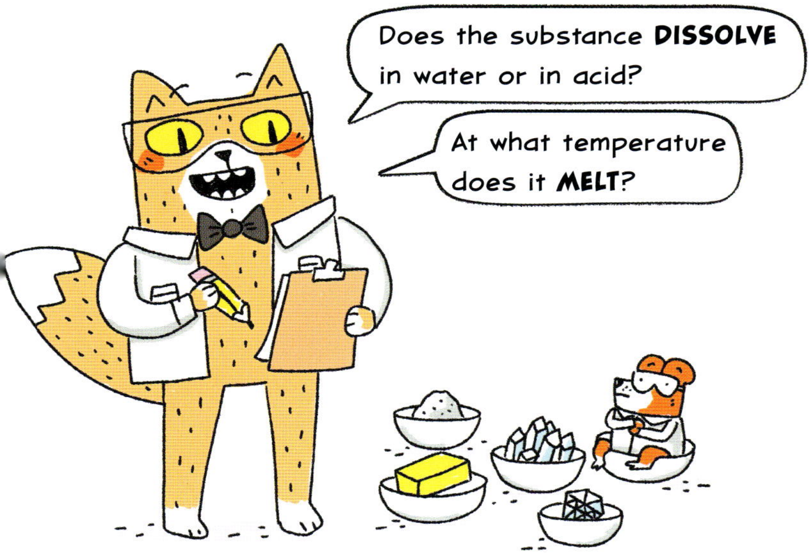
Does the substance DISSOLVE in water or in acid?
At what temperature does it MELT?

All of these properties can help identify a material. The more you learn about chemistry, the more you can predict how a material will behave.

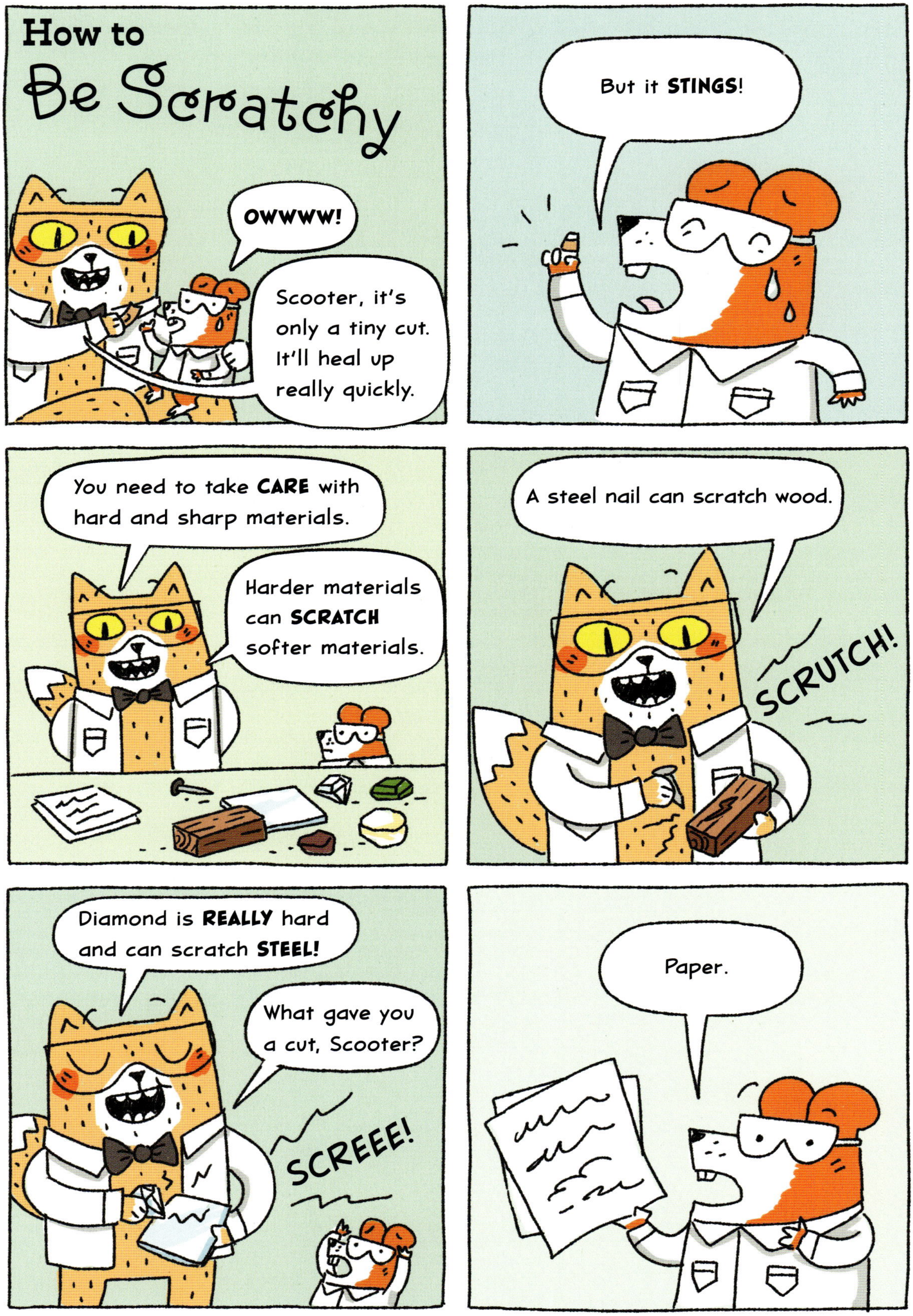
How to Be Scratchy
OWWWW!
Scooter, it's only a tiny cut. It'll heal up really quickly.
But it STINGS!
You need to take CARE with hard and sharp materials.
Harder materials can SCRATCH softer materials.
A steel nail can scratch wood.
SCRUTCH!
Diamond is REALLY hard and can scratch STEEL!
What gave you a cut, Scooter?
SCREEE!
Paper.

Hardness is a measure of how resistant a material is to being scratched or punctured. It is measured using the **Mohs scale.**

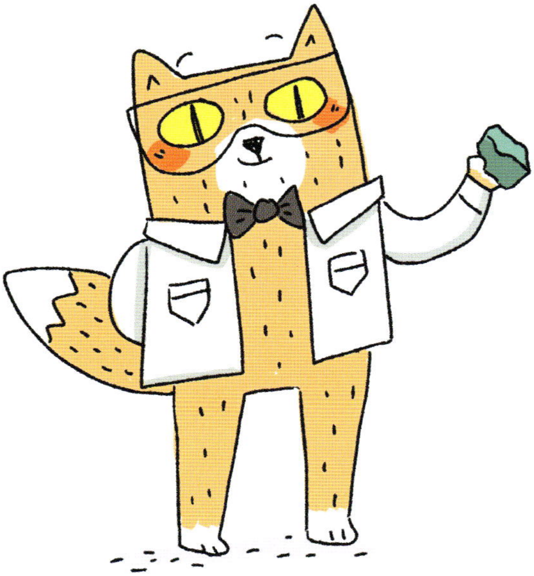

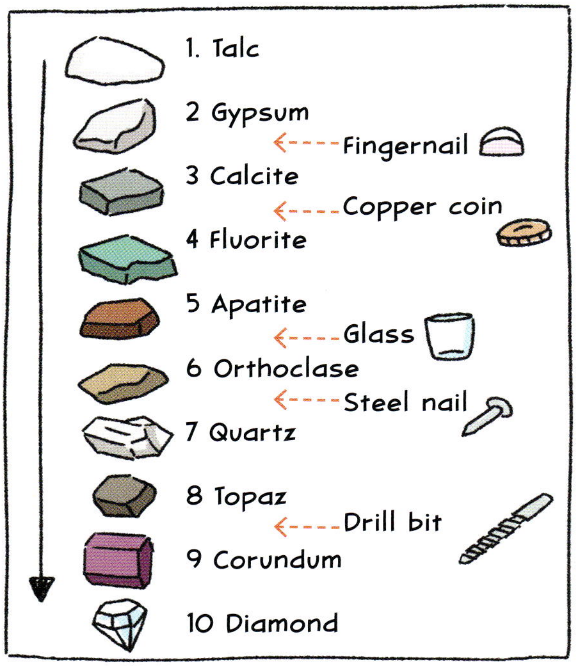
1. Talc
2 Gypsum
Fingernail
3 Calcite
Copper coin
4 Fluorite
5 Apatite
Glass
6 Orthoclase
Steel nail
7 Quartz
8 Topaz
Drill bit
9 Corundum
10 Diamond

Sample minerals are used as guides for hardness from level 1 (soft talc) to level 10 (hard diamond).

On the scale, a fingernail has a hardness between 2 and 3, while a steel nail is between 6 and 7.

Materials with higher hardness numbers can leave scratches on materials with lower hardness numbers.

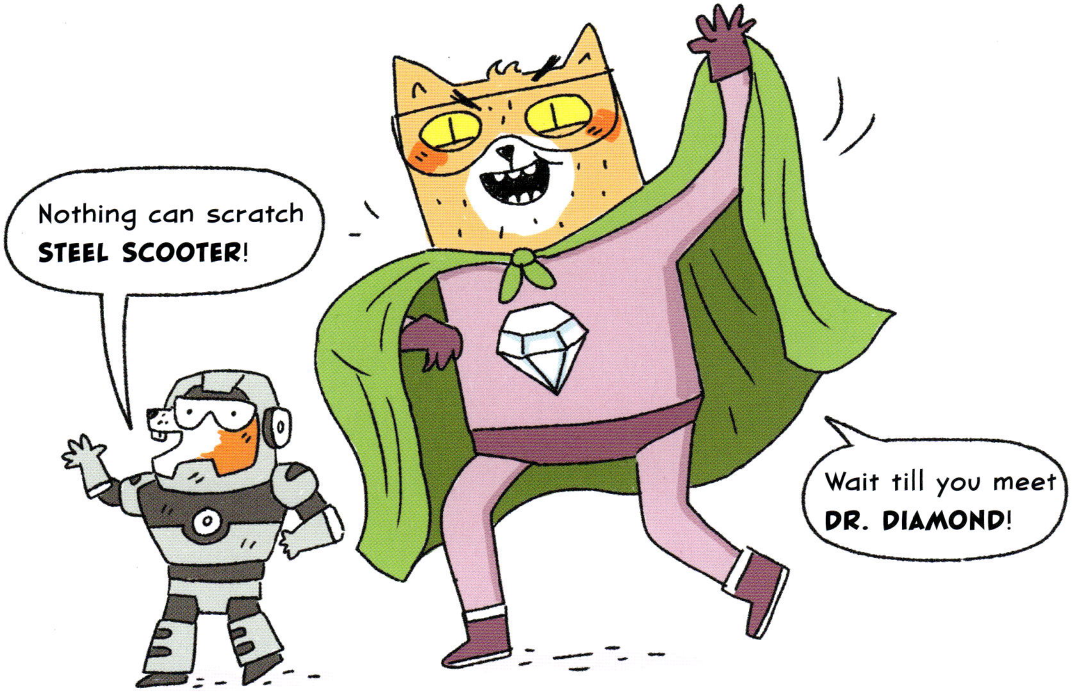
Nothing can scratch STEEL SCOOTER!
Wait till you meet DR. DIAMOND!

In a State

Materials come in three main forms or states of matter—**solids**, **liquids**, and **gases**.

The state that matter appears in depends on how strong the forces of attraction are between its atoms and molecules.

Solids have a fixed shape and volume. Their atoms or molecules are held together in a regular pattern, with strong bonds that keep them in place.

The atoms or molecules vibrate in their positions. When the solid is heated up, these particles vibrate more, and the solid expands slightly.

Solids include metals, wood, and ice.

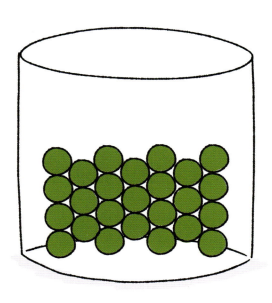

Liquids can flow and be poured into solid containers. Their atoms or molecules have weaker bonds that let them move around, though they remain close together.

Liquids include oil, water, and juice.

The liquid in thermometers expands as it gets hotter, so it can be used as a measure for temperature.

The atoms or molecules in **gases** have very weak bonds, so they can move far apart in any direction. Gases will expand to fill the space they are in, or they can be put under pressure and squeezed into small spaces.

Gases include air, oxygen, and helium.

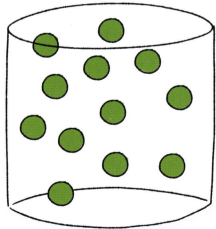

Materials can transform from solid to liquid to gas and back, through changes in temperature or pressure.

How to See Your Name in Lights
Prof A. Katzenstein Science Lab
I liked the old sign. Why did you take it DOWN?
I thought it was time to UPGRADE.
Are you READY?
What for?
Prof A. Katzenstein
TA-DA! What do you THINK?
It's, um, bright ...
CLICK
Prof A. Katzenstein & Scooter
How about NOW?
CLICK
I LOVE it!
In fact, I'm feeling a little emotional ...
Prof A. Katzenstein Science Lab

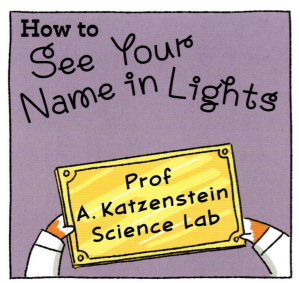

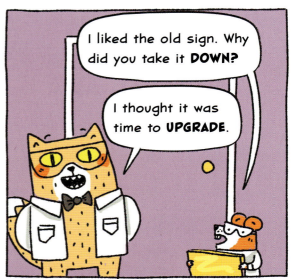

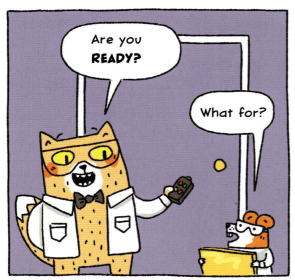

Solids, liquids, and gases are the most common states for materials found on Earth, but there is another form—**plasma**.

Plasma is a mix of high-energy charged atoms and other particles. While it is rare on Earth, plasma makes up about 99% of all matter in the Universe.

Plasma comes to Earth from the Sun. When it interacts with Earth's magnetic field, it can cause a spectacular light show called an **aurora** in the skies near the poles. These are the Northern and Southern Lights. We also see plasma as bolts of lightning.

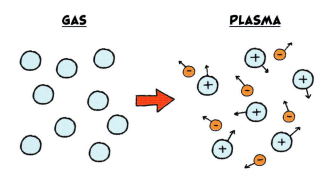

Plasma can be formed by heating a gas to a very high temperature or by passing an electric current through it. This removes electrons from their atoms.

When an electric current is used to heat **neon** in a tube, it causes the electrons in the gas to move faster and give off light. **Neon lights** are used in signs for advertising.

How to Be Supercool
I'm **READY**, Professor!
Scooter! Why have you changed your **LOOK?**
You said we were going to be **SUPERCOOL** today.
I said we were going to be **SUPERCOOLING** today.
Oh.
I'm reducing the temperature in this super-refrigerator as low as possible.
When it gets really cold, the atoms in the gas inside slow down.
How low can you go?
ABSOLUTE ZERO.
Then **THAT'S** how cool I am today!

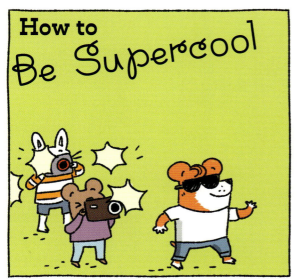

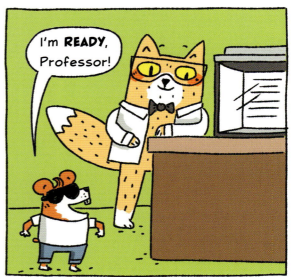

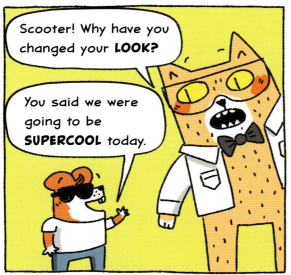

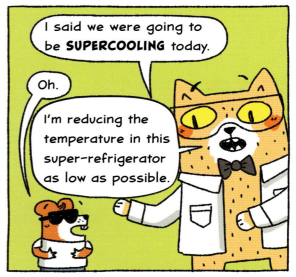

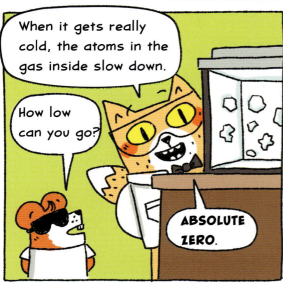

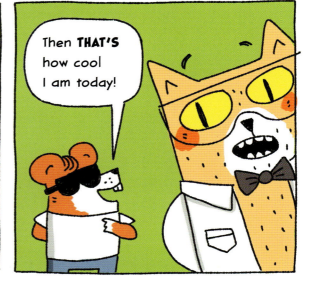

Just as heating a substance makes its atoms gain energy and move faster, cooling slows them down. But there is a limit to how cold you can go—**absolute zero.**

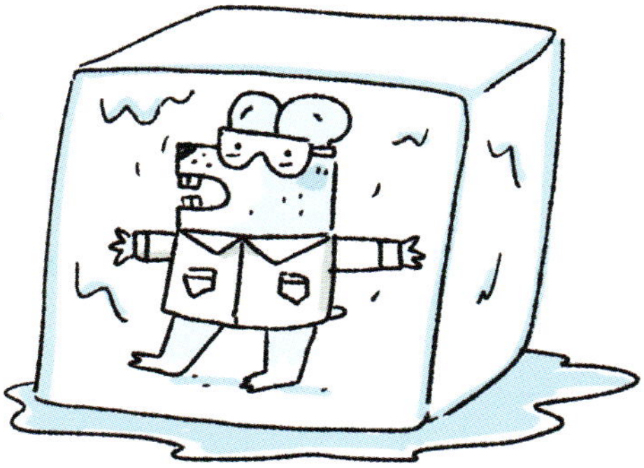

Absolute zero is −273.15 °C (−459.67 °F), a point when moving atoms almost come to a stop. It's even colder than outer space!

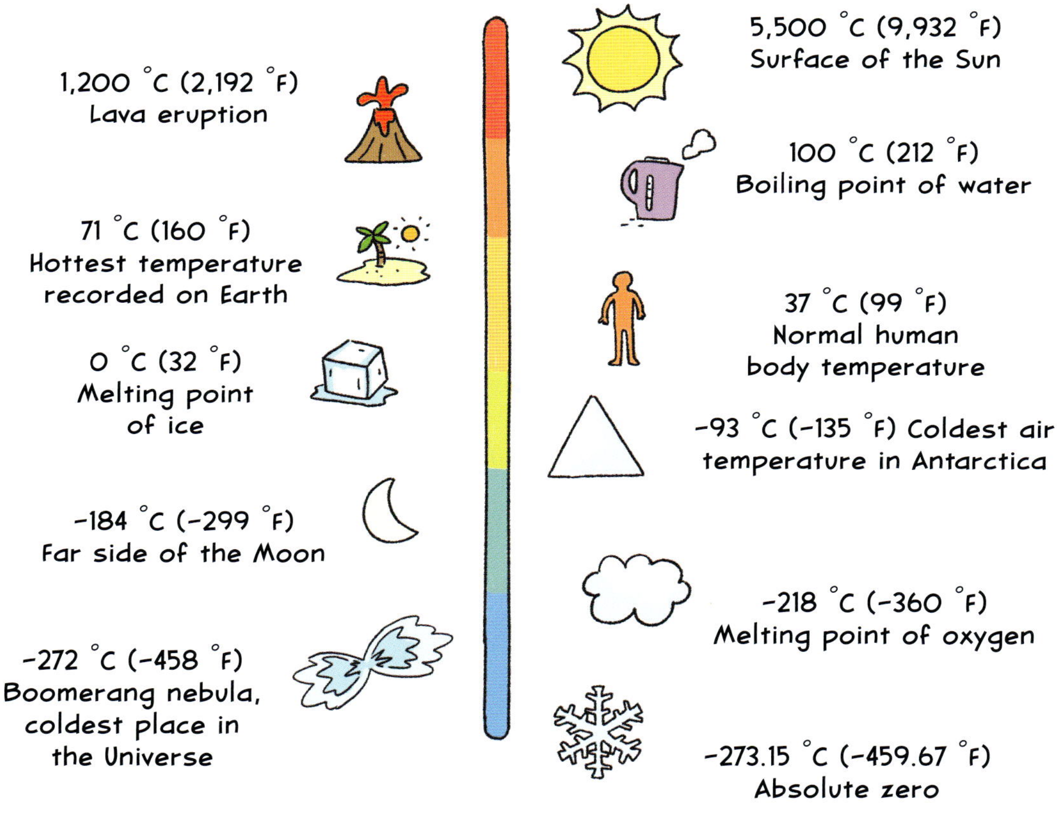

5,500 °C (9,932 °F)
Surface of the Sun
1,200 °C (2,192 °F)
Lava eruption
100 °C (212 °F)
Boiling point of water
71 °C (160 °F)
Hottest temperature recorded on Earth
37 °C (99 °F)
Normal human body temperature
0 °C (32 °F)
Melting point of ice
-93 °C (-135 °F) Coldest air temperature in Antarctica
-184 °C (-299 °F)
Far side of the Moon
-218 °C (-360 °F)
Melting point of oxygen
-272 °C (-458 °F)
Boomerang nebula, coldest place in the Universe
-273.15 °C (-459.67 °F)
Absolute zero

It's not possible to reach absolute zero, since it requires too much energy to remove all the heat from an object. But scientists have managed to reach a half-billionth of a degree above absolute zero by using lasers to slow the atoms in sodium gas.

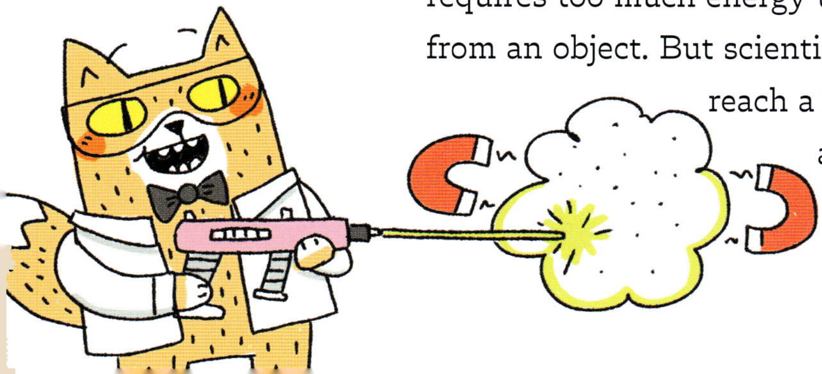

How to Let Off Steam
Cup of tea, Scooter?
I wouldn't say no.
First we need to change the STATE of the water.
What's wrong with it?
Nothing. We just need to increase its TEMPERATURE until it reaches its BOILING POINT.
Every substance has a standard state as a SOLID, LIQUID, or GAS at room temperature.
We can change this by increasing or decreasing TEMPERATURE or PRESSURE.
At room temperature, water is a liquid.
If we reduce the water's temperature to 0 °C (32 °F), the liquid FREEZES.
If we increase the temperature to water's BOILING point, it turns to a gas.
Steam!
Water boils at 100 °C (212 °F).
Then it's ready to POUR.
Correct.

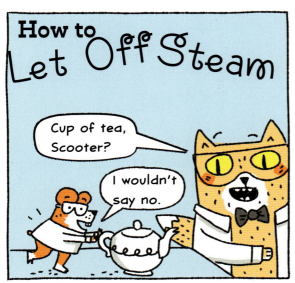

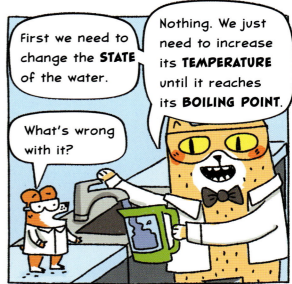

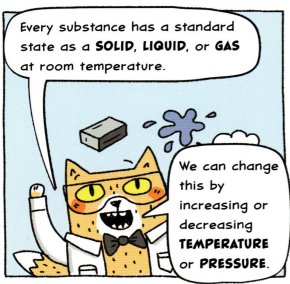

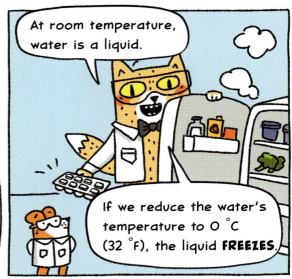

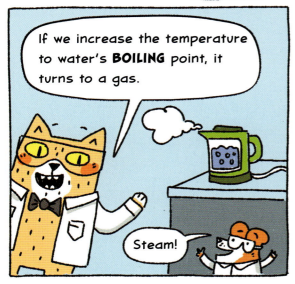

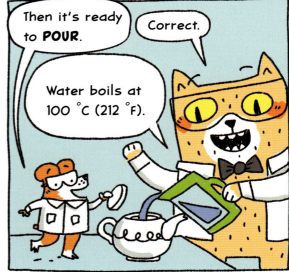

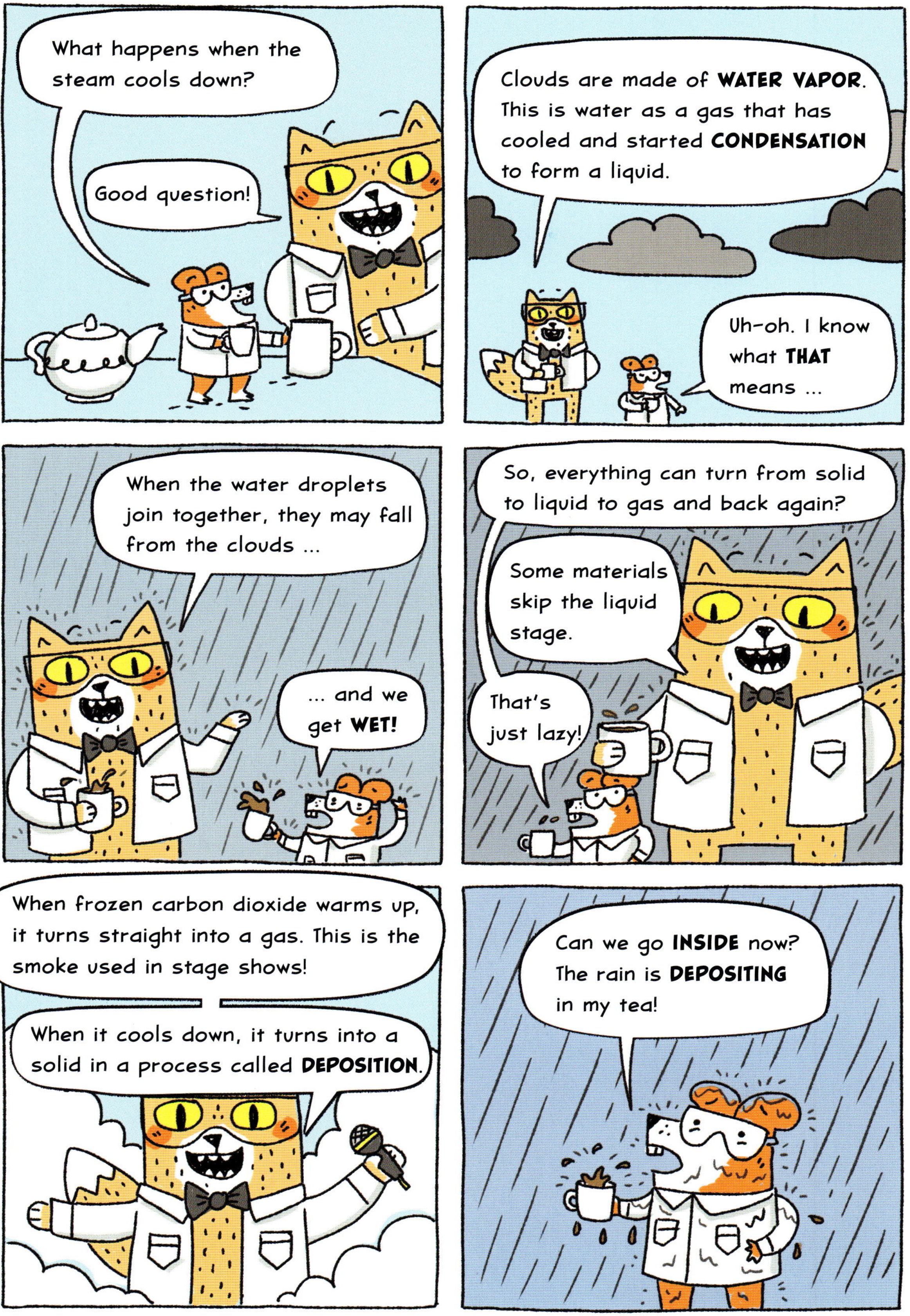
What happens when the steam cools down?
Good question!
Clouds are made of **WATER VAPOR**. This is water as a gas that has cooled and started **CONDENSATION** to form a liquid.
Uh-oh. I know what **THAT** means ...
When the water droplets join together, they may fall from the clouds ...
... and we get **WET!**
So, everything can turn from solid to liquid to gas and back again?
Some materials skip the liquid stage.
That's just lazy!
When frozen carbon dioxide warms up, it turns straight into a gas. This is the smoke used in stage shows!
When it cools down, it turns into a solid in a process called **DEPOSITION**.
Can we go **INSIDE** now? The rain is **DEPOSITING** in my tea!

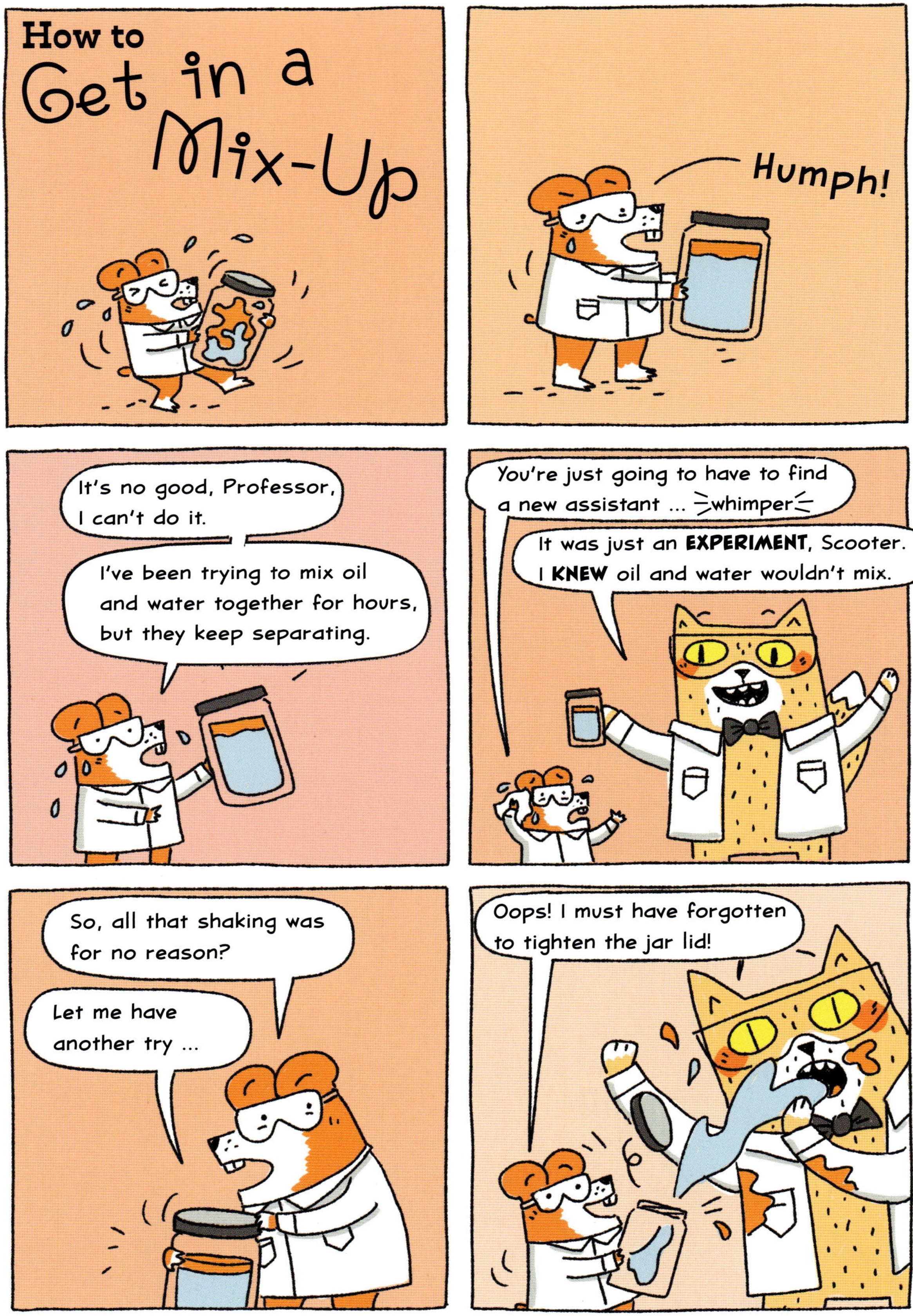
How to
Get in a Mix-Up
Humph!
It's no good, Professor, I can't do it.
I've been trying to mix oil and water together for hours, but they keep separating.
You're just going to have to find a new assistant ... whimper
It was just an **EXPERIMENT**, Scooter. I **KNEW** oil and water wouldn't mix.
So, all that shaking was for no reason?
Let me have another try ...
Oops! I must have forgotten to tighten the jar lid!

Substances made of one type of atom, such as oxygen, calcium, and iron, are called **elements**. Elements can be combined to make a **compound** or a **mixture**.

Compounds are formed when elements mix and go through a **chemical reaction**. Their atoms combine to form a new substance.

Everything in the Universe is an element, compound, or mixture.
Even ME?
I said EVERYTHING so, yes, even YOU.

Water is a compound made from hydrogen and oxygen.

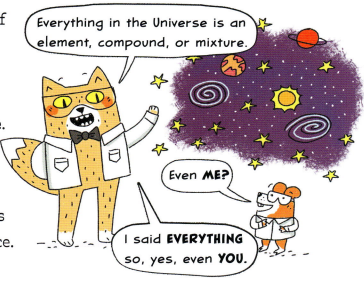

If the elements don't chemically react with each other and their atoms don't bond, they form a **mixture**.

There are three main types of mixtures—solutions, colloids, and suspensions.

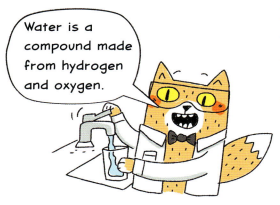

Solutions occur when one substance (a **solute**) dissolves into another (a **solvent**). Salt dissolving in water creates a solution.

SOLUTION
COLLOID
SUSPENSION
Microscopic particles
Dust-sized particles

Colloids are mixtures made up of particles too small to see that are evenly spread out. Milk is a colloid.

Suspensions contain visible particles that can settle in their container.

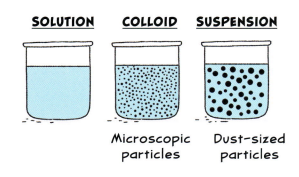

Not all substances mix well. Some liquids have molecules that repel each other. These are called **immiscible liquids.** Oil and water are one example.

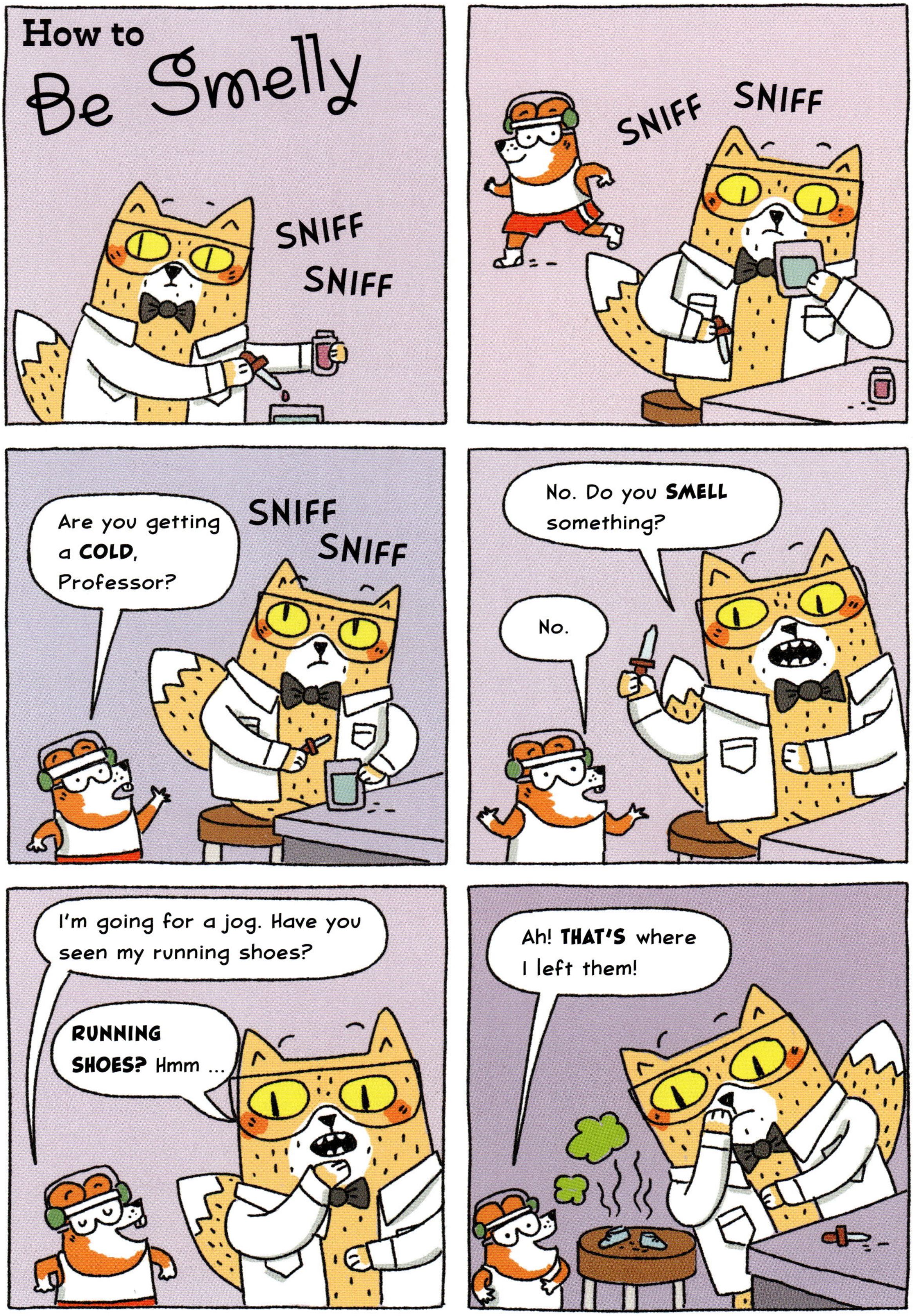
How to Be Smelly
SNIFF SNIFF
SNIFF SNIFF
Are you getting a COLD, Professor?
SNIFF SNIFF
No. Do you SMELL something?
No.
I'm going for a jog. Have you seen my running shoes?
RUNNING SHOES? Hmm ...
Ah! THAT'S where I left them!

The tiny particles that make up gases and liquids move around in a random way to fill their container.

If a gas or liquid of one substance is added to another, the particles of the new substance spread out through the first substance, moving from areas of high **concentration** to areas of low concentration.

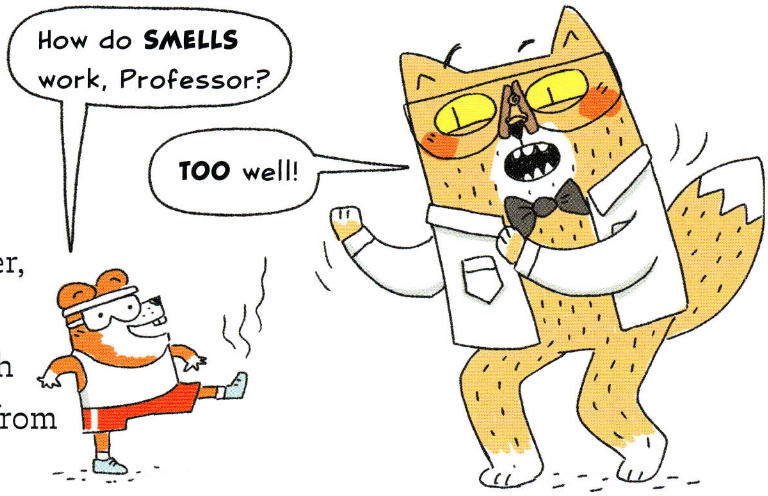
How do SMELLS work, Professor?
TOO well!

This process is called **diffusion**.

Diffusion can be seen by adding a dye to a beaker of water. When the colored drops enter the water, they spread out.

The tiny particles in the dye bump into the tiny particles in the water until they are evenly mixed and the water appears a new, even color.

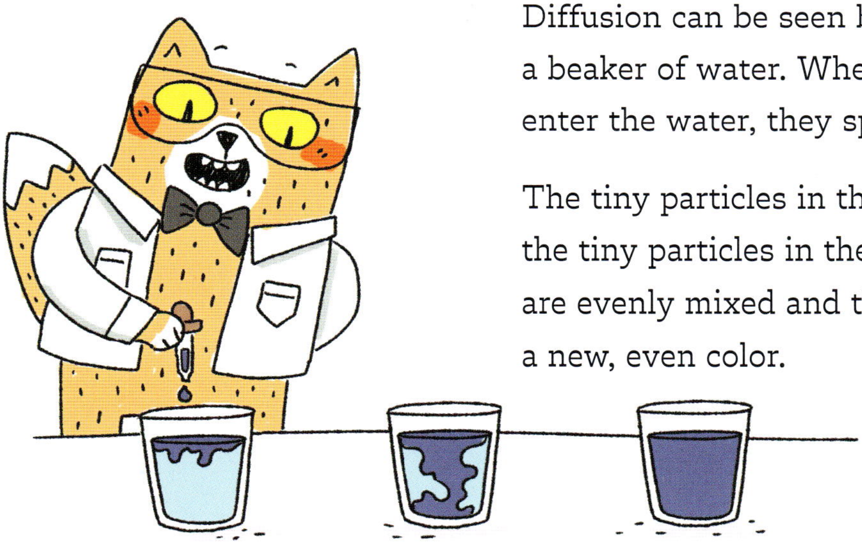

The mixing process can be speeded up by shaking or heating the water.

The same happens when gases are mixed. Perfumes and smells spread in the same way, with the smelly particles bouncing into air particles. When these reach our nose, we can detect them.

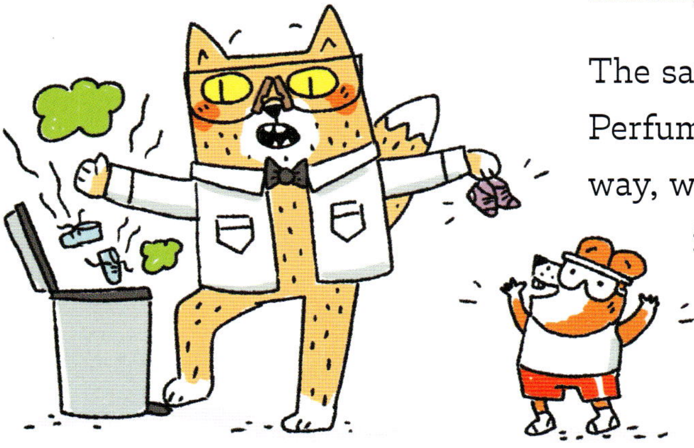

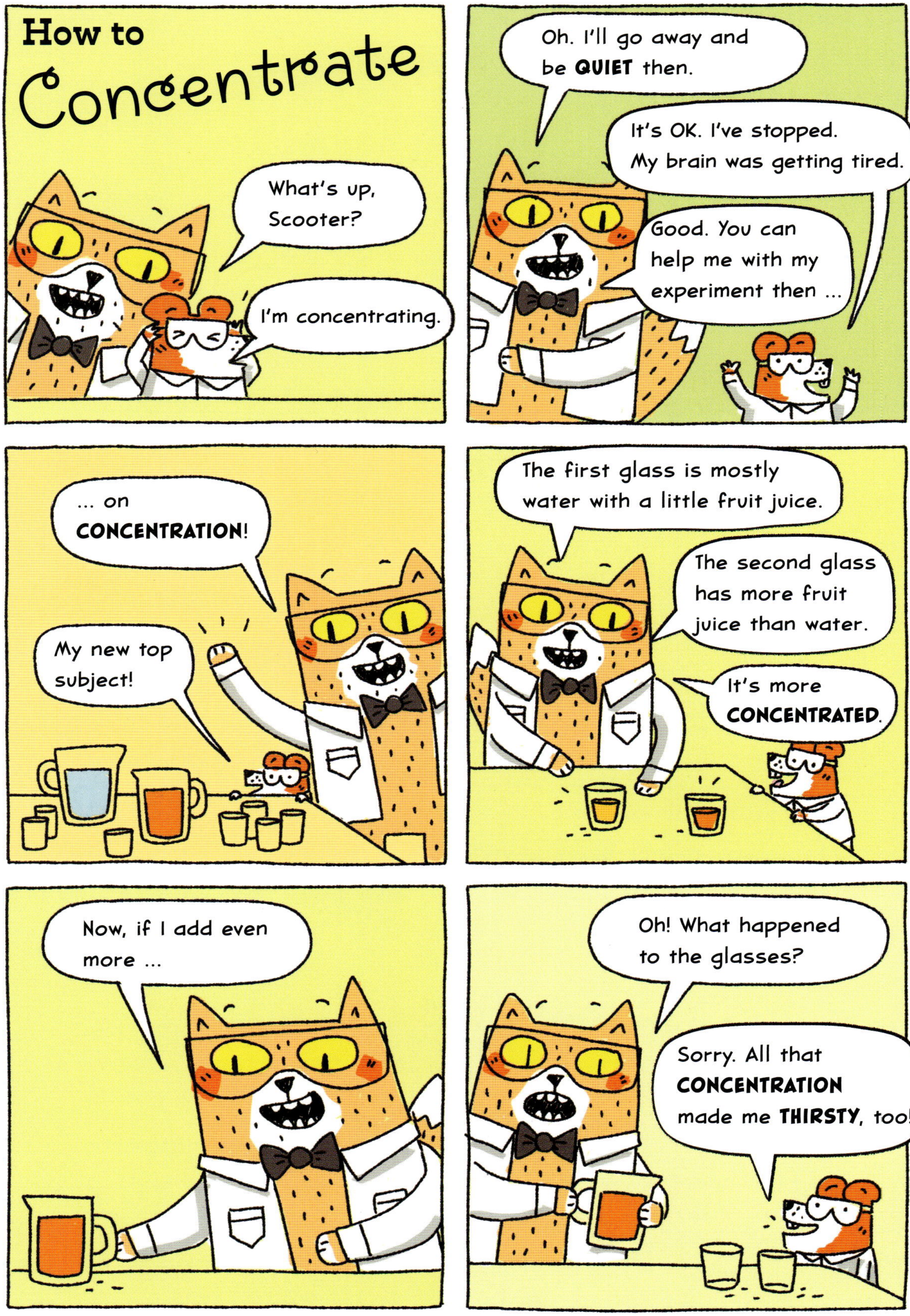
How to Concentrate
What's up, Scooter?
I'm concentrating.
Oh. I'll go away and be QUIET then.
It's OK. I've stopped. My brain was getting tired.
Good. You can help me with my experiment then ...
... on CONCENTRATION!
My new top subject!
The first glass is mostly water with a little fruit juice.
The second glass has more fruit juice than water.
It's more CONCENTRATED.
Now, if I add even more ...
Oh! What happened to the glasses?
Sorry. All that CONCENTRATION made me THIRSTY, too!

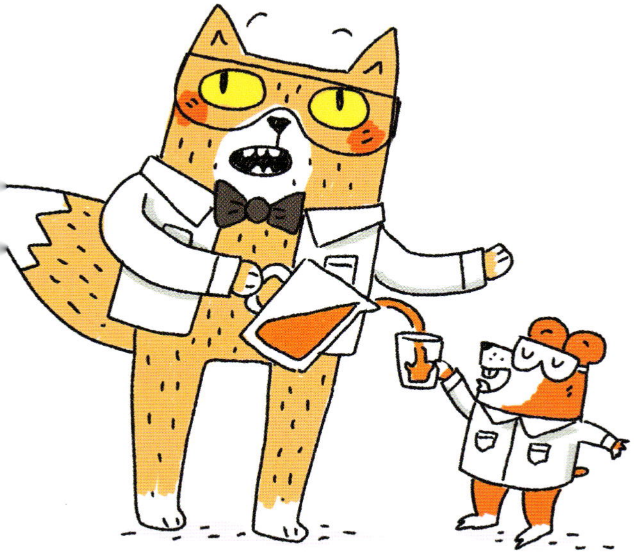

Concentration is a measure of how much of a substance is in an amount of a mixture.

To make a **solution**, one substance (the **solute**) is added to another substance (the **solvent**). The more solute in a volume of a solution, the greater its concentration.

With a high concentration, the particles for each substance will bump into each other more often. If the substances being mixed can undergo a chemical reaction, a high concentration will make it happen faster.

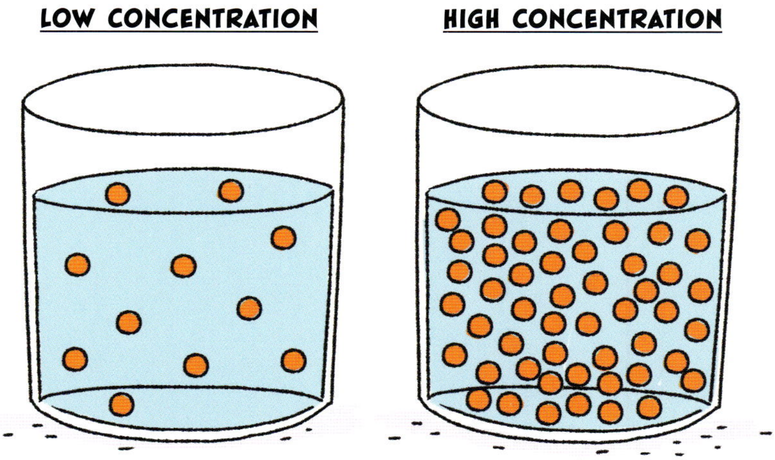
LOW CONCENTRATION
HIGH CONCENTRATION

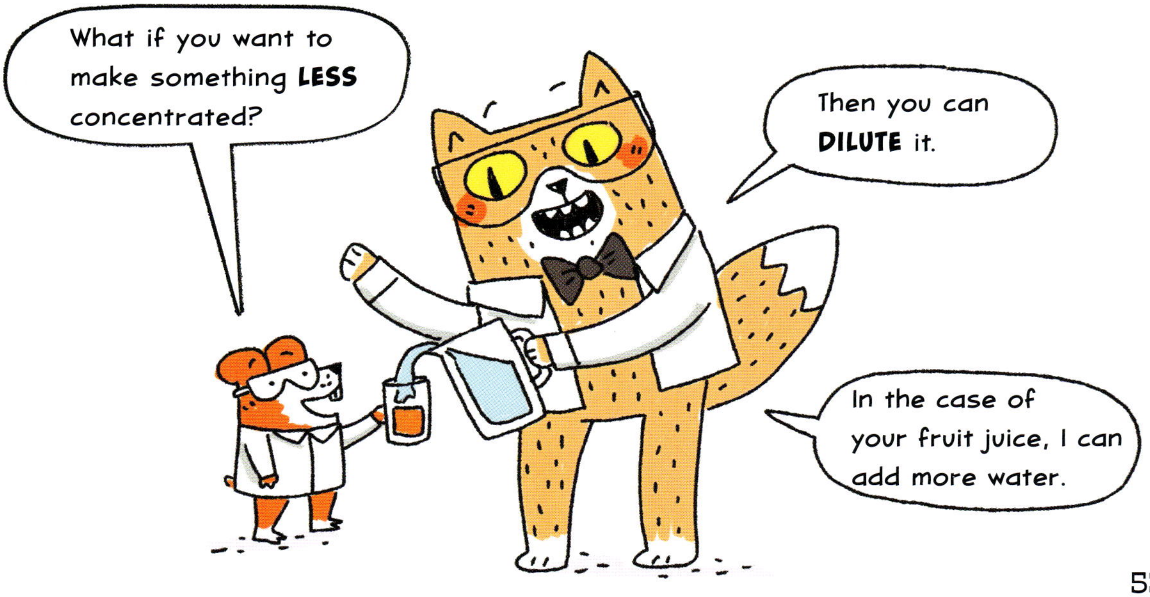
What if you want to make something LESS concentrated?
Then you can DILUTE it.
In the case of your fruit juice, I can add more water.

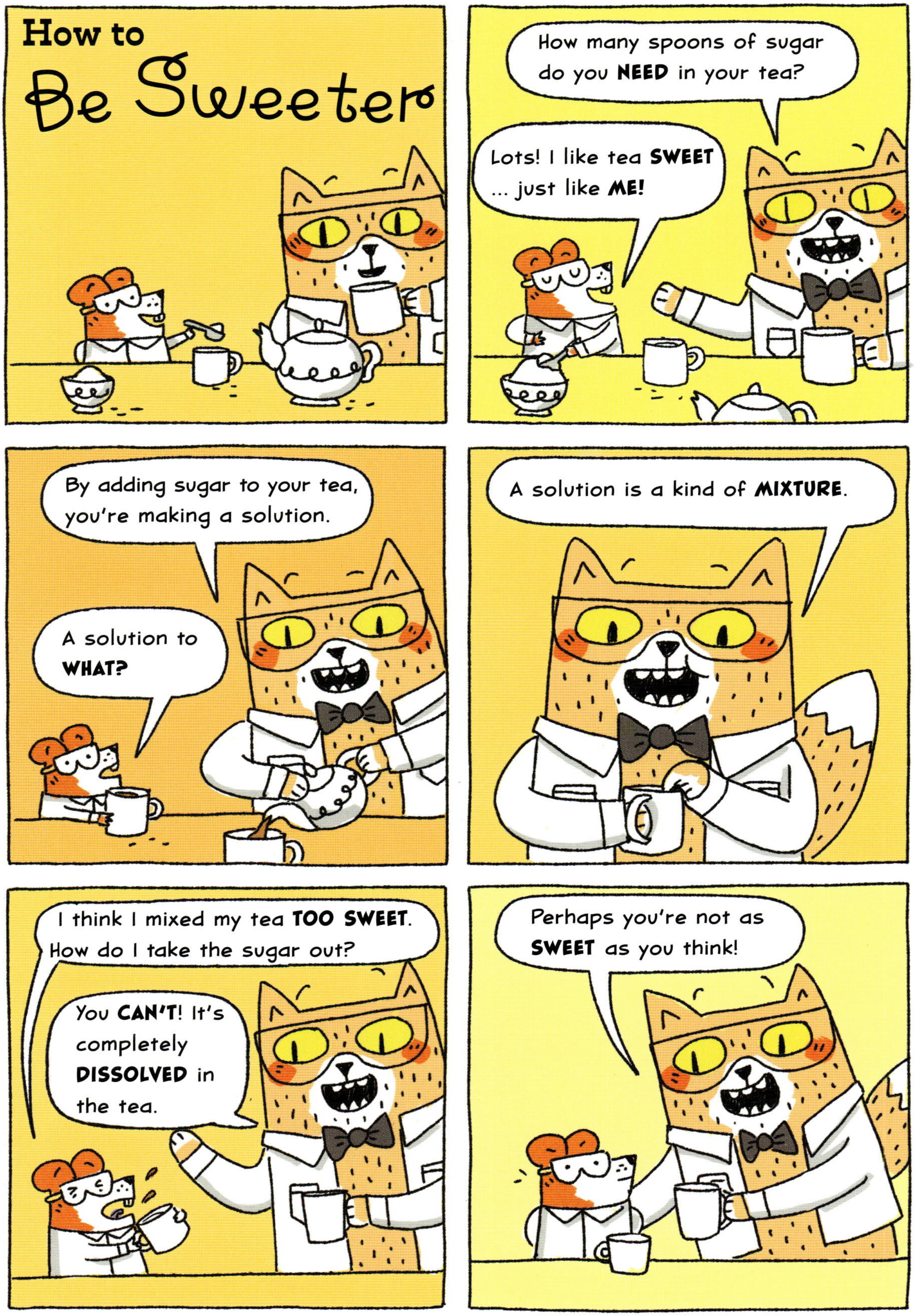
How to
Be Sweeter
How many spoons of sugar do you NEED in your tea?
Lots! I like tea SWEET ... just like ME!
By adding sugar to your tea, you're making a solution.
A solution to WHAT?
A solution is a kind of MIXTURE.
I think I mixed my tea TOO SWEET. How do I take the sugar out?
You CAN'T! It's completely DISSOLVED in the tea.
Perhaps you're not as SWEET as you think!

When sugar is added to water (or tea) it **dissolves** to form a **solution.**

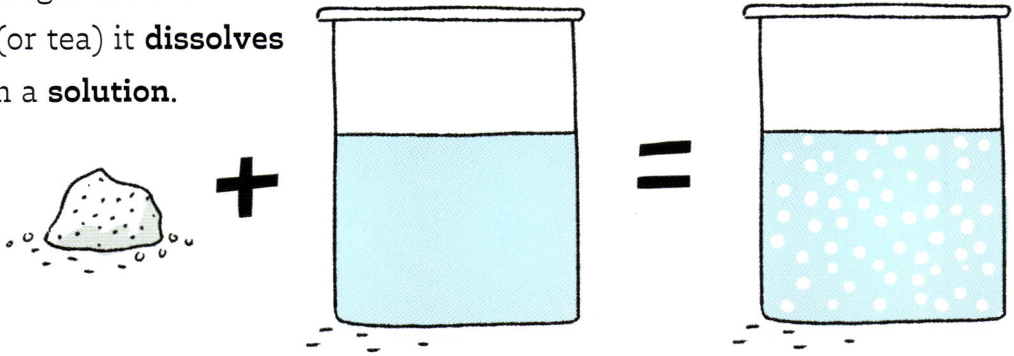

In this case, sugar is the **solute**, and water is the **solvent.**

The tiny sugar particles or **molecules** mix with the water molecules, but they do not **react** with each other. They are chemically unchanged by the process.

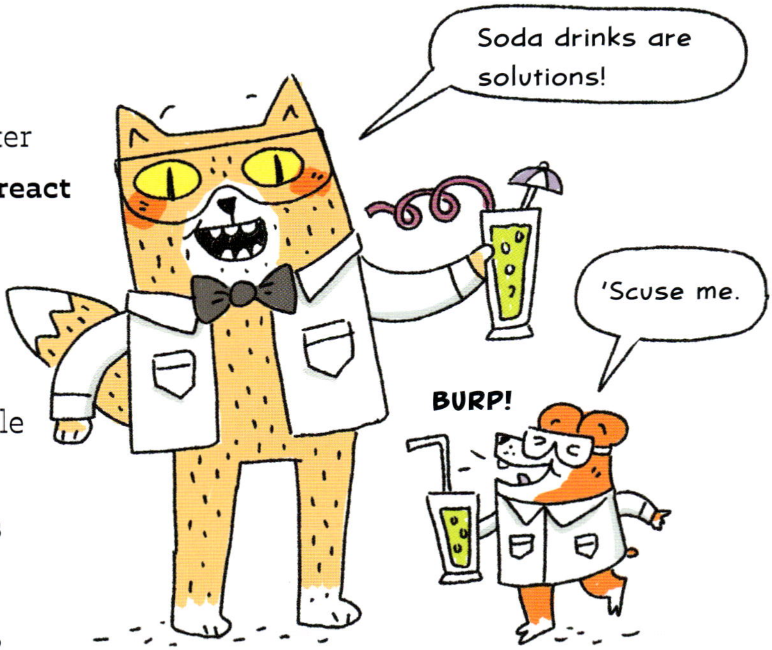
Soda drinks are solutions!
'Scuse me.
BURP!

Sugar in water is an example of a **solid in liquid**. Other solutions include **gas in gas** (such as air), **gas in liquid** (such as carbonated water), and even **solid in solid.**

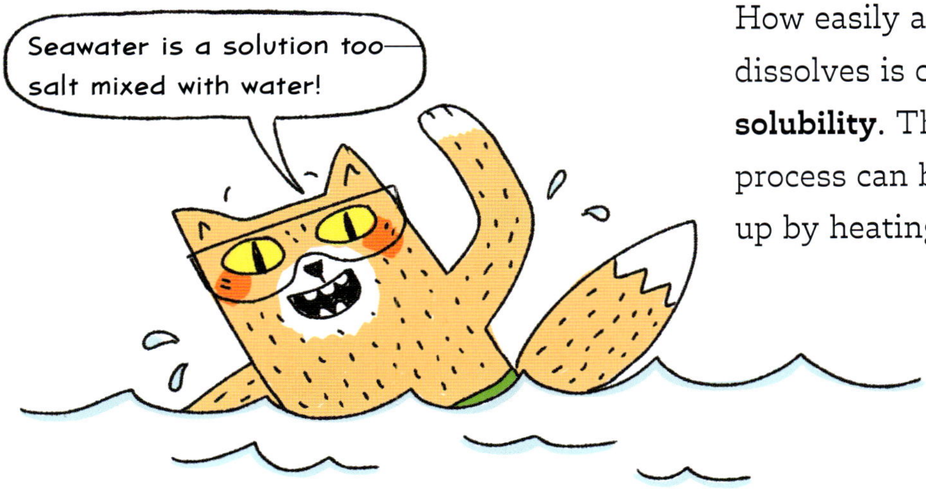
Seawater is a solution too—
salt mixed with water!

How easily a substance dissolves is called its **solubility**. The dissolving process can be speeded up by heating the liquid.

How to Split Up

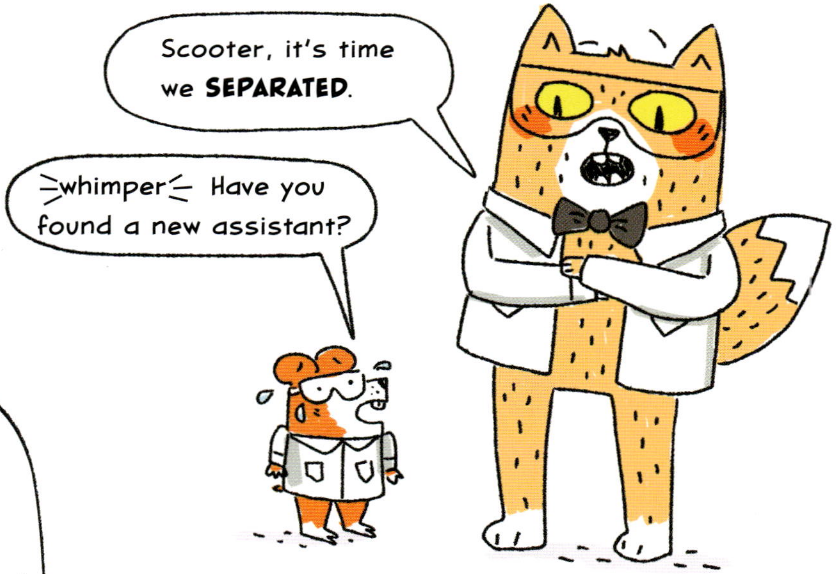

Scooter, it's time we **SEPARATED**.
⋛whimper⋚ Have you found a new assistant?

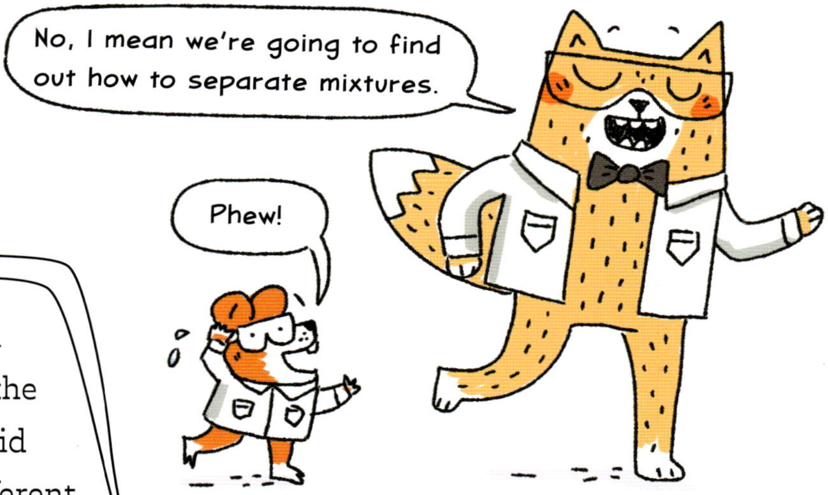

No, I mean we're going to find out how to separate mixtures.
Phew!

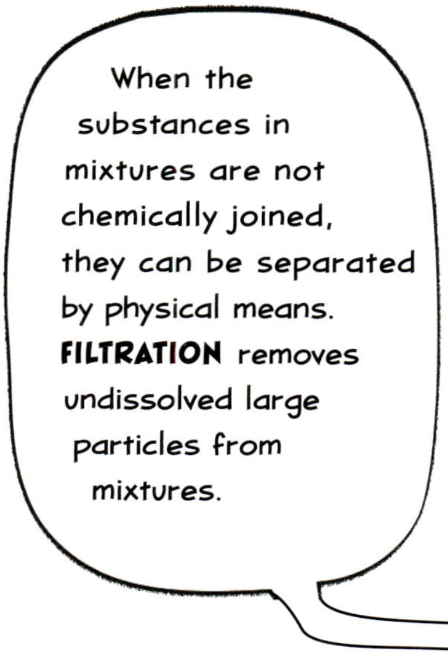

When the substances in mixtures are not chemically joined, they can be separated by physical means. **FILTRATION** removes undissolved large particles from mixtures.

A **filter** is a material with tiny pores that lets only the smallest particles of a solid through. You can use different filters to trap different-sized particles.

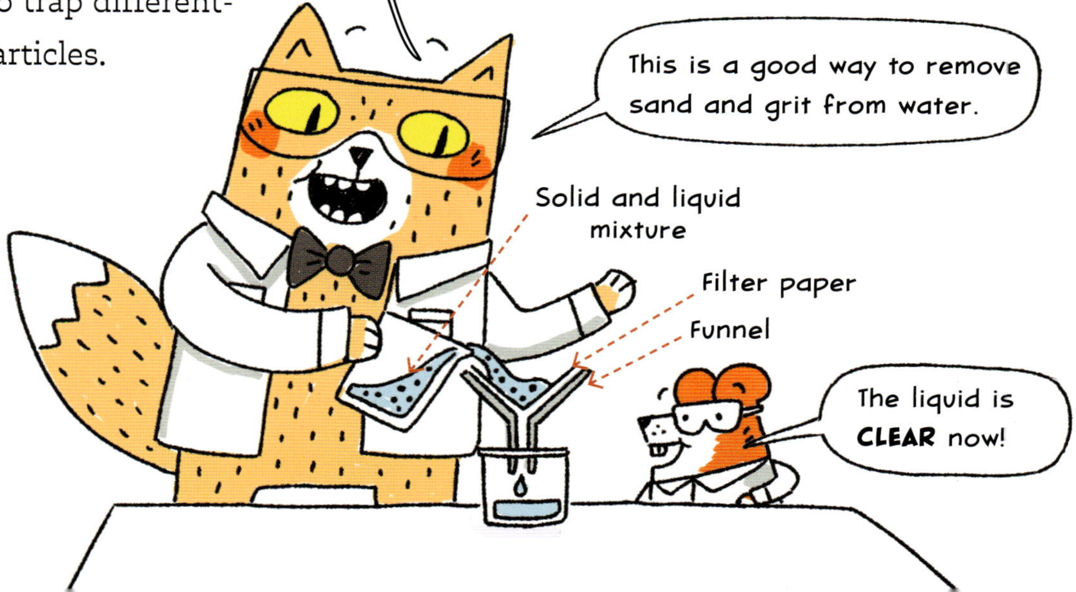

This is a good way to remove sand and grit from water.
Solid and liquid mixture
Filter paper
Funnel
The liquid is **CLEAR** now!

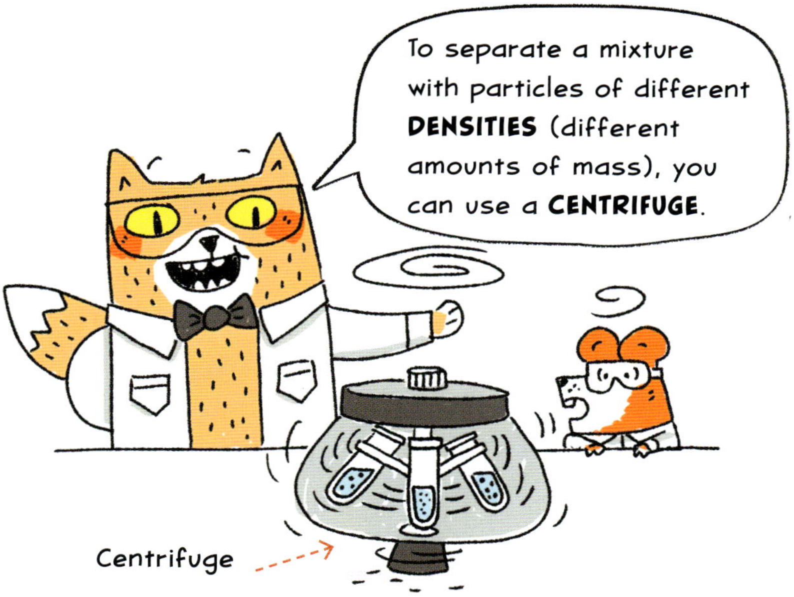
To separate a mixture with particles of different **DENSITIES** (different amounts of mass), you can use a **CENTRIFUGE**.
Centrifuge

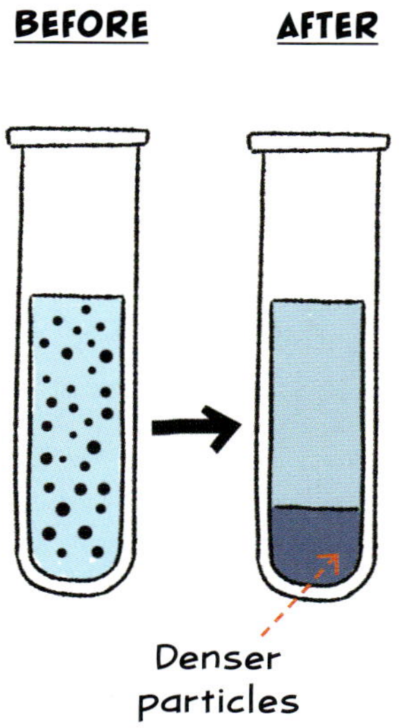
BEFORE
AFTER
Denser particles

A centrifuge is a machine that spins test tubes containing a liquid mixture. **Centrifugal force** pushes undissolved denser particles to the bottom of the test tube.

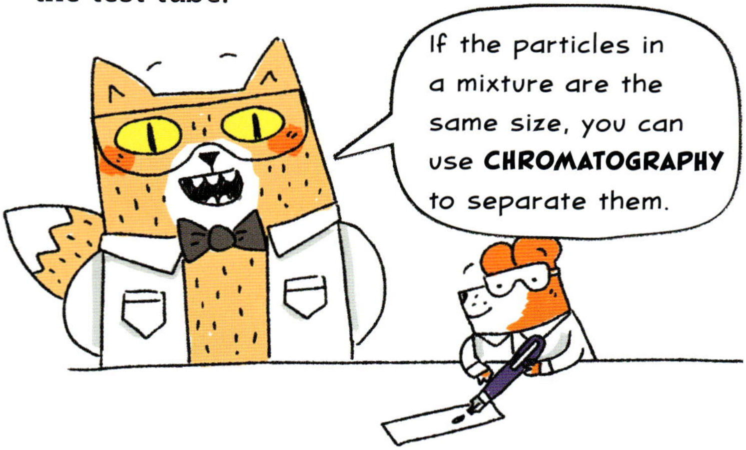
If the particles in a mixture are the same size, you can use **CHROMATOGRAPHY** to separate them.

For a simple **paper chromatography** test, add drops of black ink to a strip of **filter paper**.

Suspend the paper over a beaker of water, just dipping it in below the ink.

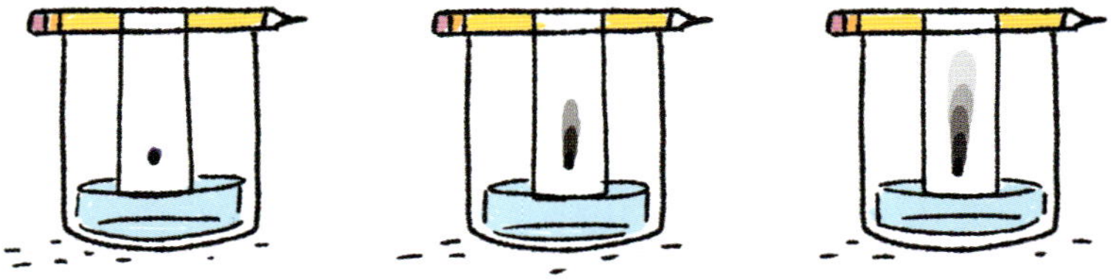

As the water soaks into the paper, it passes the ink, and the different dyes in the black ink move up the paper at different speeds. The result is a pattern of dyes called a **chromatogram**.

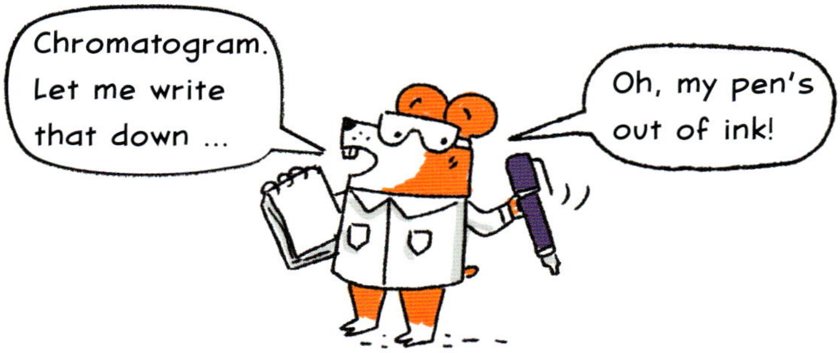
Chromatogram. Let me write that down ...
Oh, my pen's out of ink!

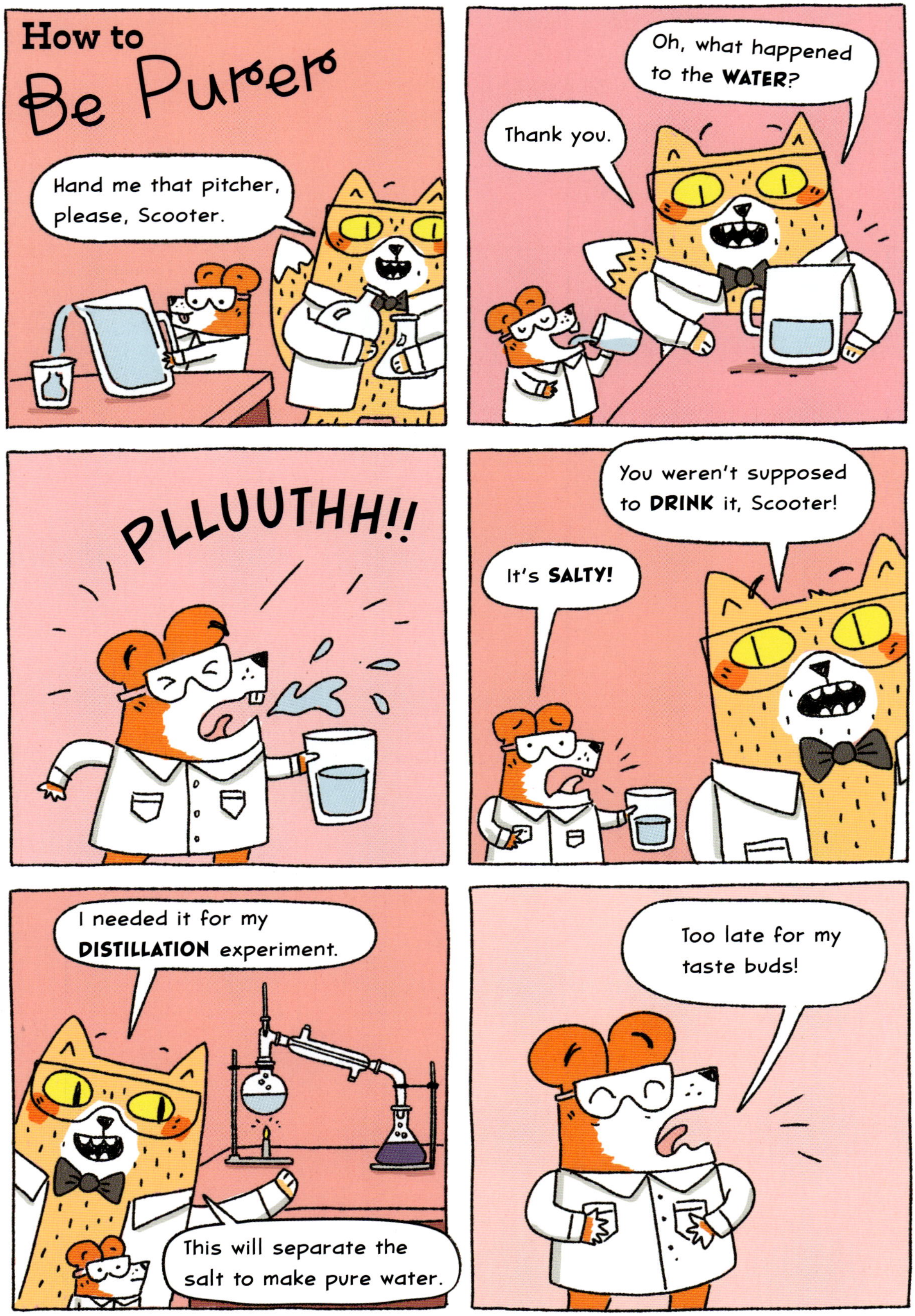

How to Be Purer
Hand me that pitcher, please, Scooter.
Oh, what happened to the WATER?
Thank you.
PLLUUTHH!!
You weren't supposed to DRINK it, Scooter!
It's SALTY!
I needed it for my DISTILLATION experiment.
This will separate the salt to make pure water.
Too late for my taste buds!

Liquid mixtures made up of substances with different **boiling points** can be separated using **distillation**.

First, the mixture is heated up using the setup below.

Thermometer
The thermometer measures the **BOILING POINT** of each liquid.
Cold water out
Condenser
This is **PURE** chemistry!
Cold water in
Liquid evaporates
Distilling flask
Mixture of liquids
Heat
Flask
Pure liquid

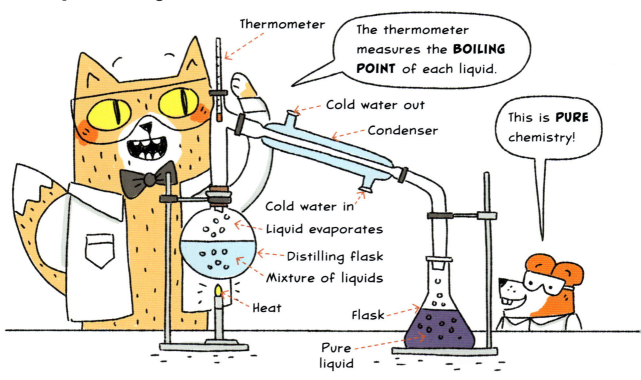

The liquid with the lowest boiling point **evaporates** (changes from a liquid to a gas or **vapor**) first.

The vapor rises and is collected in a **condenser.** This is a glass tube surrounded by another tube filled with cold water. The water cools the vapor, turning it back into a liquid.

This **pure liquid** is then collected in a flask.

Distillation can be used to remove salt from water. It can be used to separate a mixture of more than one liquid, with each turning to vapor at different temperatures.

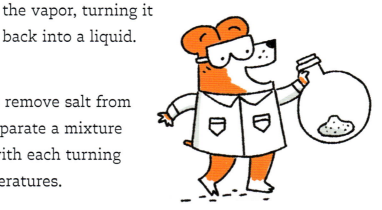

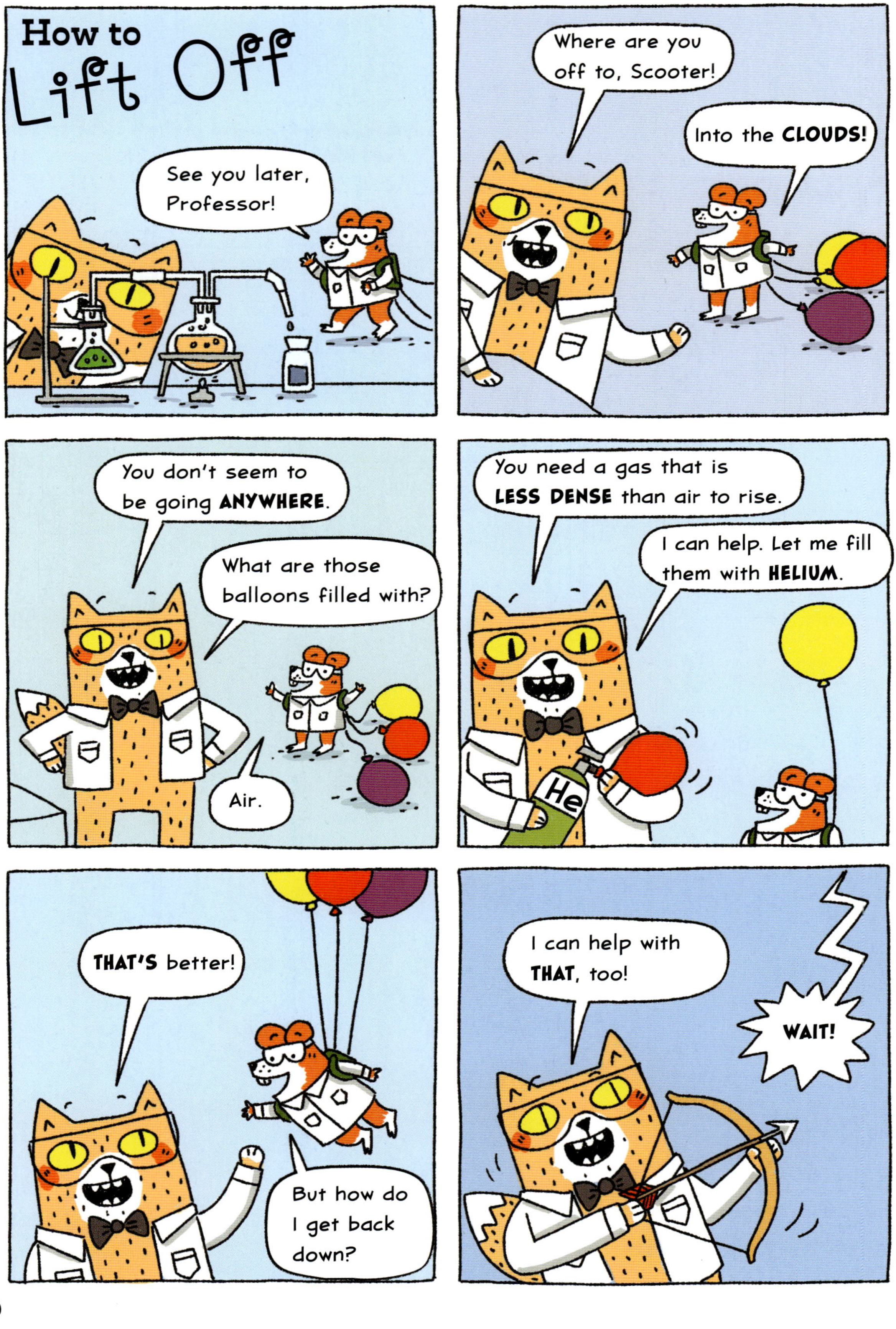

How to
Lift Off
See you later, Professor!
Where are you off to, Scooter!
Into the CLOUDS!
You don't seem to be going ANYWHERE.
What are those balloons filled with?
Air.
You need a gas that is LESS DENSE than air to rise.
I can help. Let me fill them with HELIUM.
He
THAT'S better!
But how do I get back down?
I can help with THAT, too!
WAIT!

Getting a Reaction

(Reactions, Tests, Energy Changes)

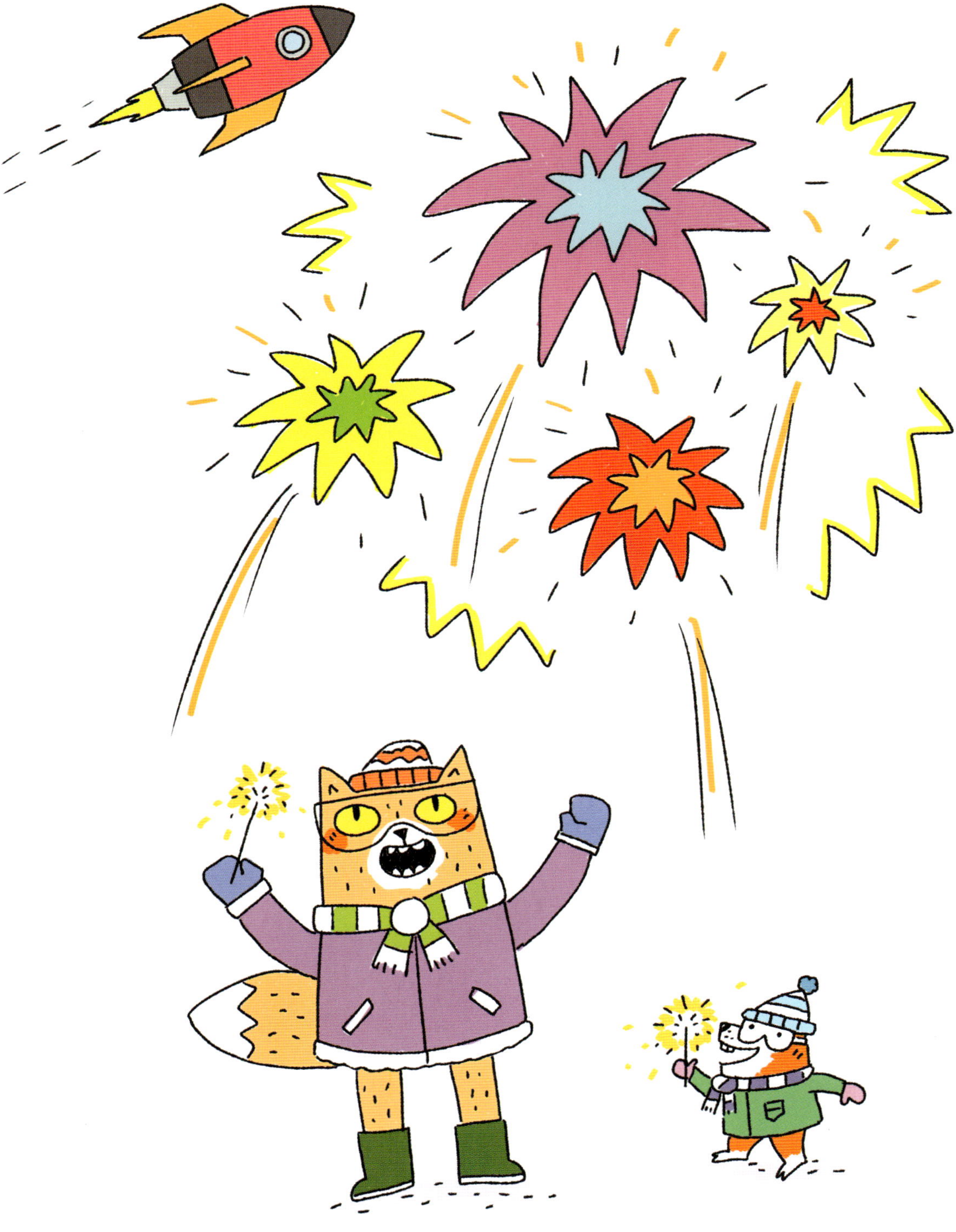

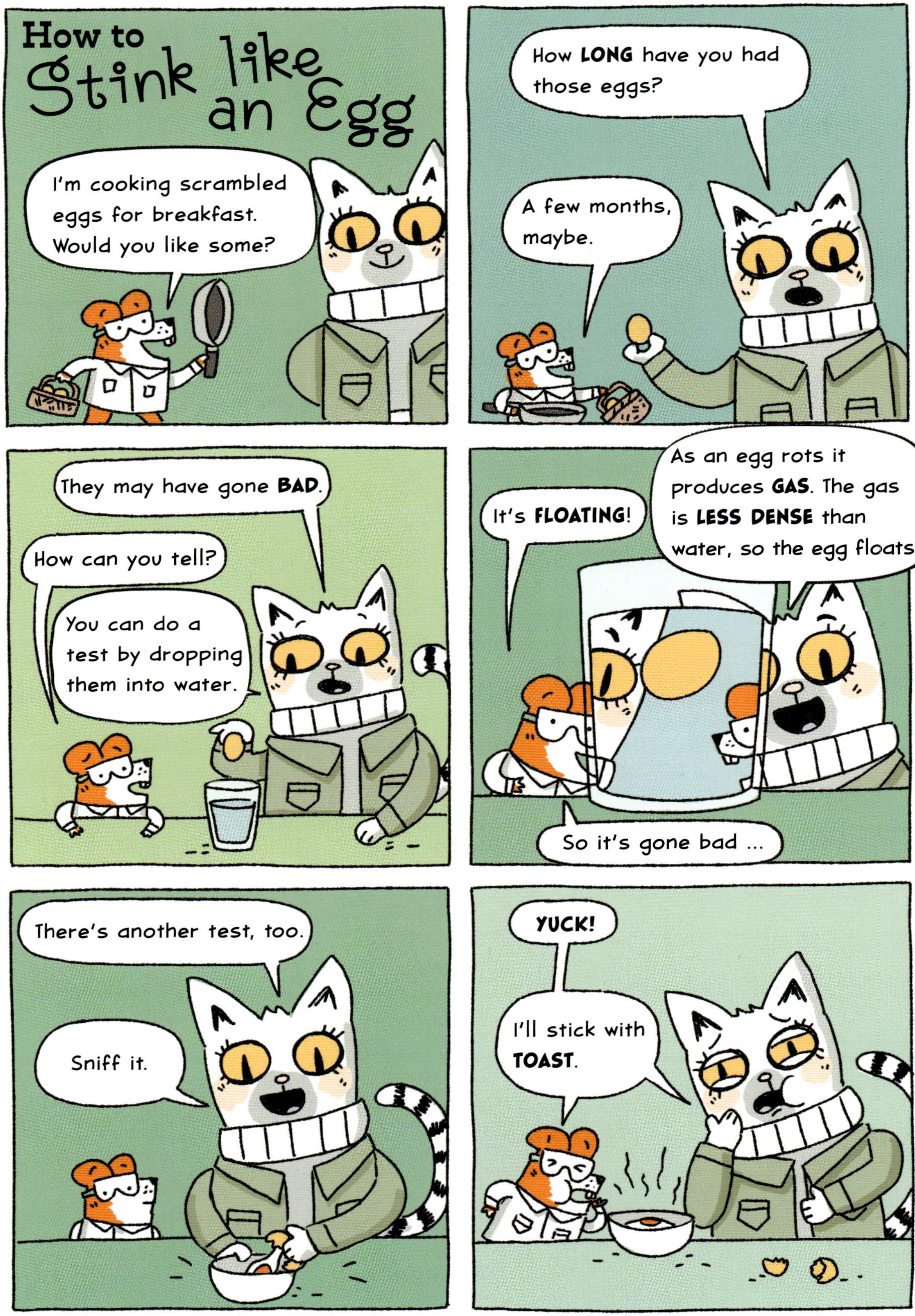
How to Stink like an Egg
I'm cooking scrambled eggs for breakfast. Would you like some?
How LONG have you had those eggs?
A few months, maybe.
They may have gone BAD.
How can you tell?
You can do a test by dropping them into water.
It's FLOATING!
As an egg rots it produces GAS. The gas is LESS DENSE than water, so the egg floats.
So it's gone bad ...
There's another test, too.
Sniff it.
YUCK!
I'll stick with TOAST.

Sulfur is a chemical found in many horrid smells, such as rotten eggs, bad breath, and even skunk spray.

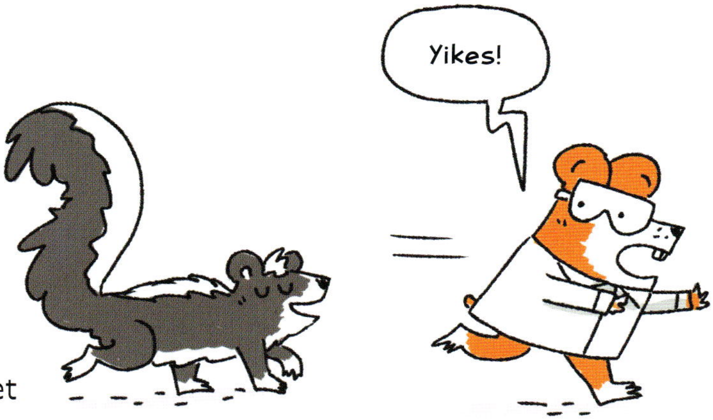
Yikes!

This soft, nonmetal element is yellow in color and found in volcanic rock. Sulfur is easily set alight and burns with a blue flame.

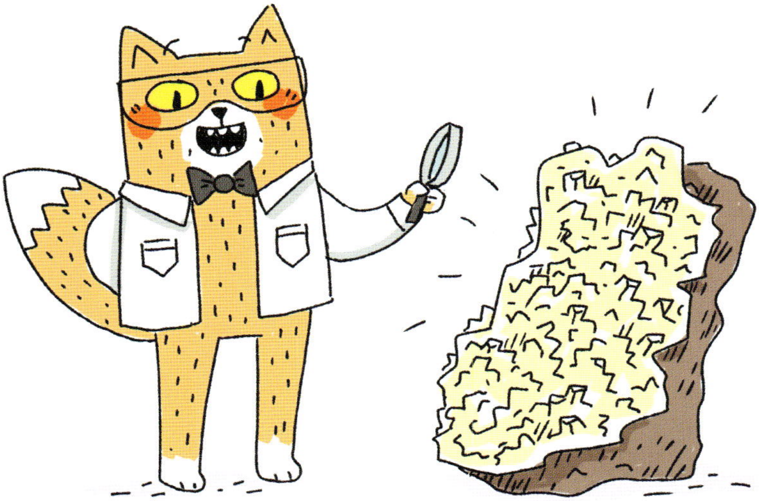

Sulfur reacts easily with hydrogen to produce the gas **hydrogen sulfide**. This is the smelly gas produced by rotten eggs. Beware, it can be toxic even in small doses!

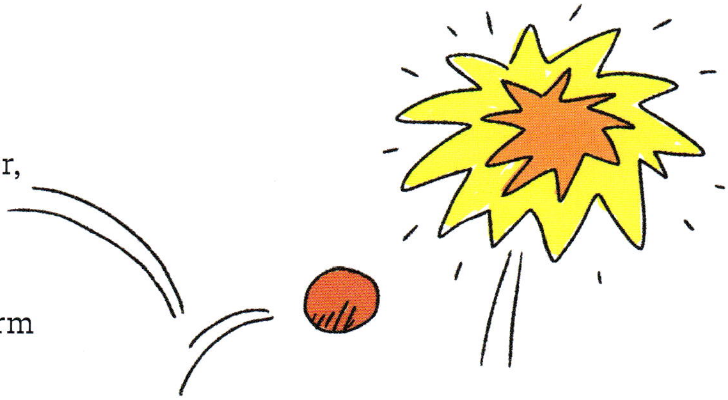

Sulfur is used to make **sulfuric acid** for car batteries. It is also used in making concrete, rubber, and fireworks. Sulfur plays an important role in the human body, too, helping us form fats, build strong bones, and grow nails and hair.

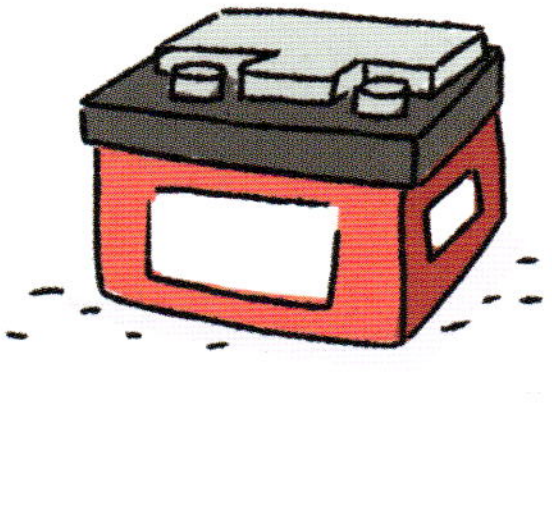

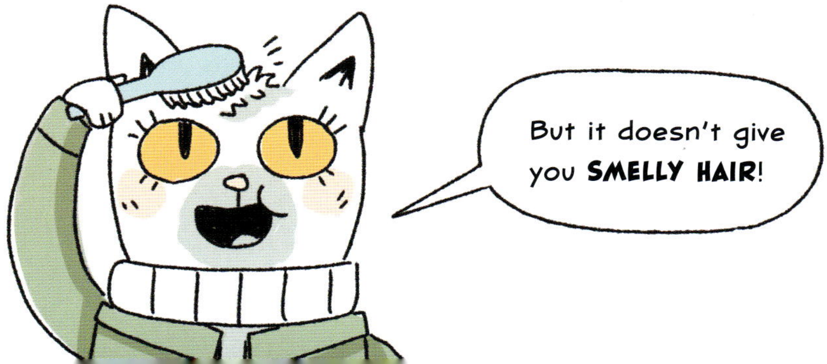
But it doesn't give you **SMELLY HAIR**!

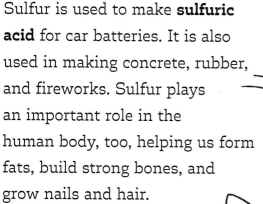

How to Be Unstable

Why are we **DRESSING UP**, Professor?
These suits are to protect us while we study a **RADIOACTIVE ELEMENT**.
It's not **STABLE**.
Correct, Scooter!
Radioactive elements are **UNSTABLE**. They produce **RADIATION**.
It's not **STABLE**.
Indeed.
This radioactive element is safely stored in a lead-lined container.
It's not **STABLE**.
Yes, I heard you.
OOF!
WHUMP
I tried to tell you—the **STOOL'S** not **STABLE**!

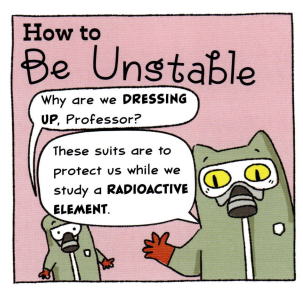

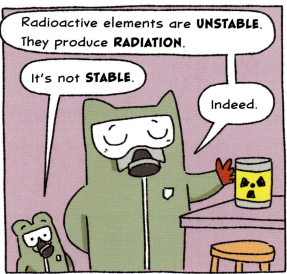

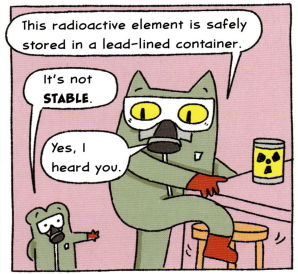

Most atoms are **stable** and do not change over time. **Radioactive** elements, however, have **unstable nuclei** that release energy called **radiation** until they change into a new stable form. This process, called **decay**, can take seconds or even millions of years.

Radioactive elements include **uranium**, **radium**, and **polonium**. The radiation they give off is in the form of **alpha particles**, **beta particles**, and **gamma rays**.

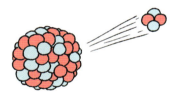

Alpha particles are two protons and two neutrons.

Beta particles are freed electrons.

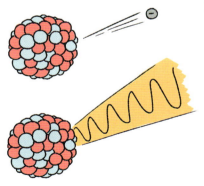

Gamma rays are dangerous high-energy waves.

Radioactive particles and waves can knock electrons from other atoms, including those in your body, damaging your living cells. So, radioactive materials carry a warning sign.

65

All Change!

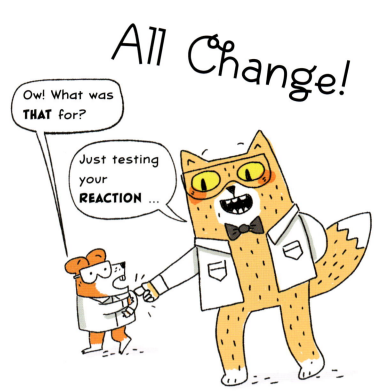

Ow! What was THAT for?
Just testing your REACTION ...

Chemical reactions are processes that change substances. The reactions happen at the atomic level with atoms rearranged, bonds broken, and new bonds made.

Chemicals that react together are called **reactants.**

The new substance they make is called the **product.**

REACTANTS
PRODUCT

Chemical reactions don't just happen in the lab. Batteries work using a chemical reaction. Metal turning rusty and leaves changing color with the seasons are also the result of chemical reactions.

This process also gives you **energy** to power your muscles and brain.

Chemical reactions even happen in your BODY!
No, thanks.
It's perfectly NORMAL, Scooter. When you breath in air, OXYGEN reacts with sugars in your body to produce CARBON DIOXIDE and WATER VAPOR.

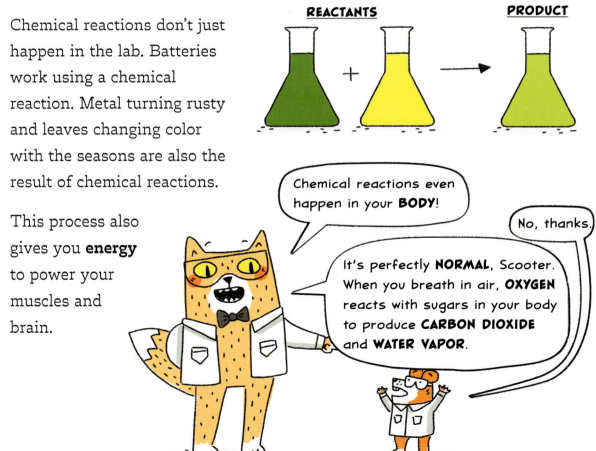

Chemical reactions can take in or give off energy such as light or heat. Some reactions happen quickly, like explosions ...

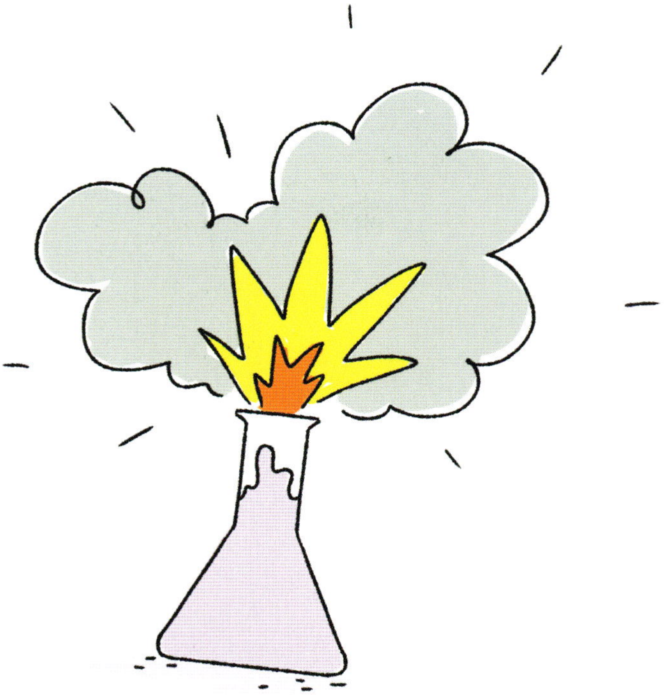

Some take a long time. Reaction speeds can be increased by adding energy in the form of heat or electricity, or by increasing the **concentration** of a reactant.

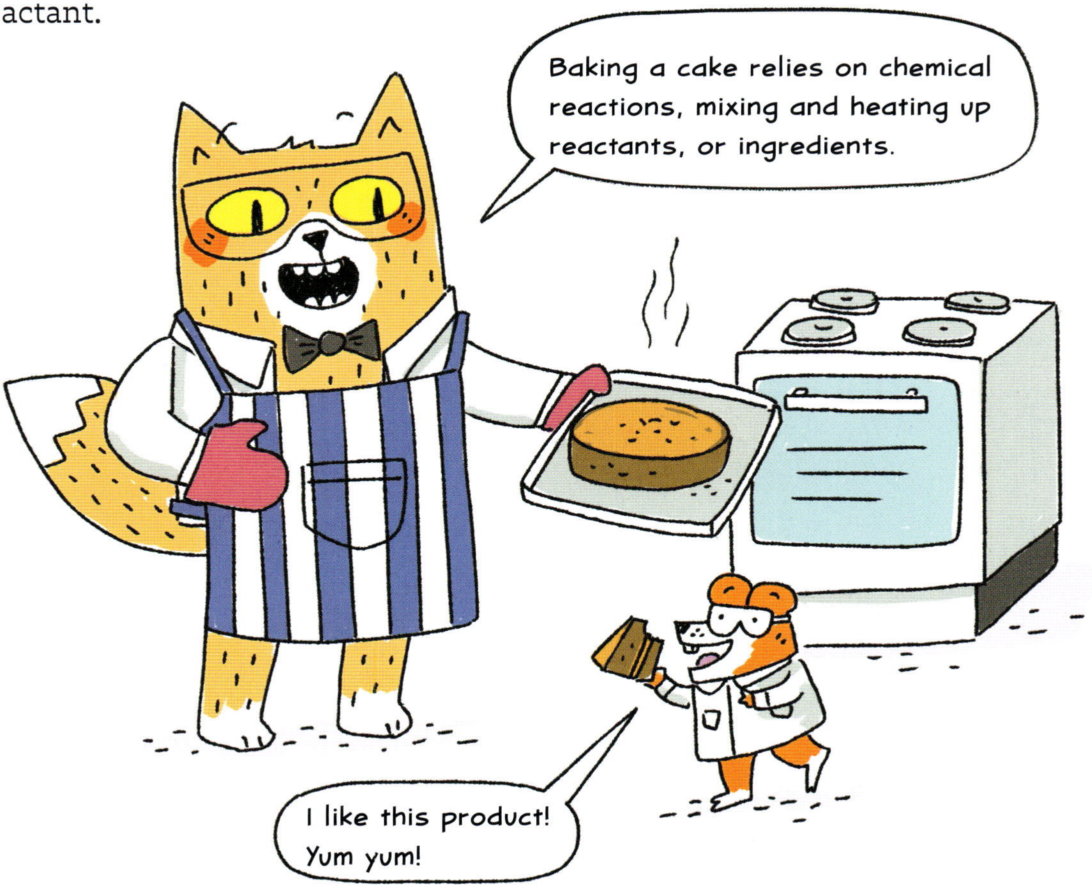
Baking a cake relies on chemical reactions, mixing and heating up reactants, or ingredients.
I like this product! Yum yum!

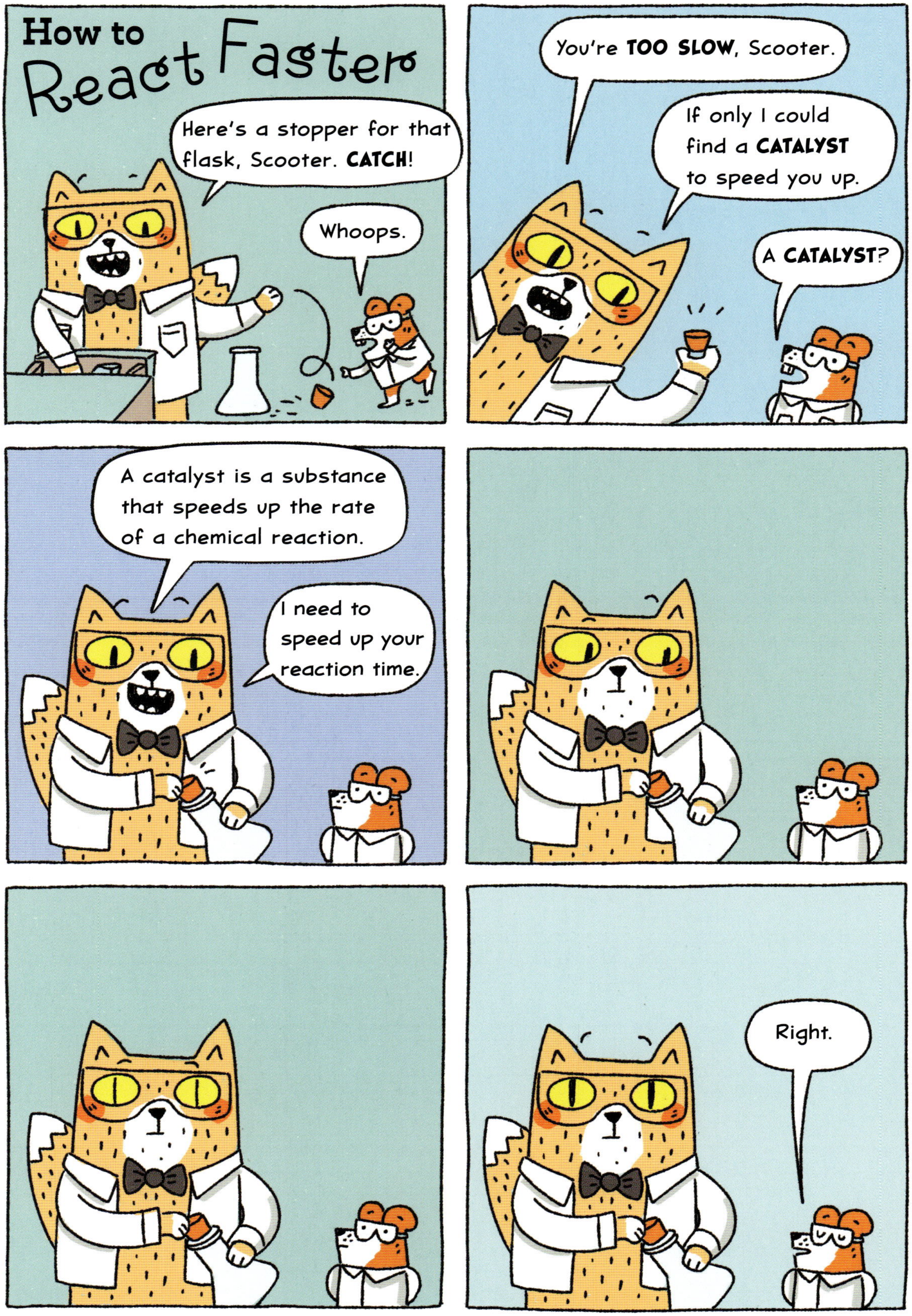
How to React Faster
Here's a stopper for that flask, Scooter. CATCH!
Whoops.
You're TOO SLOW, Scooter.
If only I could find a CATALYST to speed you up.
A CATALYST?
A catalyst is a substance that speeds up the rate of a chemical reaction.
I need to speed up your reaction time.
Right.

Chemical reactions can be sped up by adding a **catalyst**.

The energy needed for a chemical reaction to occur is called the **activation energy**. A catalyst lowers the amount needed for **reactants** to start reacting.

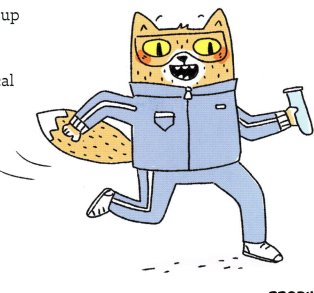

Catalysts are not changed or used up during the process. They can even be collected and used again.

Iron is used as a catalyst to help hydrogen and nitrogen react to form ammonia, which is used in crop fertilizers.

REACTANTS
PRODUCT
CATALYST

Chomp chomp!

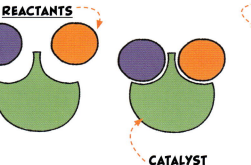

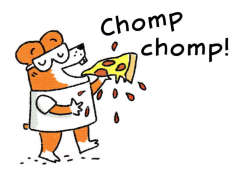

Biological catalysts are called **enzymes**. Enzymes are found in saliva and help your body digest food.

Enzymes are also used in detergents to help remove greasy stains in clothes.

Chemical reactions can be slowed down or stopped by adding an **inhibitor**. Inhibitors help make reactions more controllable. Chemical inhibitors are used to stop metals from turning rusty.

Whoops.

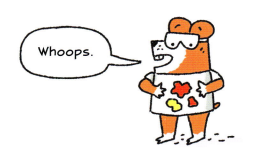

How to Power a Rocket
Good luck, Ted. Be BRAVE.
Are you DONE?
I'm gonna miss him.
You know, we don't NEED a passenger in this rocket. It's only a TEST LAUNCH.
He INSISTED.
OK. First, we need to check the FUEL.
Rockets burn a mix of HYDROGEN GAS with OXYGEN in a chemical process called COMBUSTION.
Like when wood, coal, and oil are burned?
Yes. The combustion produces a lot of heat and light.

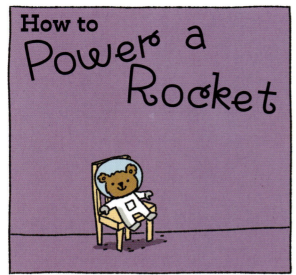

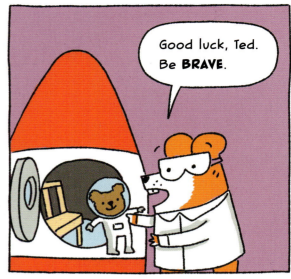

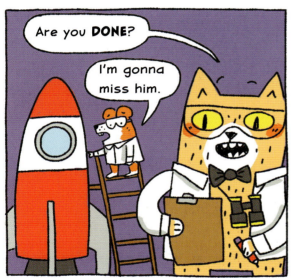

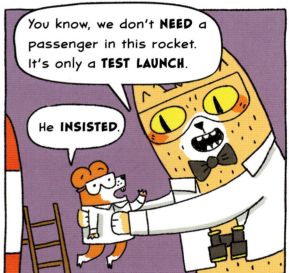

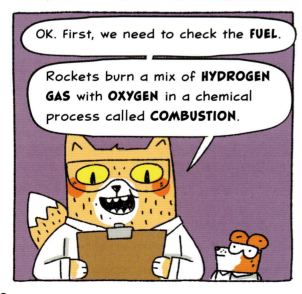

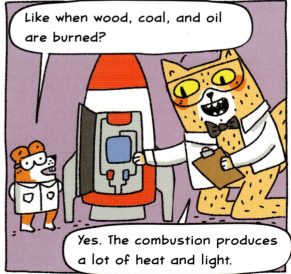

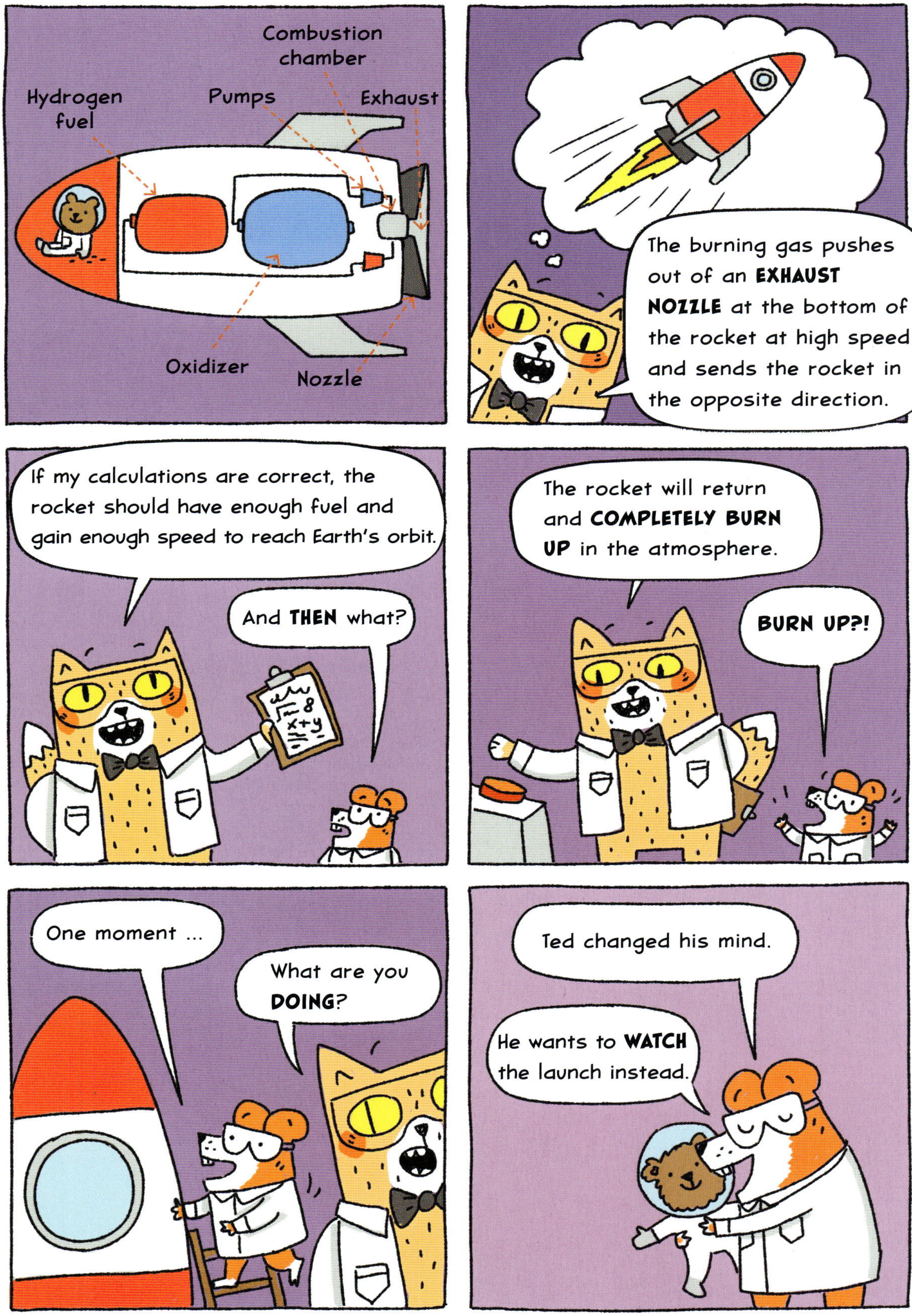
Combustion chamber
Hydrogen fuel
Pumps
Exhaust
Oxidizer
Nozzle
The burning gas pushes out of an EXHAUST NOZZLE at the bottom of the rocket at high speed and sends the rocket in the opposite direction.
If my calculations are correct, the rocket should have enough fuel and gain enough speed to reach Earth's orbit.
And THEN what?
The rocket will return and COMPLETELY BURN UP in the atmosphere.
BURN UP?!
One moment ...
What are you DOING?
Ted changed his mind.
He wants to WATCH the launch instead.

How to Put On a Fireworks Display
Pak!
Wow!
WOW!
What are we CELEBRATING?
The power of CHEMISTRY.
Poof!
Is it NATIONAL CHEMISTRY DAY?
Every day is Chemistry Day!
We wouldn't have FIREWORKS if it weren't for a combination of metal compounds and an oxidizer gaining and losing electrons in a REDOX REACTION.
Can't you just say the fireworks look PRETTY?
OK, Scooter. Yes, they DO look pretty.
Poof!
Bang!

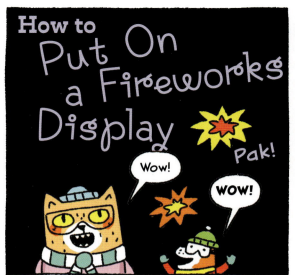

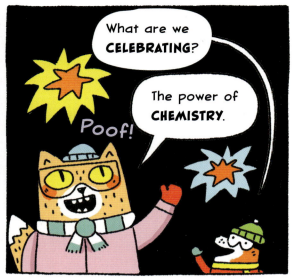

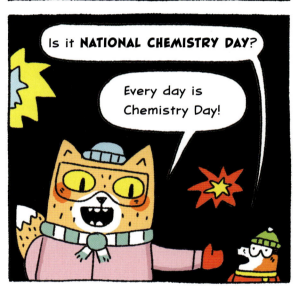

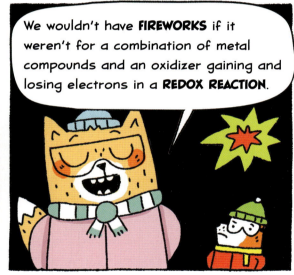

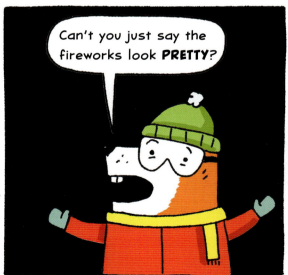

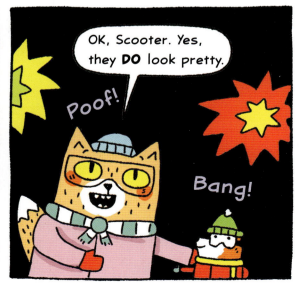

Fireworks are the result of a **redox reaction.**

Redox is short for **reduction** and **oxidation.** In this reaction, one reactant loses electrons (oxidation), while the other gains them (reduction).

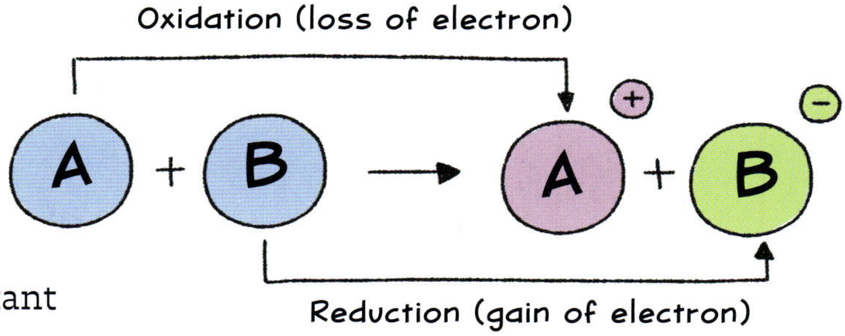
Oxidation (loss of electron)
A + B → A + B
+
−
Reduction (gain of electron)

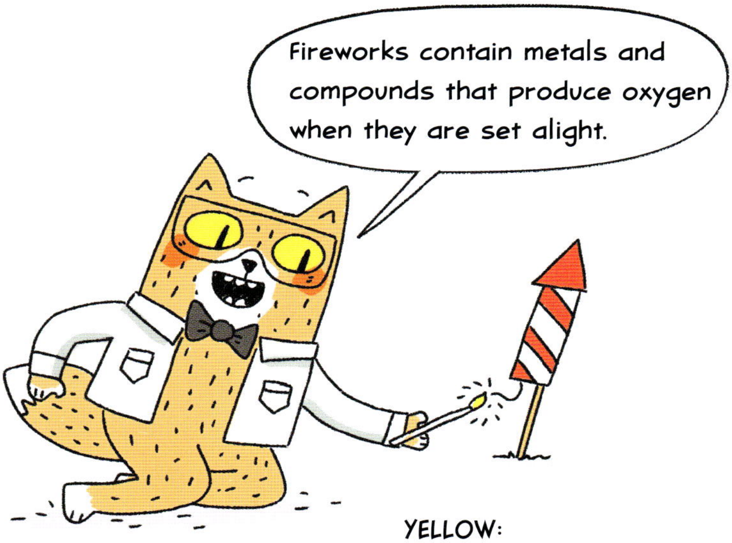
Fireworks contain metals and compounds that produce oxygen when they are set alight.

The redox reaction in fireworks produces oxygen, which quickly combines with the firework's fuel, releasing a lot of heat and light energy.

Metals in the firework burn brightly, each producing a different color.

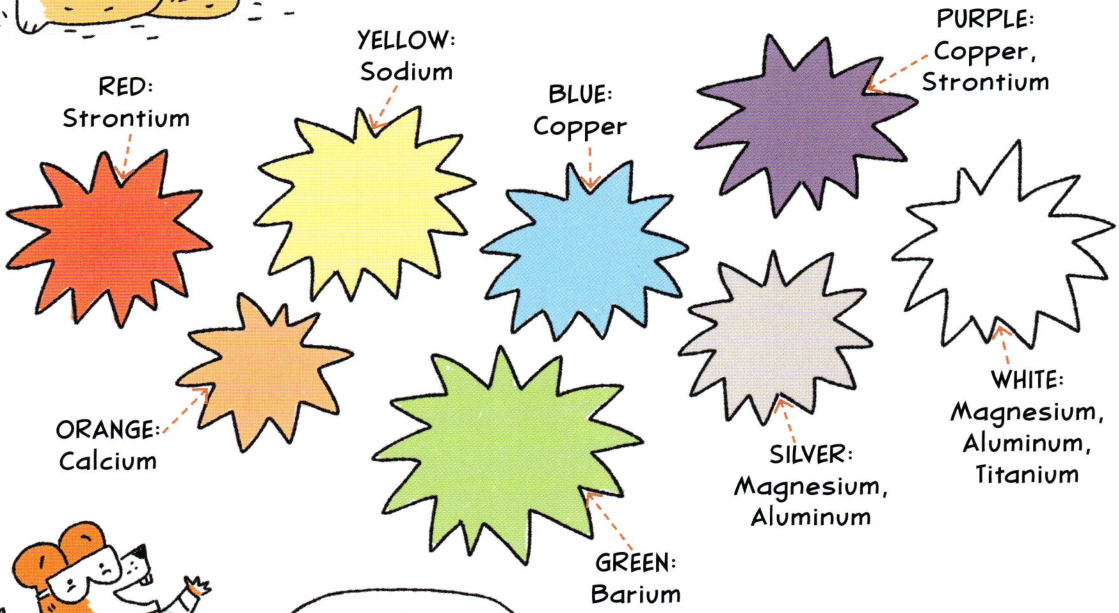
RED: Strontium
YELLOW: Sodium
BLUE: Copper
PURPLE: Copper, Strontium
ORANGE: Calcium
GREEN: Barium
SILVER: Magnesium, Aluminum
WHITE: Magnesium, Aluminum, Titanium

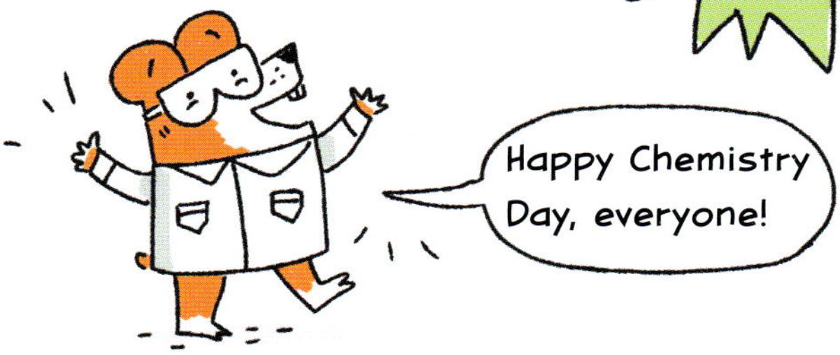
Happy Chemistry Day, everyone!

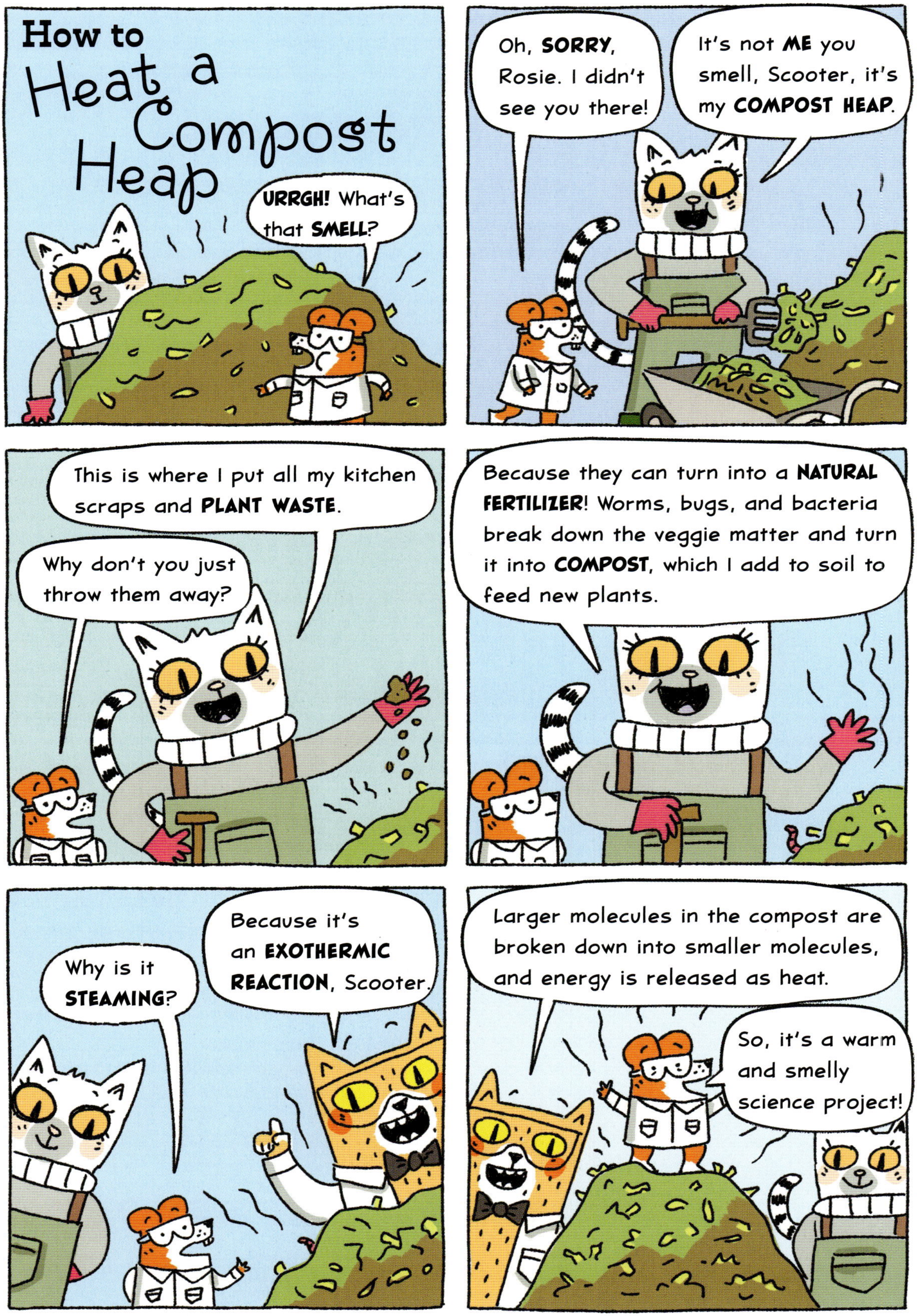
How to Heat a Compost Heap
URRGH! What's that SMELL?
Oh, SORRY, Rosie. I didn't see you there!
It's not ME you smell, Scooter, it's my COMPOST HEAP.
This is where I put all my kitchen scraps and PLANT WASTE.
Why don't you just throw them away?
Because they can turn into a NATURAL FERTILIZER! Worms, bugs, and bacteria break down the veggie matter and turn it into COMPOST, which I add to soil to feed new plants.
Why is it STEAMING?
Because it's an EXOTHERMIC REACTION, Scooter.
Larger molecules in the compost are broken down into smaller molecules, and energy is released as heat.
So, it's a warm and smelly science project!

Chemicals contain energy. During **exothermic reactions**, some of that energy is released, usually in the form of heat.

Heat
Combustion

Exothermic reactions include fuel **combustion** and the decomposing of plant waste. In the case of burning fuels, a lot of heat energy is produced.

Hand warmers are one example of an exothermic reaction since chemicals are mixed and produce heat as they react together. **Glow sticks** are another example, with light released instead of heat.

Alkali
Acid
Heat
Heat

Exothermic reactions also occur when some **alkalis** are added to **acids** such as sodium hydroxide and hydrochloric acid.

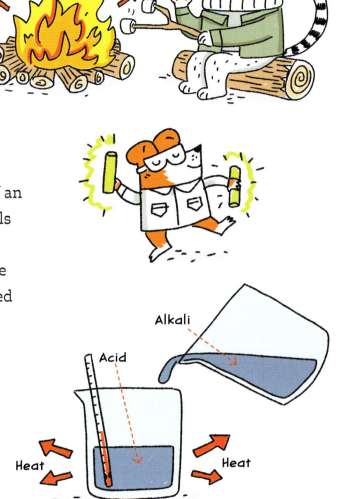

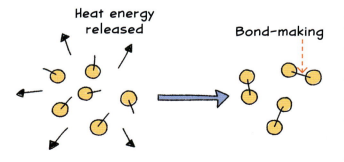

Heat energy released
Bond-making

Exothermic reactions involve the making and breaking of bonds between molecules. Bond-making uses less energy than the bond-breaking. The leftover energy is released as heat or light.

How to Chill Out
THIS is the life!
Lemonade?
Yes, please.
Would you like an ENDOTHERMIC REACTION with your lemonade?
No, thanks. I just like to drink it.
I mean, would you like some ICE?
Oh! Yes, please, LOTS of ice.
Here you go.
CLINK! CLINK!
Slurp!
Ooh! Cold!
I thought you didn't WANT a reaction!

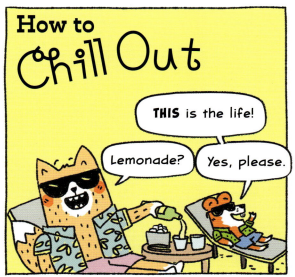

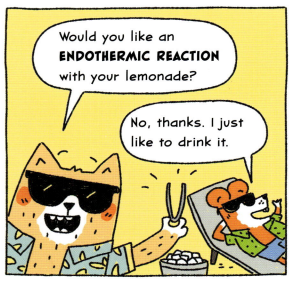

Heat
taken in

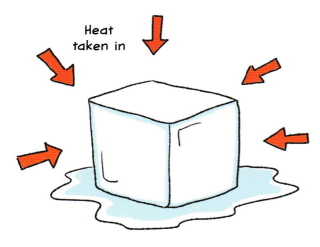

While **exothermic reactions** give off energy, **endothermic reactions** take in energy.

This energy can include heat, reducing the temperature of the environment. A melting ice cube is an example of an endothermic process. The ice takes in heat and makes its surroundings feel colder.

Cold packs used to help with sports injuries make use of **endothermic reactions.** The same chemical reactions are used in packs to keep drinks and picnic food cool.

AH! I've got BRAIN FREEZE!

WHOA!
Vinegar
Baking Soda

Another example of an endothermic reaction is when baking soda (sodium bicarbonate) is added to vinegar (acetic acid). The reaction between the two chemicals takes in energy and makes the surrounding temperature drop.

It also causes a lot of foam!

How to Build a Battery

Oh, my phone is out of power!
That's something **CHEMISTRY** can't fix!
But it's **EVERYTHING** to do with chemistry, Scooter!

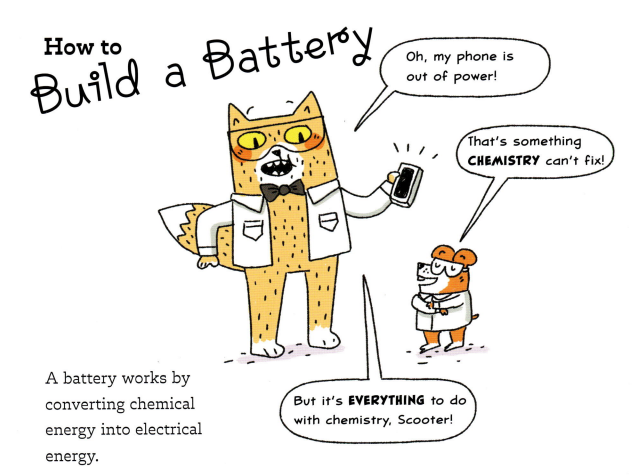

A battery works by converting chemical energy into electrical energy.

Positive terminal
+
Anode
Cathode
Electrolyte
−
Negative terminal

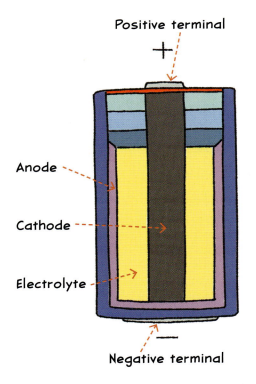

A simple battery has two **electrodes**, an **anode** (negative) and **cathode** (positive). These are made of different metals placed in a paste called an **electrolyte**.

A chemical reaction between the anode and the electrolyte frees **electrons.** A reaction between the cathode and electrolyte makes it ready to receive electrons. When the battery's terminals are joined by a wire in a **circuit**, the electrons flow through the electrolyte.

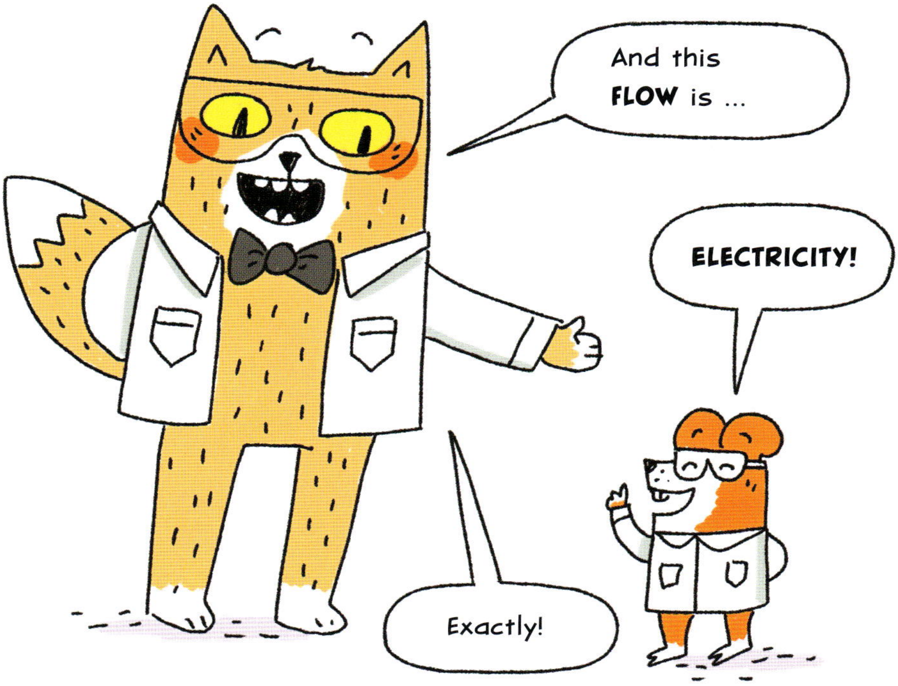
And this **FLOW** is ...
ELECTRICITY!
Exactly!

Just like the burning of fuels to produce heat, this is an **exothermic reaction.**

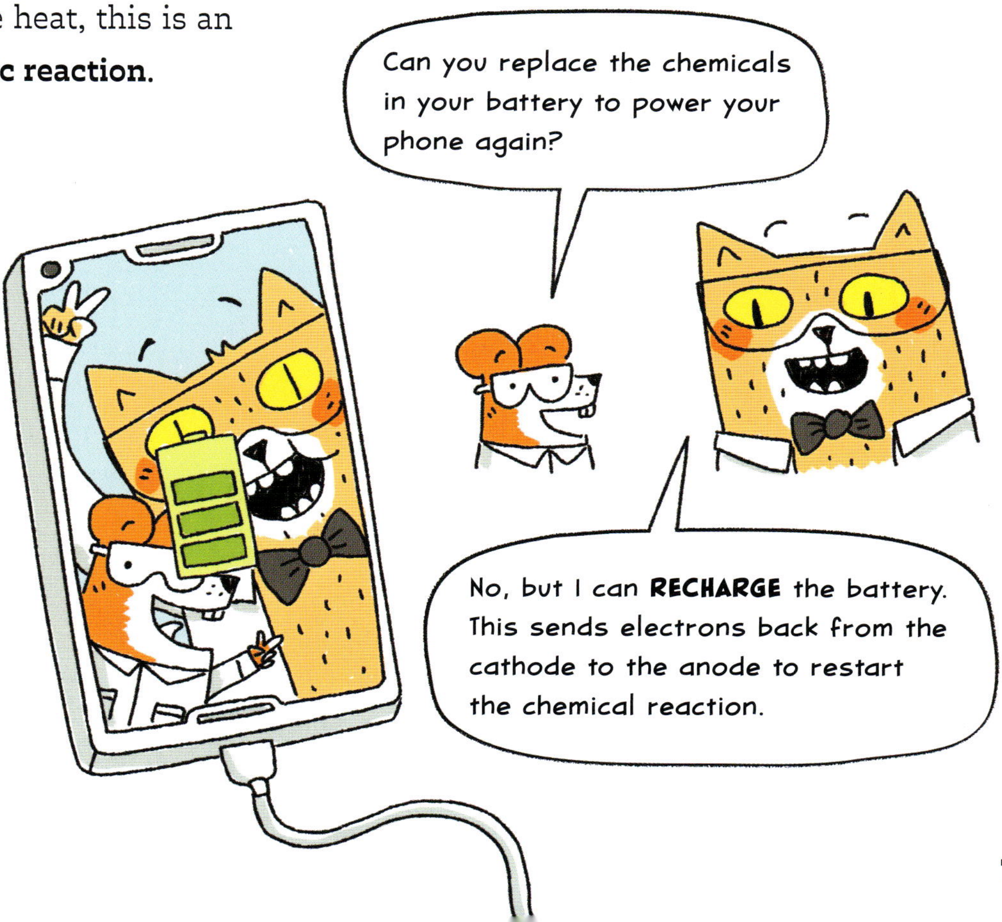
Can you replace the chemicals in your battery to power your phone again?
No, but I can **RECHARGE** the battery. This sends electrons back from the cathode to the anode to restart the chemical reaction.

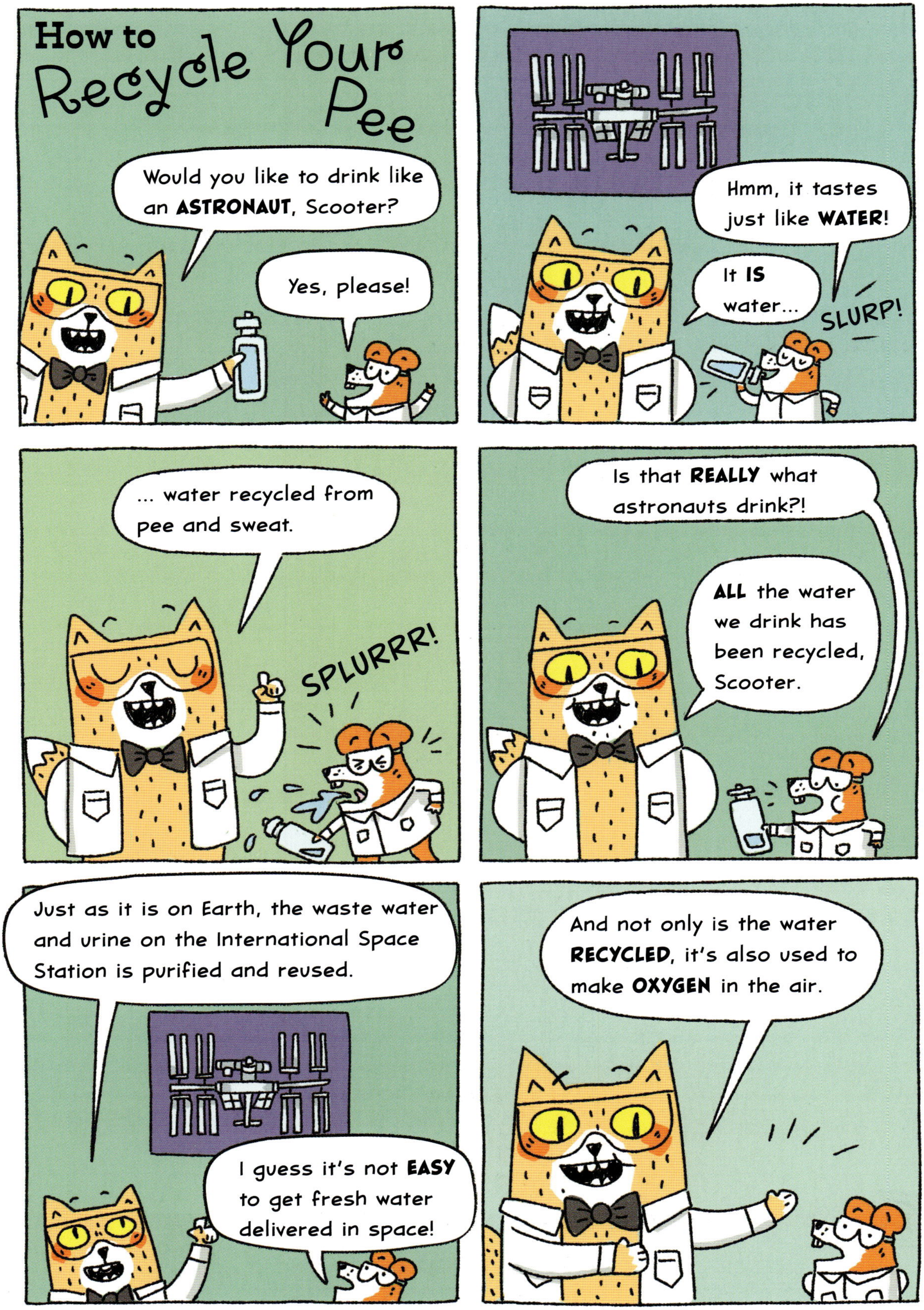
How to Recycle Your Pee
Would you like to drink like an ASTRONAUT, Scooter?
Yes, please!
Hmm, it tastes just like WATER!
It IS water...
SLURP!
... water recycled from pee and sweat.
SPLURRR!
Is that REALLY what astronauts drink?!
ALL the water we drink has been recycled, Scooter.
Just as it is on Earth, the waste water and urine on the International Space Station is purified and reused.
I guess it's not EASY to get fresh water delivered in space!
And not only is the water RECYCLED, it's also used to make OXYGEN in the air.

Battery
Anode
Cathode
Oxygen
(O_2)
Hydrogen
(H_2)
Water
(H_2O)

Water is precious aboard the International Space Station (ISS). It can't be replaced easily. Waste water and urine have to be recycled and made drinkable. It can even be used to provide **oxygen** for astronauts to breathe. After the water is purified, it can be put through a process called **electrolysis**.

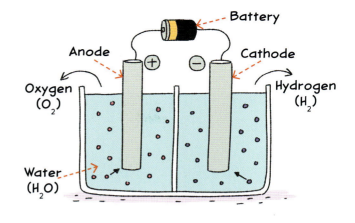

As in a battery, electrolysis features **electrodes** in an **electrolyte**. In this case, the electrolyte is water (H_2O).

When an electric current is passed through it, the water's **hydrogen** (H_2) and **oxygen** (O_2) **molecules** lose or gain electrons. They become charged atoms called **ions**.

The chemical formula for this is ...
$2H_2O$
↓
$2H_2$ and O_2

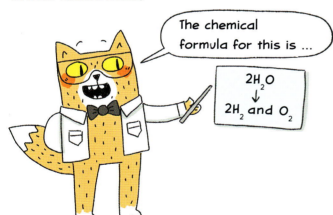

The positively charged hydrogen ions are attracted to the negative electrode.

The negatively charged oxygen ions are attracted to the positive electrode.

At the electrodes, the hydrogen and oxygen lose or gain electrons to become H_2 and O_2 atoms with no overall charge. They are collected as gases.

Aboard the ISS, the separated oxygen is pumped into the space station's air supply, while the hydrogen is used to make clean water for drinking.

SLURP!

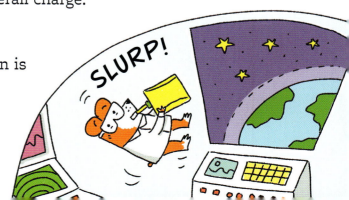

How to
Walk on Water
What are you looking at, Rosie?
A WATER STRIDER.
A water WHAT?!
It's an insect that can WALK ON WATER.
How is that POSSIBLE? I fall in if I try.
Even though you're quite small, you're still too HEAVY to walk on water.
The water strider, or pond skater, does it by spreading its weight over what appears to be a skin on the water's surface.
Water doesn't have SKIN!
No, but what it DOES have is SURFACE TENSION!

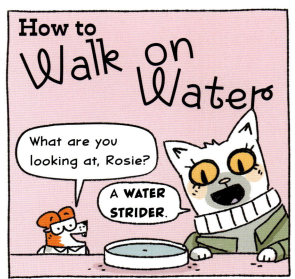

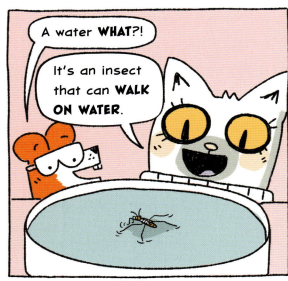

The molecules in liquids tend to pull together. In water this results in **surface tension**, with water molecules more attracted to each other than to air molecules.

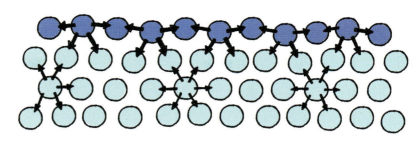

Below the surface, the molecules are pulled in every direction. With no water molecules above them, the surface molecules exert a stronger force on those to the sides and below. This creates a thin, transparent "skin" over the surface that is strong enough to support a tiny insect.

Now, that's just **SHOWING OFF**!

You don't need a bug to test surface tension. Carefully drop a paper clip flat on to water, and even though it is more **dense** than water, it should float.

Surface tension is the reason water droplets are rounded, with the water molecules pulling in toward each other. You can see rounded water droplets when they land on a waxy surface.

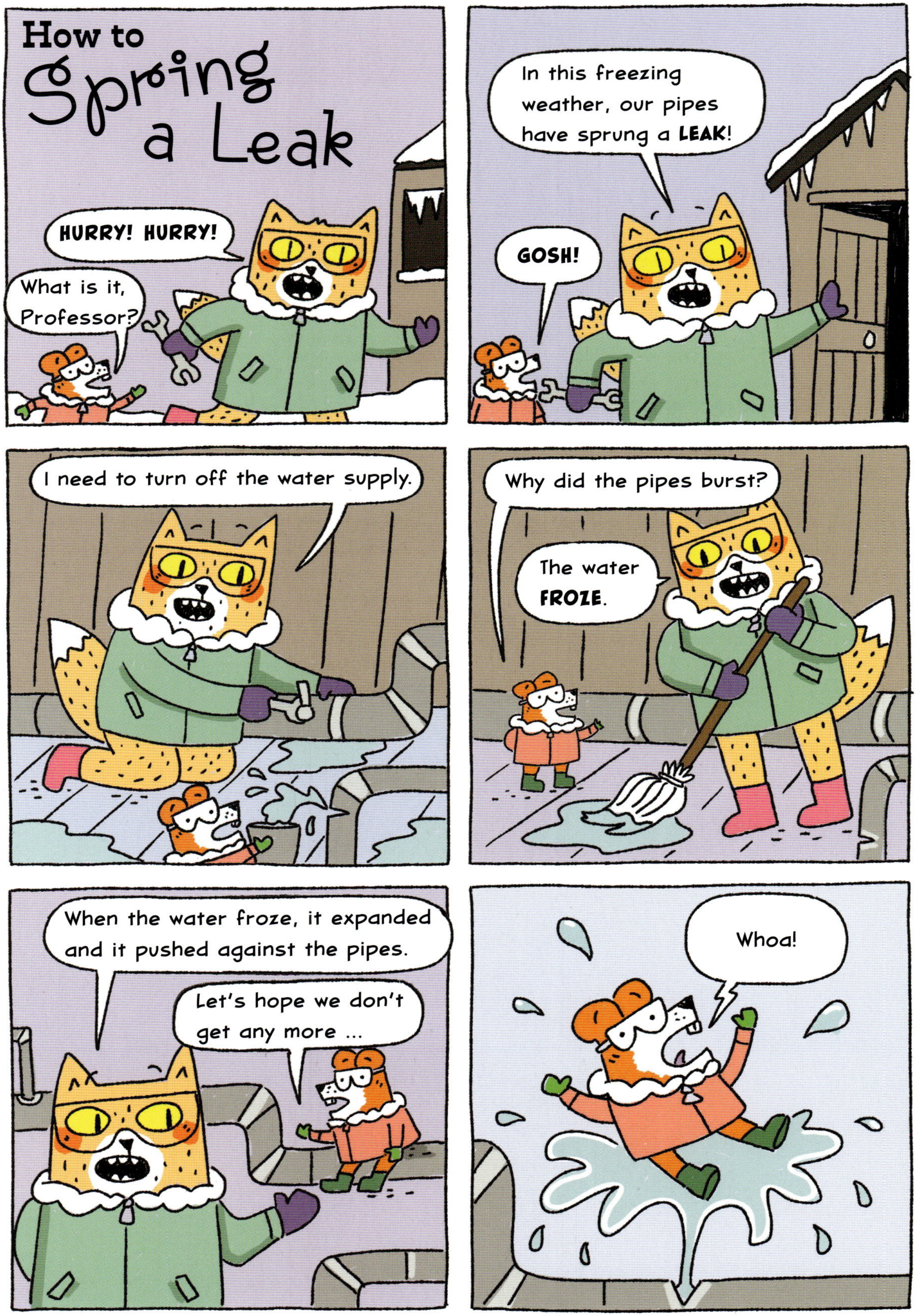
How to Spring a Leak
HURRY! HURRY!
What is it, Professor?
In this freezing weather, our pipes have sprung a LEAK!
GOSH!
I need to turn off the water supply.
Why did the pipes burst?
The water FROZE.
When the water froze, it expanded and it pushed against the pipes.
Let's hope we don't get any more ...
Whoa!

Water is unusual in that it can be found as a gas, a liquid, and a solid under average temperatures and pressures.

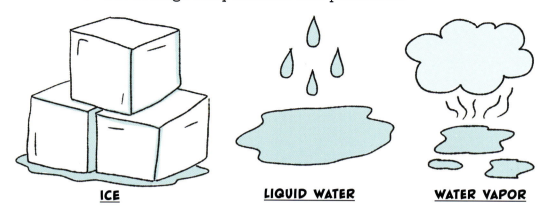

ICE   LIQUID WATER   WATER VAPOR

When it changes from a liquid to a solid, it also **expands**.

Water is made from hydrogen and oxygen (H_2O) and it freezes at 0°C (32°F). Water molecules are held together by **hydrogen bonds.** When water freezes, the molecules bond in a crystal-like structure with larger gaps.

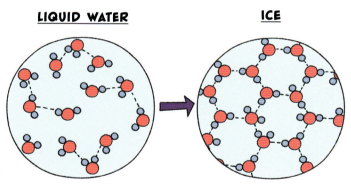

So, as the water turns to ice, it expands. The strength of the expanding water can burst a metal pipe.

This is **COOL**.

This expansion also means that ice is less dense than liquid water and will float in it.

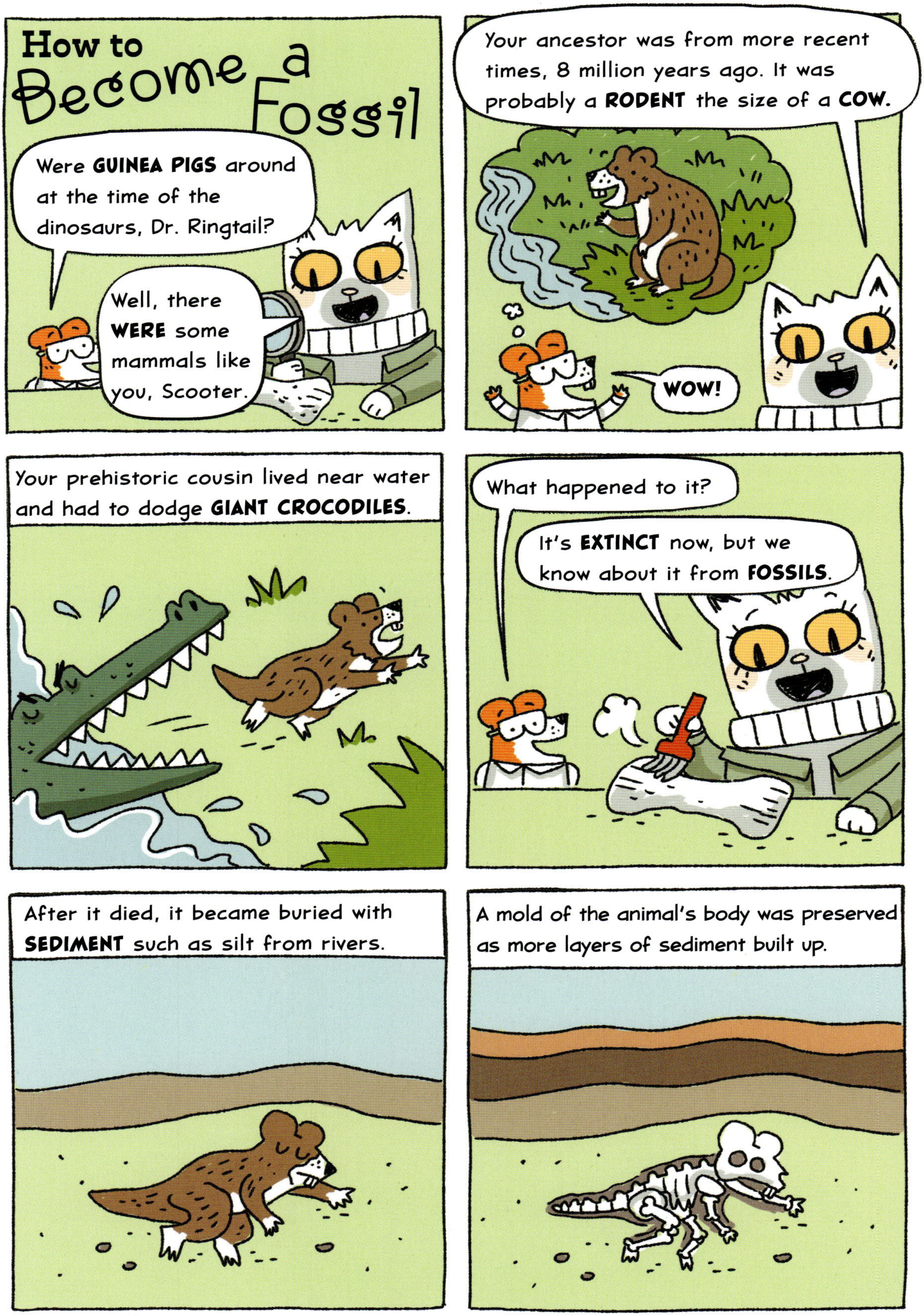
How to Become a Fossil
Were GUINEA PIGS around at the time of the dinosaurs, Dr. Ringtail?
Well, there WERE some mammals like you, Scooter.
Your ancestor was from more recent times, 8 million years ago. It was probably a RODENT the size of a COW.
WOW!
Your prehistoric cousin lived near water and had to dodge GIANT CROCODILES.
What happened to it?
It's EXTINCT now, but we know about it from FOSSILS.
After it died, it became buried with SEDIMENT such as silt from rivers.
A mold of the animal's body was preserved as more layers of sediment built up.

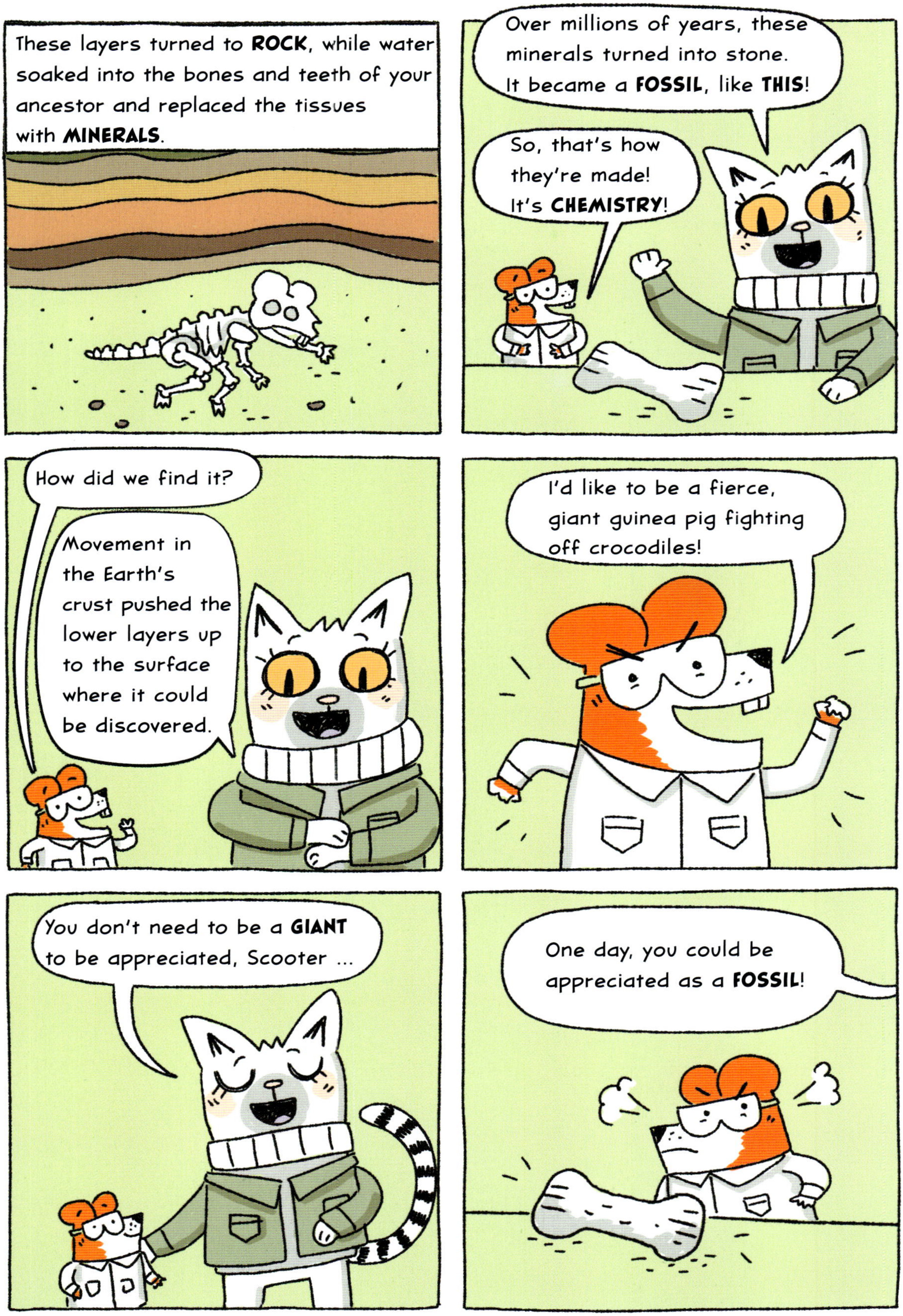
These layers turned to ROCK, while water soaked into the bones and teeth of your ancestor and replaced the tissues with MINERALS.
Over millions of years, these minerals turned into stone. It became a FOSSIL, like THIS!
So, that's how they're made! It's CHEMISTRY!
How did we find it?
Movement in the Earth's crust pushed the lower layers up to the surface where it could be discovered.
I'd like to be a fierce, giant guinea pig fighting off crocodiles!
You don't need to be a GIANT to be appreciated, Scooter ...
One day, you could be appreciated as a FOSSIL!

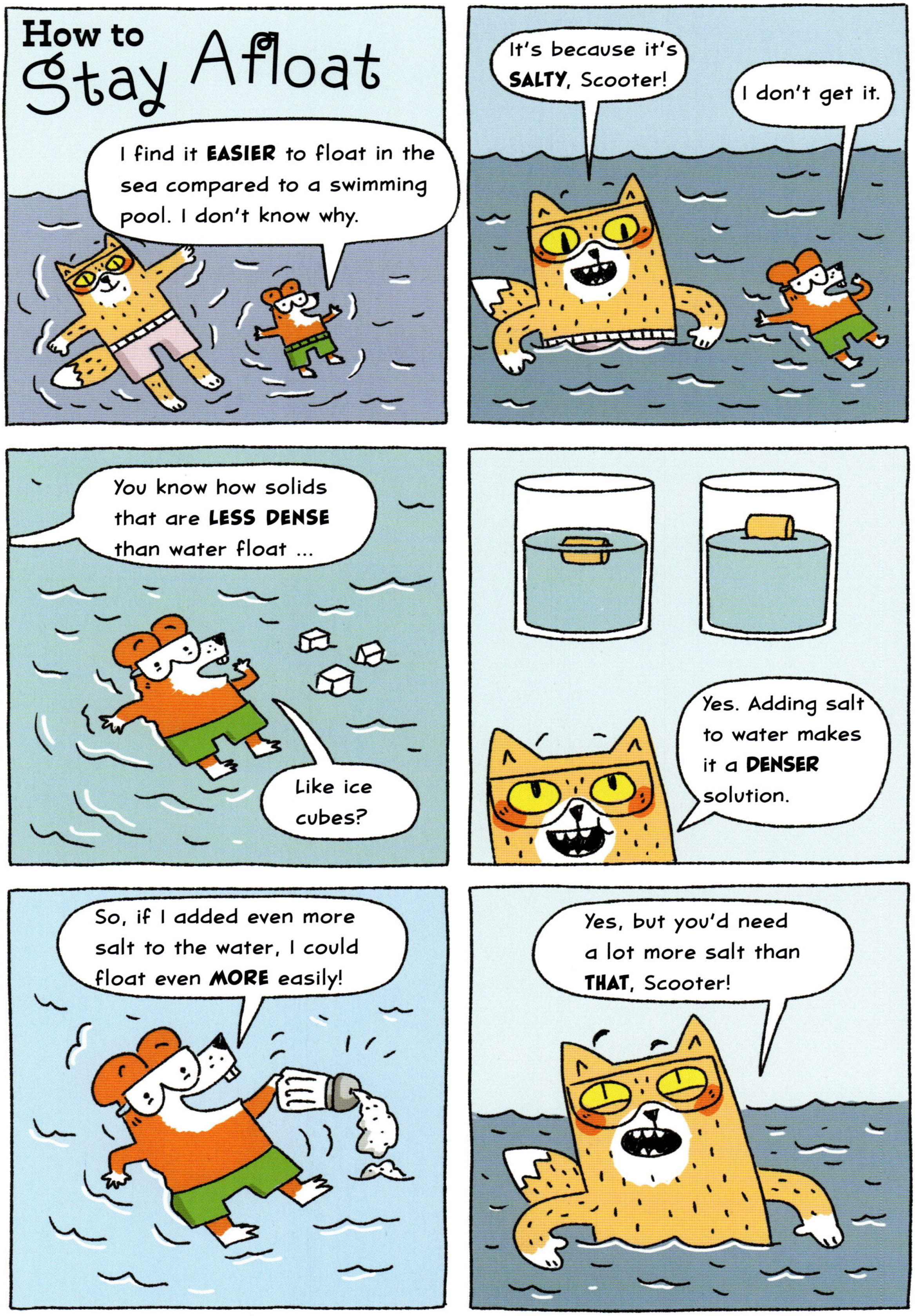
How to Stay Afloat
I find it EASIER to float in the sea compared to a swimming pool. I don't know why.
It's because it's SALTY, Scooter!
I don't get it.
You know how solids that are LESS DENSE than water float ...
Like ice cubes?
Yes. Adding salt to water makes it a DENSER solution.
So, if I added even more salt to the water, I could float even MORE easily!
Yes, but you'd need a lot more salt than THAT, Scooter!

The Acid Test

(Acids, Alkalis, Bases)

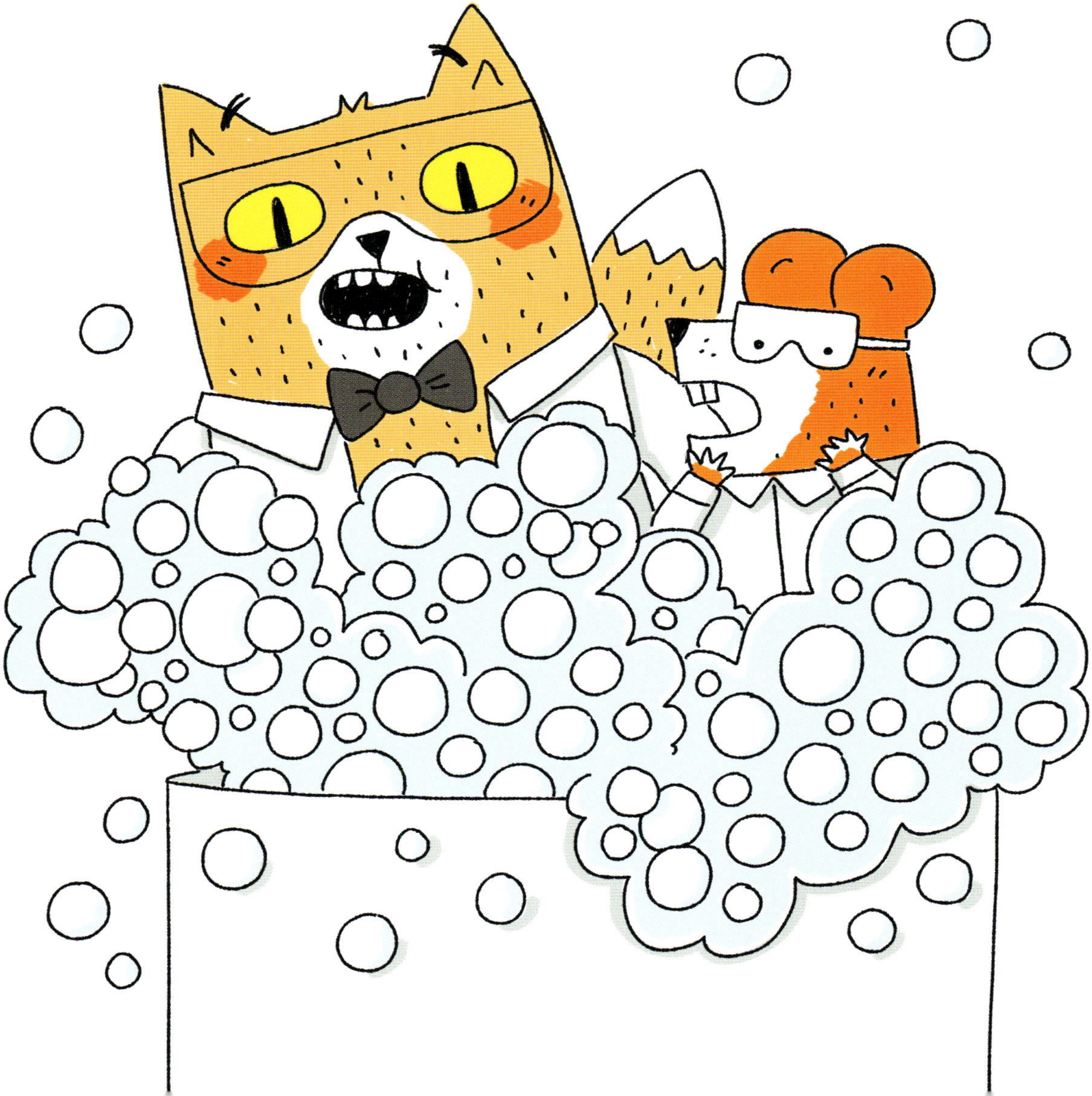

How to Top a Pancake
How do you like your PANCAKES?
Simple, with a spoon of FRUCTOSE and a splash of CITRIC ACID.
It's the KITCHEN, not the LAB, Professor.
OK, honey and lemon juice.
Is lemon juice an ACID?
Yes, a weak one. The juice of lots of fruits—lemons, limes, oranges, and grapefruits—contains citric acid.
Acids are compounds that make HYDROGEN IONS when dissolved in water.
If you say so.
One flip and your pancake's on its way!
Oh.

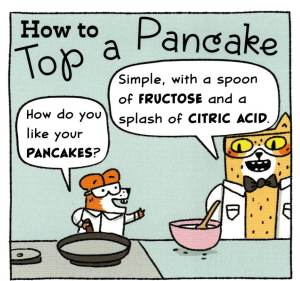

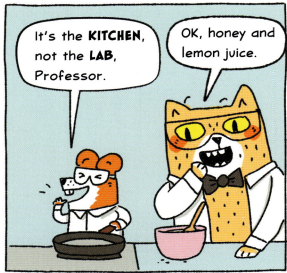

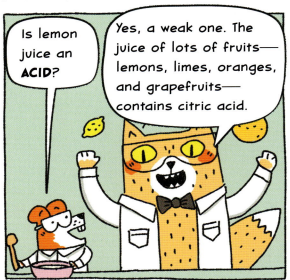

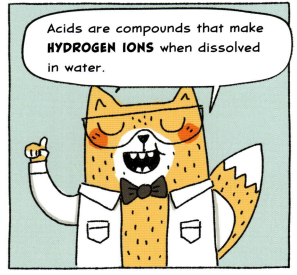

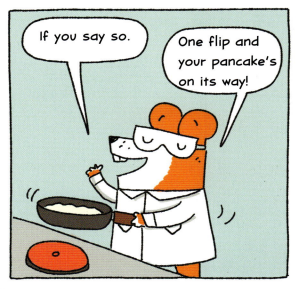

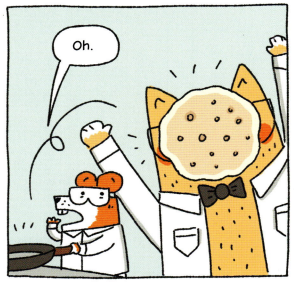

Acids are **compounds** that may have a sour taste (lemon juice or vinegar) or the ability to cause burning (car battery acid). The opposite of an acid is a **base.**

In chemical terms, an acid is a substance that forms positively charged **hydrogen ions** when dissolved in water.

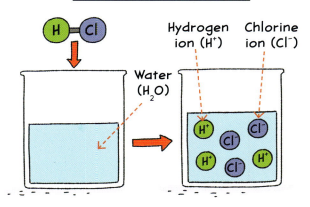

HYDROGEN CHLORIDE (HCL)
H
Cl
Water (H_2O)
Hydrogen ion (H^+)
Chlorine ion (Cl^-)
H^+
Cl^-

The more ions released by the acid, the stronger it is.

One example is the gas **hydrogen chloride.** When this is added to water it produces **hydrochloric acid**, an acid a thousand times stronger than the citric acid in fruit.

You have have hydrochloric acid in your **STOMACH**, Scooter.
OH, NO! Fetch a **DOCTOR!**
No need. Your stomach is protected by mucus and bicarbonate.

Acids can be **corrosive**, which means they can burn, but if a lot of water is added, they become less **concentrated** and less dangerous.

EXAMPLES OF STRONG ACIDS:
Sulfuric acid, used in car batteries
Hydrochloric acid, used in refining metals
Nitric acid, used to make fertilizers

EXAMPLES OF WEAK ACIDS:
Citric acid, in fruit
Acetic acid, in vinegar
Formic acid, in ant stings

How to Make Your Cake Rise
Thanks, Scooter. I need two teaspoons of that **BAKING SODA** for my cake.
What's baking soda?
Baking soda is **SODIUM BICARBONATE**. It's a weak **BASE**, the opposite of an acid.
Does it taste nice?
I'm not adding it to my cake mix for **FLAVOR** but for what it **DOES**.
The baking soda reacts with acids in the cake mix, such as yogurt or juice, and produces bubbles of **CARBON DIOXIDE**.
The gas makes the cake lighter and rise in the tin.
It needs to. The mix looks very flat.
Just you wait ...
50 minutes later ...
TA-DA!
It **WORKED**!

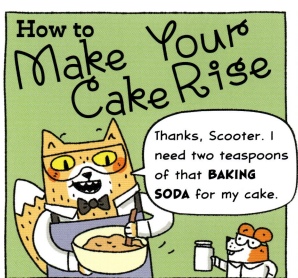

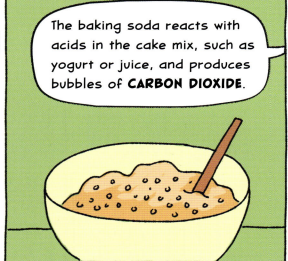

Bases are the opposite of **acids**. When added to water they make negatively charged **hydroxide** ions (OH^-).

Hydrochloric acid (HCl)
+
Sodium hydroxide (NaOH)
Water (H_2O)
Table salt (NaCl)

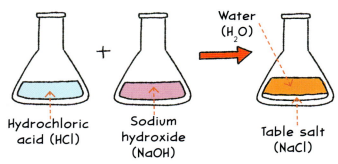

Bases can also be strong or weak, depending on how many hydroxide ions they make. Strong bases, such as sodium hydroxide, can also be **corrosive** like acids. A base that dissolves in water is also called an **alkali**.

Acids and bases react together in a process called **neutralization**, which produces a salt and water. The result is neither acid nor alkali. For example, hydrochloric acid reacts with sodium hydroxide to make table salt and water.

My stomach HURTS. I think I ate TOO MUCH CAKE ...
Would you like an INDIGESTION TABLET?
I don't think I have space.

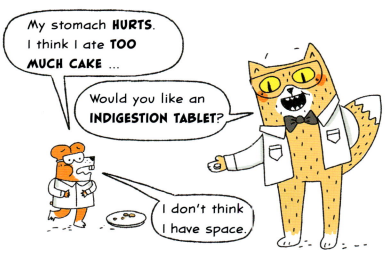

Another example is **magnesium hydroxide**, which is used in indigestion tablets. Indigestion is caused by stomach acids. The alkali in the tablet neutralizes the acids, turning them into harmless salts.

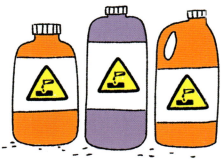

EXAMPLES OF STRONG BASES:
Sodium hydroxide, used as a drain cleaner
Potassium hydroxide, used in soap
Calcium hydroxide, used in cement

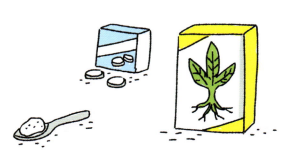

EXAMPLES OF WEAK BASES:
Sodium bicarbonate, baking soda
Magnesium hydroxide, used in indigestion tablets
Ammonia, used in fertilizers

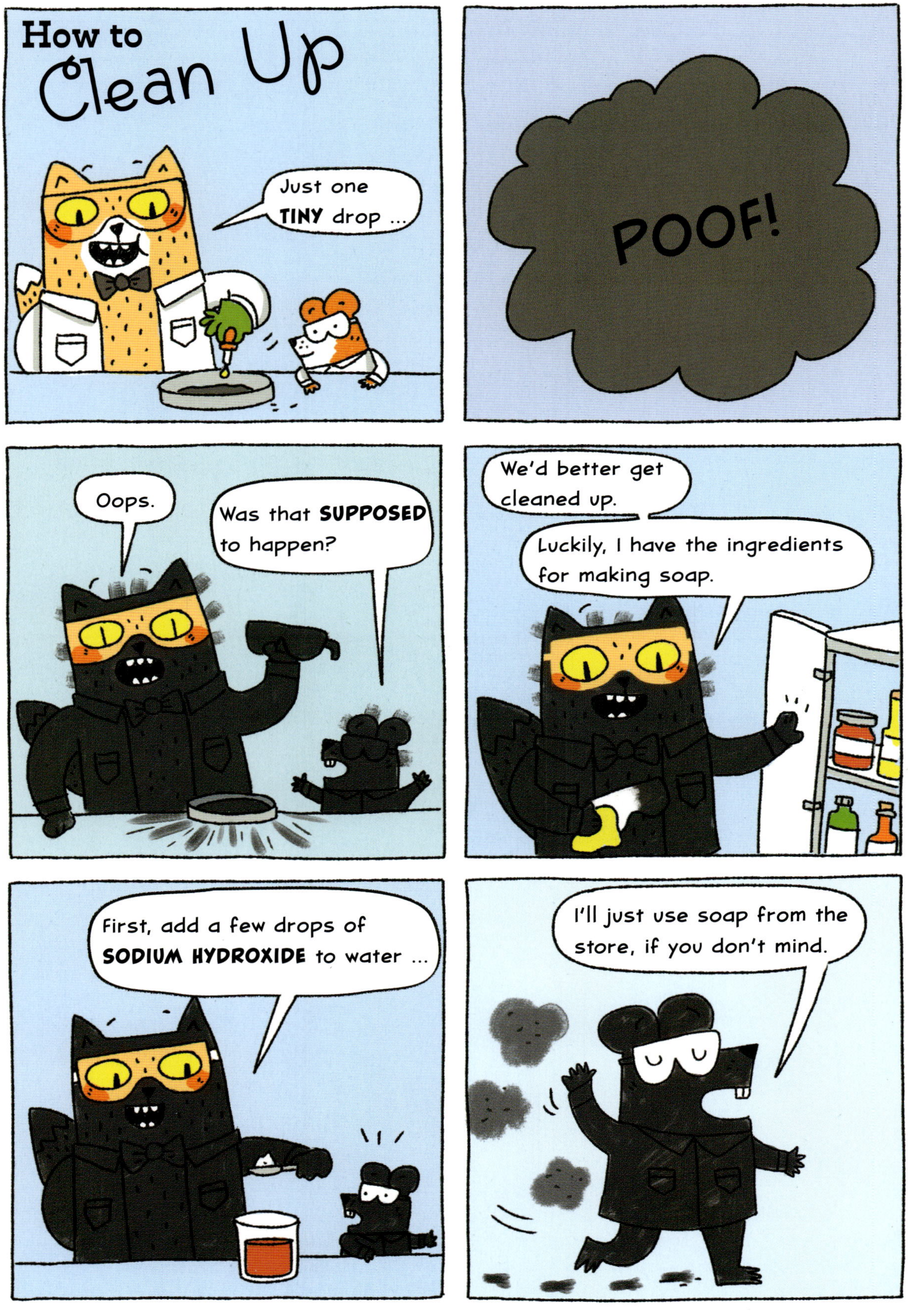
How to Clean Up
Just one TINY drop ...
POOF!
Oops.
Was that SUPPOSED to happen?
We'd better get cleaned up.
Luckily, I have the ingredients for making soap.
First, add a few drops of SODIUM HYDROXIDE to water ...
I'll just use soap from the store, if you don't mind.

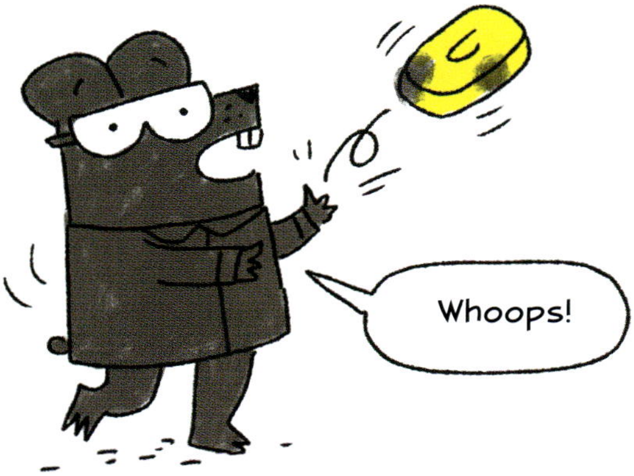
Whoops!

Soap is made from a mix of an **alkali** with oils. Oil and water do not normally mix, but soap manages to do this because of the nature of its molecules.

Soap is made up of chains of molecules with a head and tail. The tail end is **hydrophobic**, which means it will join to oils but not water, while the "head" is **hydrophilic** and bonds with water.

When you use soap with dirty, greasy hands, the dirty grease is attracted to the soap molecules. You can then use water to wash away both the soap and the grease from your hands.

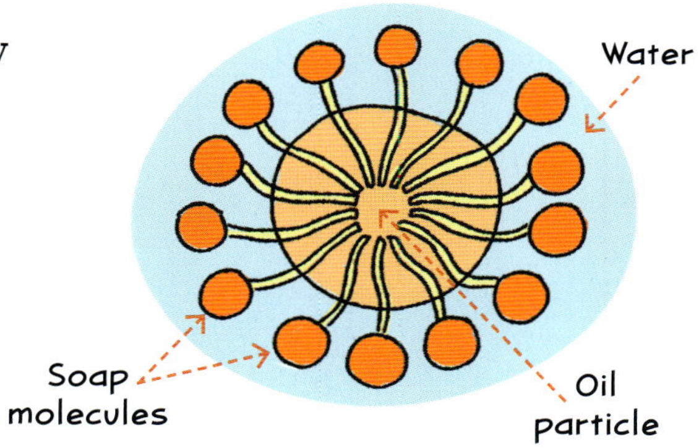
Water
Soap molecules
Oil particle

Soap also helps remove any germs that get caught up in the oils on your skin. So don't forget to use soap!

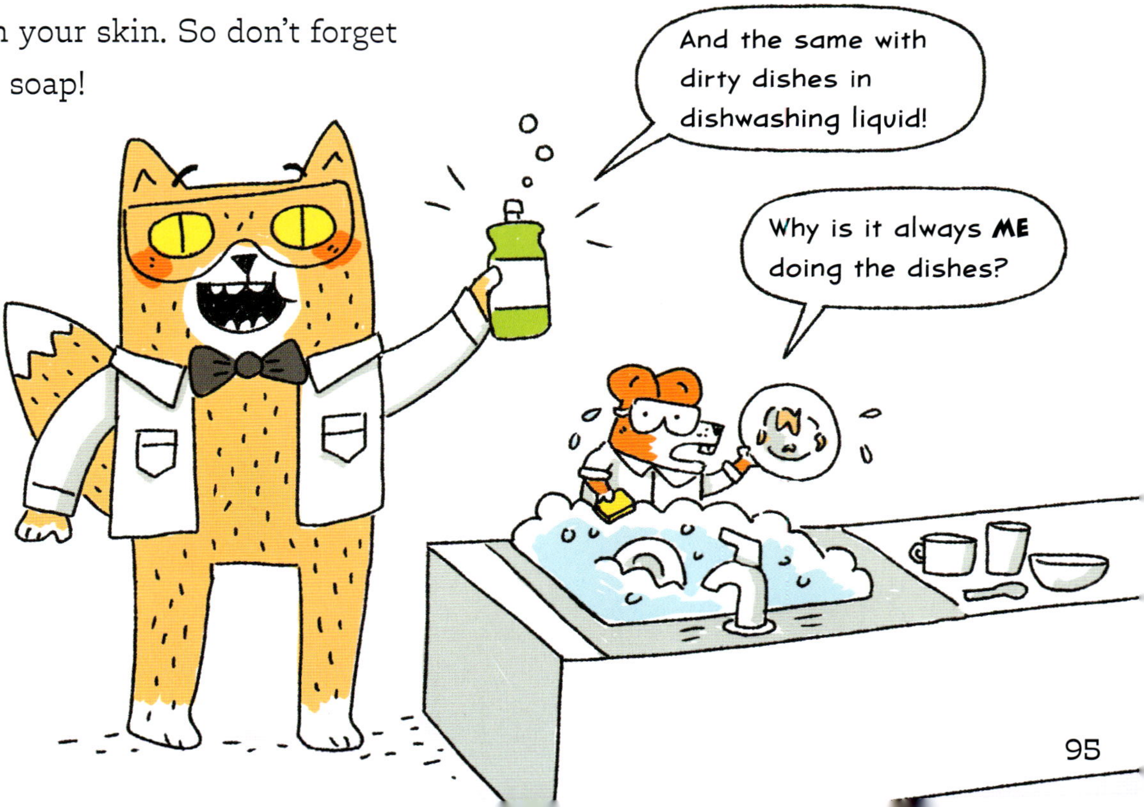
And the same with dirty dishes in dishwashing liquid!
Why is it always **ME** doing the dishes?

Taking the Measure

So, we have **acids** and **bases**, but how do we know which is which?

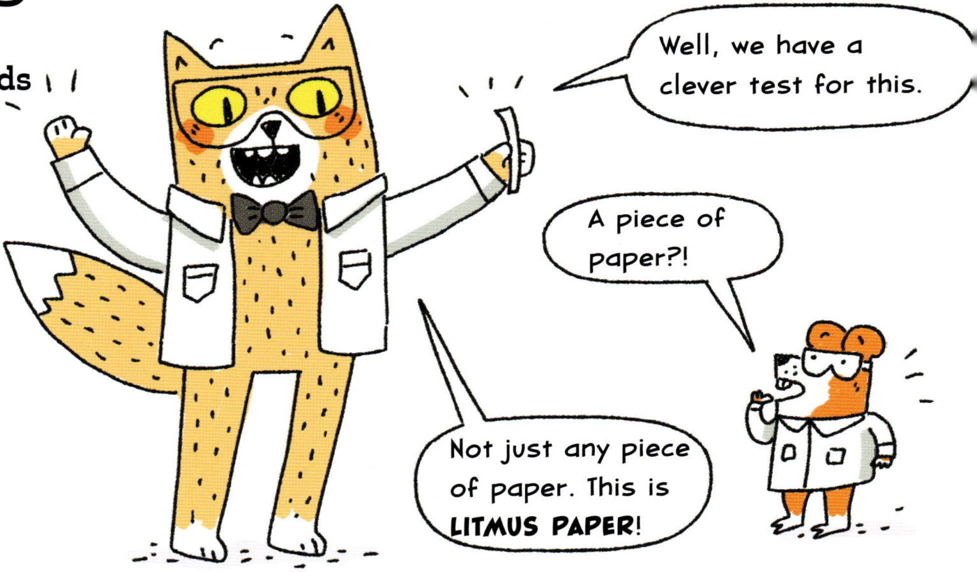

Well, we have a clever test for this.
A piece of paper?!
Not just any piece of paper. This is **LITMUS PAPER**!

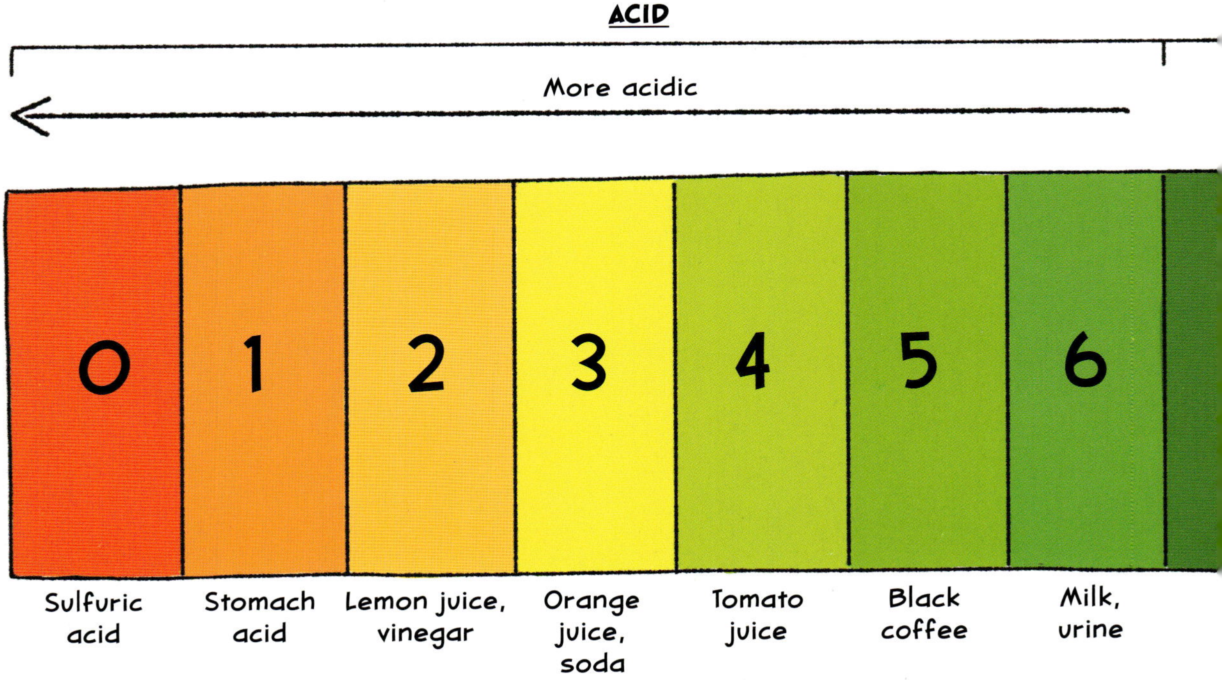

ACID
More acidic
0
1
2
3
4
5
6
Sulfuric acid
Stomach acid
Lemon juice, vinegar
Orange juice, soda
Tomato juice
Black coffee
Milk, urine

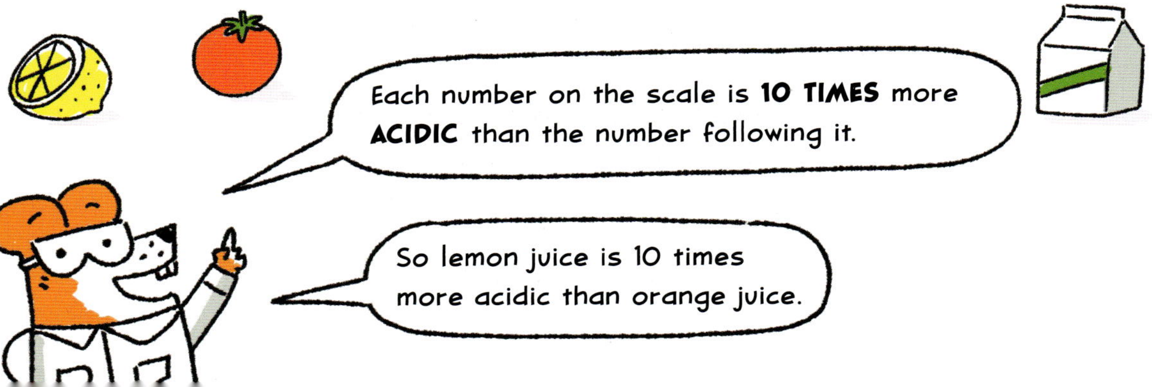

Each number on the scale is **10 TIMES** more **ACIDIC** than the number following it.
So lemon juice is 10 times more acidic than orange juice.

Litmus paper is an **indicator**. When dipped in a liquid it will change color to show whether the liquid is an acid or a base.

Universal indicator is a chemical that does the same job but with more detailed results. It changes to a color of the rainbow that indicates whether a substance is an acid or a base and even how strong it is.

The color chart that indicates acids and bases is called the **pH scale**.

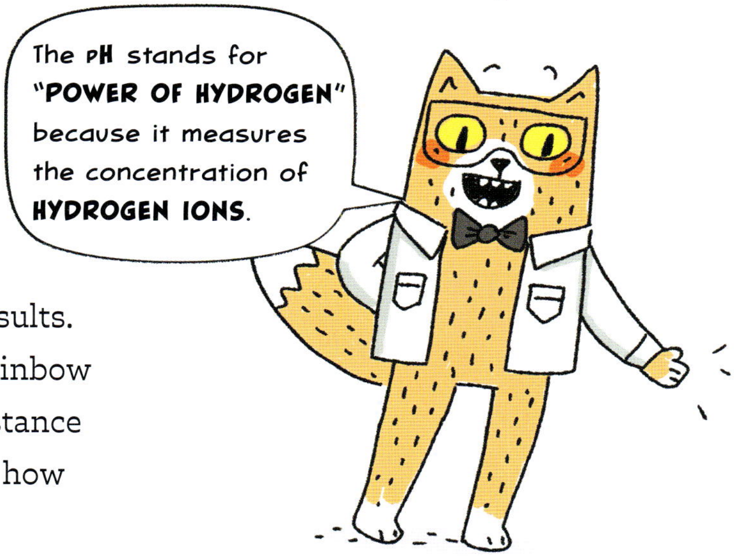
The pH stands for "POWER OF HYDROGEN" because it measures the concentration of HYDROGEN IONS.

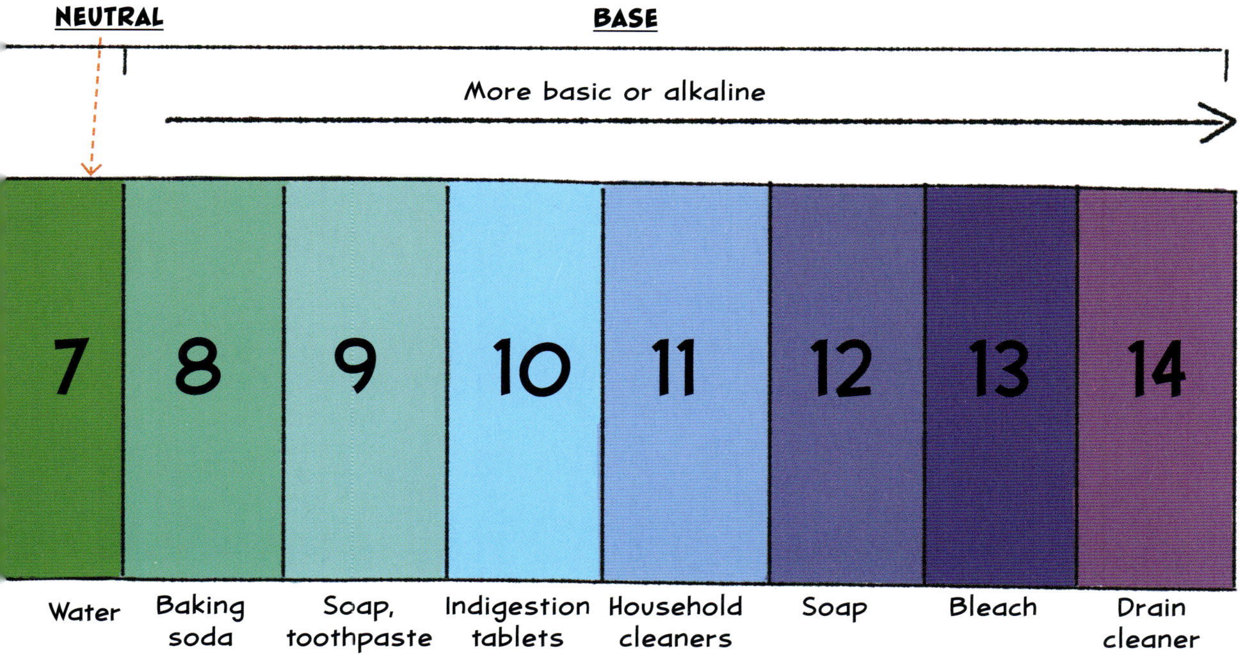
NEUTRAL
BASE
More basic or alkaline
7
8
9
10
11
12
13
14
Water
Baking soda
Soap, toothpaste
Indigestion tablets
Household cleaners
Soap
Bleach
Drain cleaner

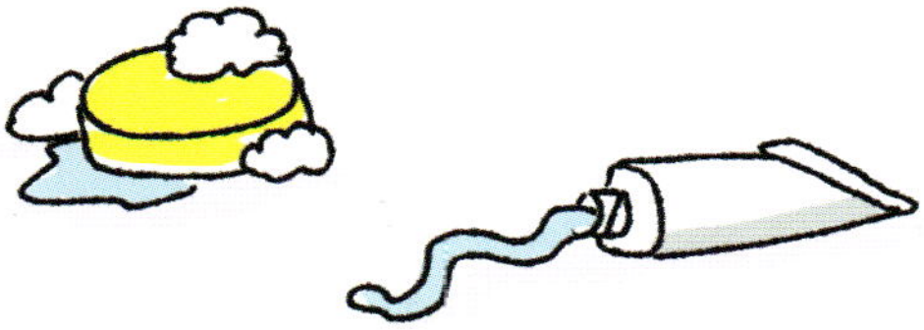

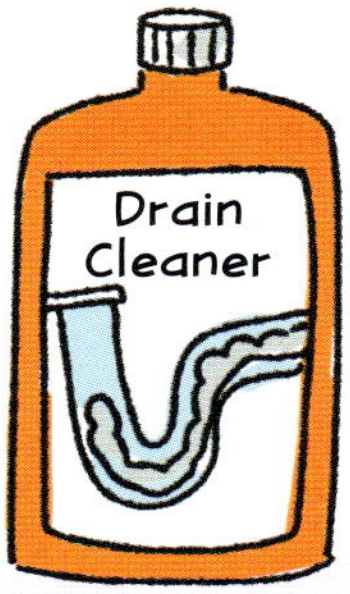
Drain Cleaner

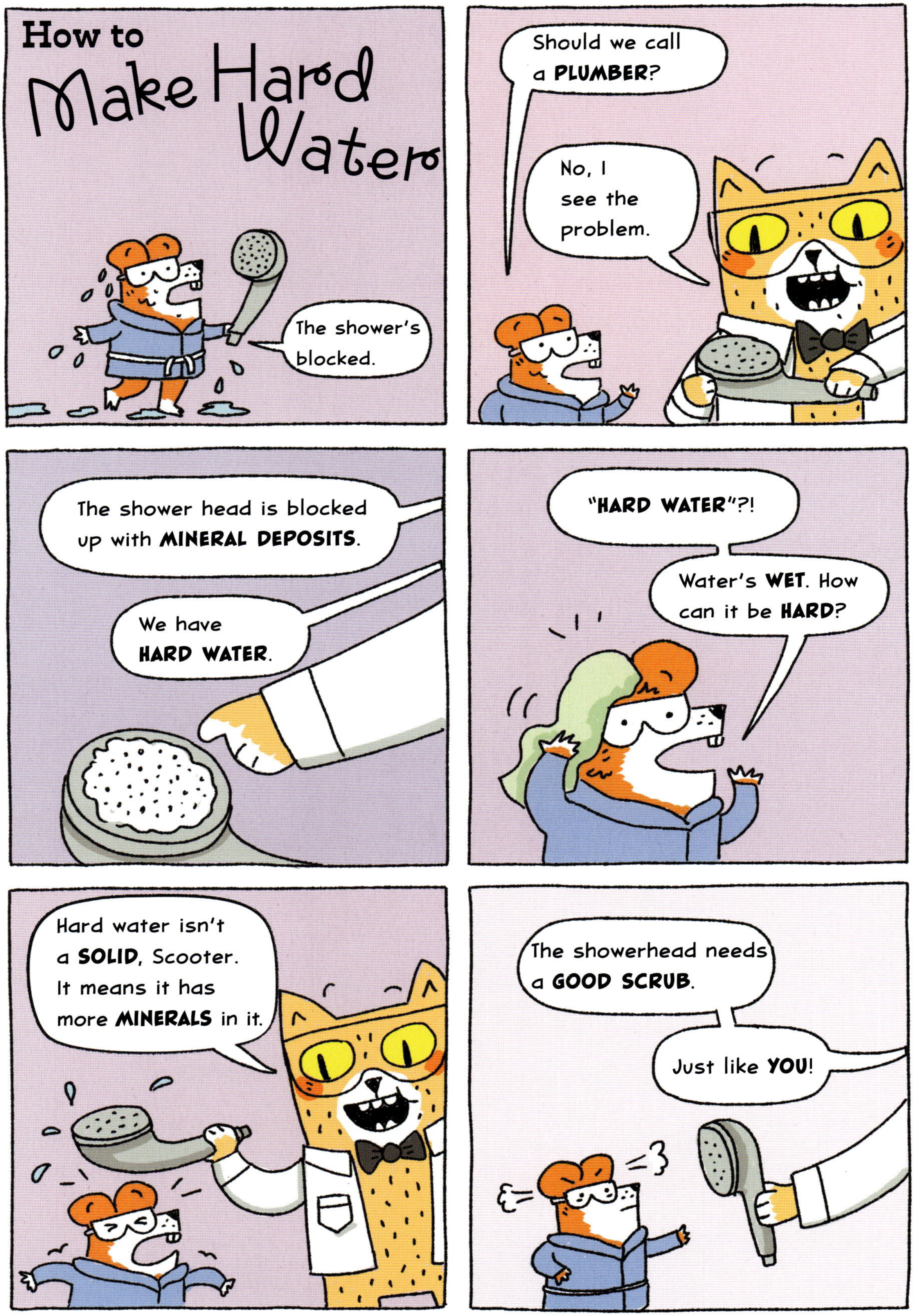
How to Make Hard Water
The shower's blocked.
Should we call a PLUMBER?
No, I see the problem.
The shower head is blocked up with MINERAL DEPOSITS.
We have HARD WATER.
"HARD WATER"?!
Water's WET. How can it be HARD?
Hard water isn't a SOLID, Scooter. It means it has more MINERALS in it.
The showerhead needs a GOOD SCRUB.
Just like YOU!

When rain falls, carbon dioxide and other gases dissolve in the water. This makes it slightly **acidic.**

When rainwater soaks through rocks such as limestone, minerals present in the rock, such as **magnesium carbonate** and **calcium carbonate**, are dissolved in the water.

Rain
Magnesium
Hard water
Calcium

Feels soft to me.

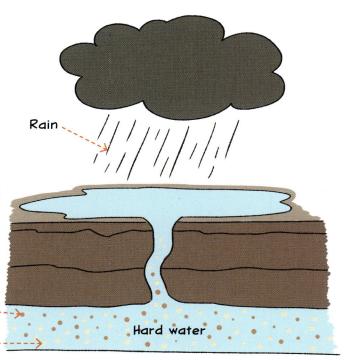

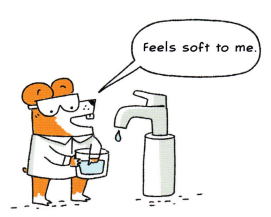

Water with these minerals in it is called **hard water**. The more calcium and magnesium present in the water the "harder" it is. Hard water isn't harmful. In fact, your body needs a small amount of magnesium and calcium.

But hard water can result in mineral deposits called **limescale** clogging up pipes and fixtures, such as showerheads. You may also find a grimy ring left around the bathtub after you've washed.

The salts can be removed through boiling water or by using a water filter.

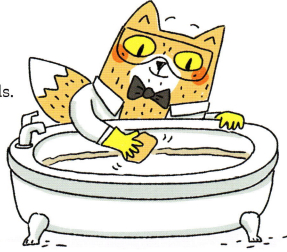

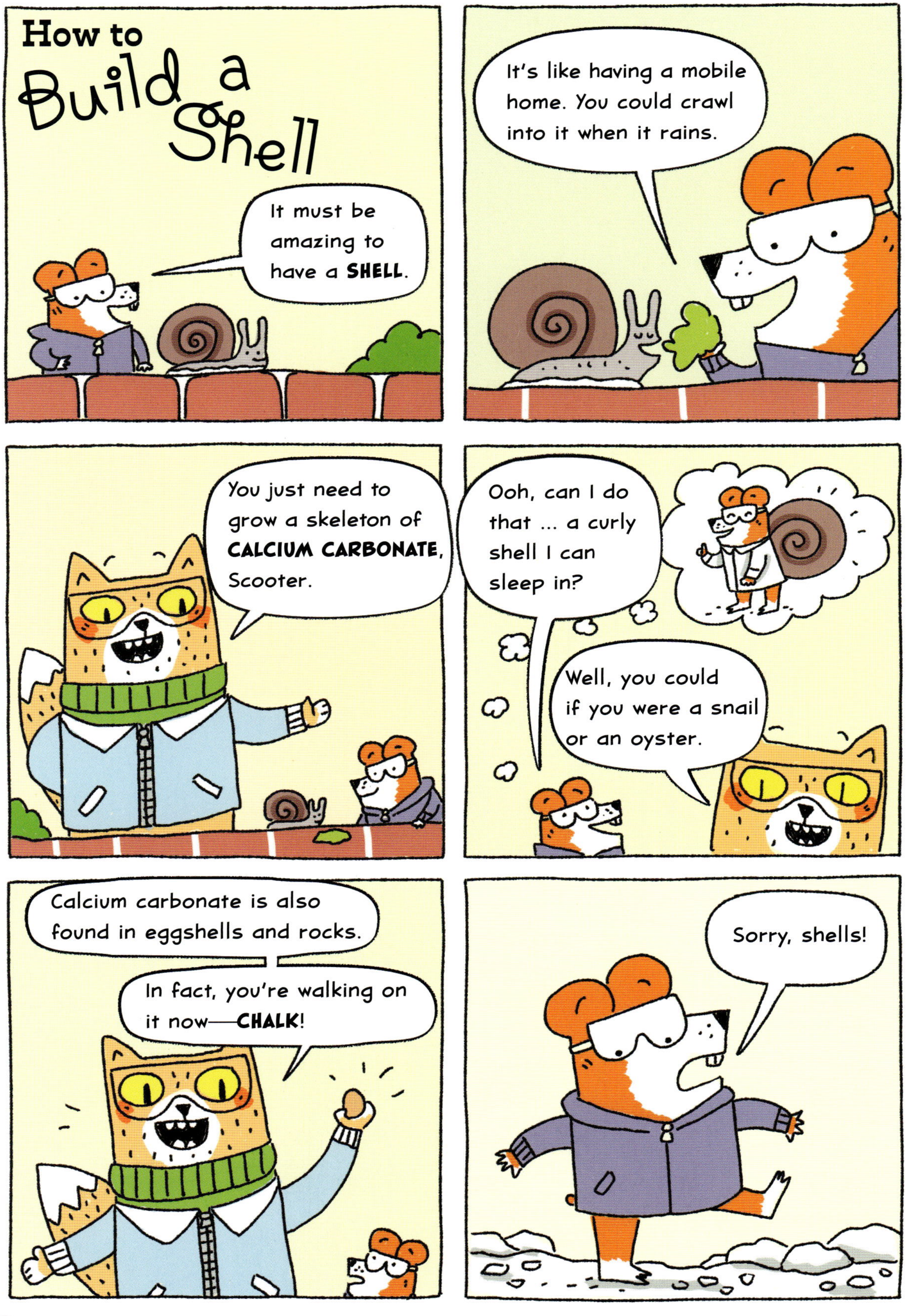
How to Build a Shell
It must be amazing to have a SHELL.
It's like having a mobile home. You could crawl into it when it rains.
You just need to grow a skeleton of CALCIUM CARBONATE, Scooter.
Ooh, can I do that ... a curly shell I can sleep in?
Well, you could if you were a snail or an oyster.
Calcium carbonate is also found in eggshells and rocks.
In fact, you're walking on it now—CHALK!
Sorry, shells!

Calcium carbonate is a **compound**. It's chemical formula is $CaCO_3$, so you can probably work out it contains the elements **calcium** (Ca), **carbon** (C), and **oxygen** (O).

This common compound is found in rocks, including limestone, aragonite, and chalk.

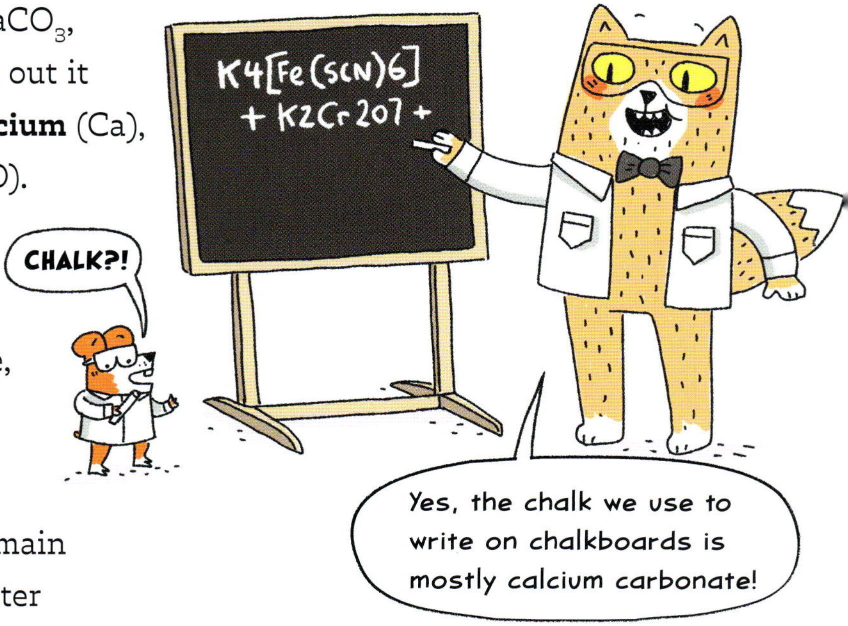

K4[Fe(SCN)6] + K2Cr207 +
CHALK?!
Yes, the chalk we use to write on chalkboards is mostly calcium carbonate!

Calcium carbonate is the main ingredient of **coral**, the outer skeleton of tiny sea creatures called polyps. It is also used in the shells of oysters, mussels, sea urchins, and other shellfish.

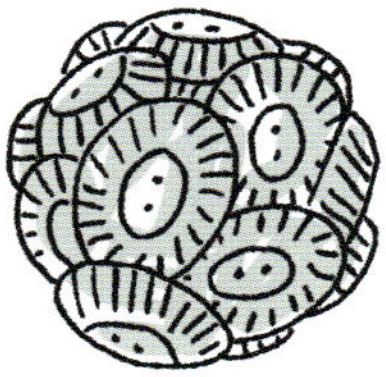

Chalk is mostly made from the fossilized scales of tiny organisms called coccoliths.

Animals, including humans, have a lot of calcium in their bodies, too. A different compound called **calcium phosphate** is used to make bones and teeth. Calcium is the most common metal in the human body!

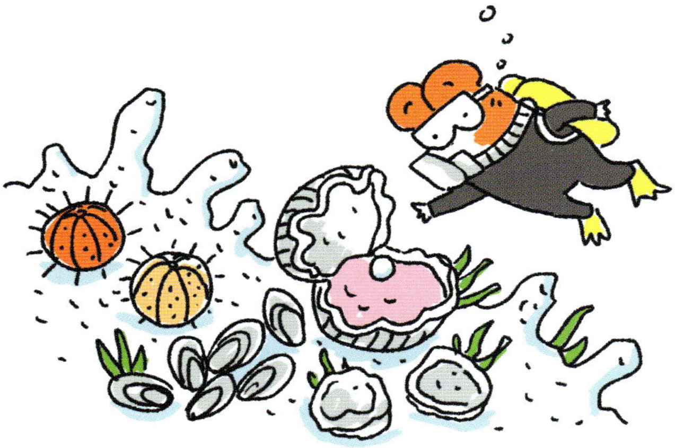

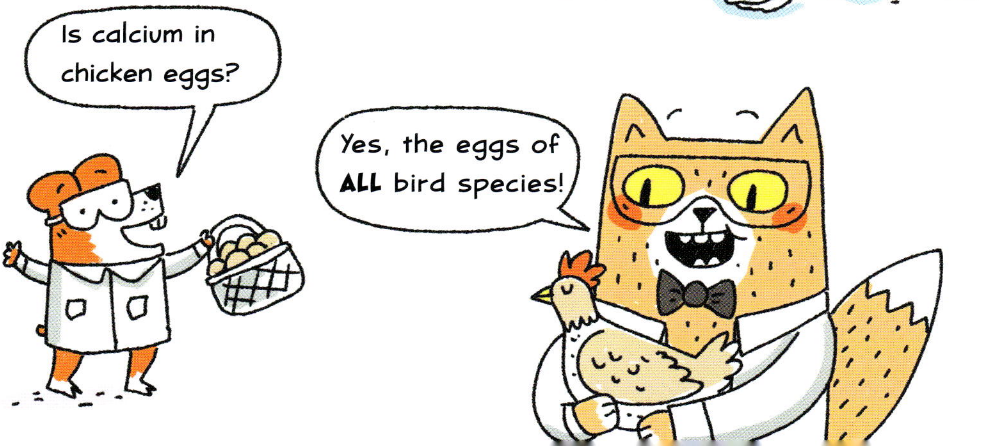

Is calcium in chicken eggs?
Yes, the eggs of **ALL** bird species!

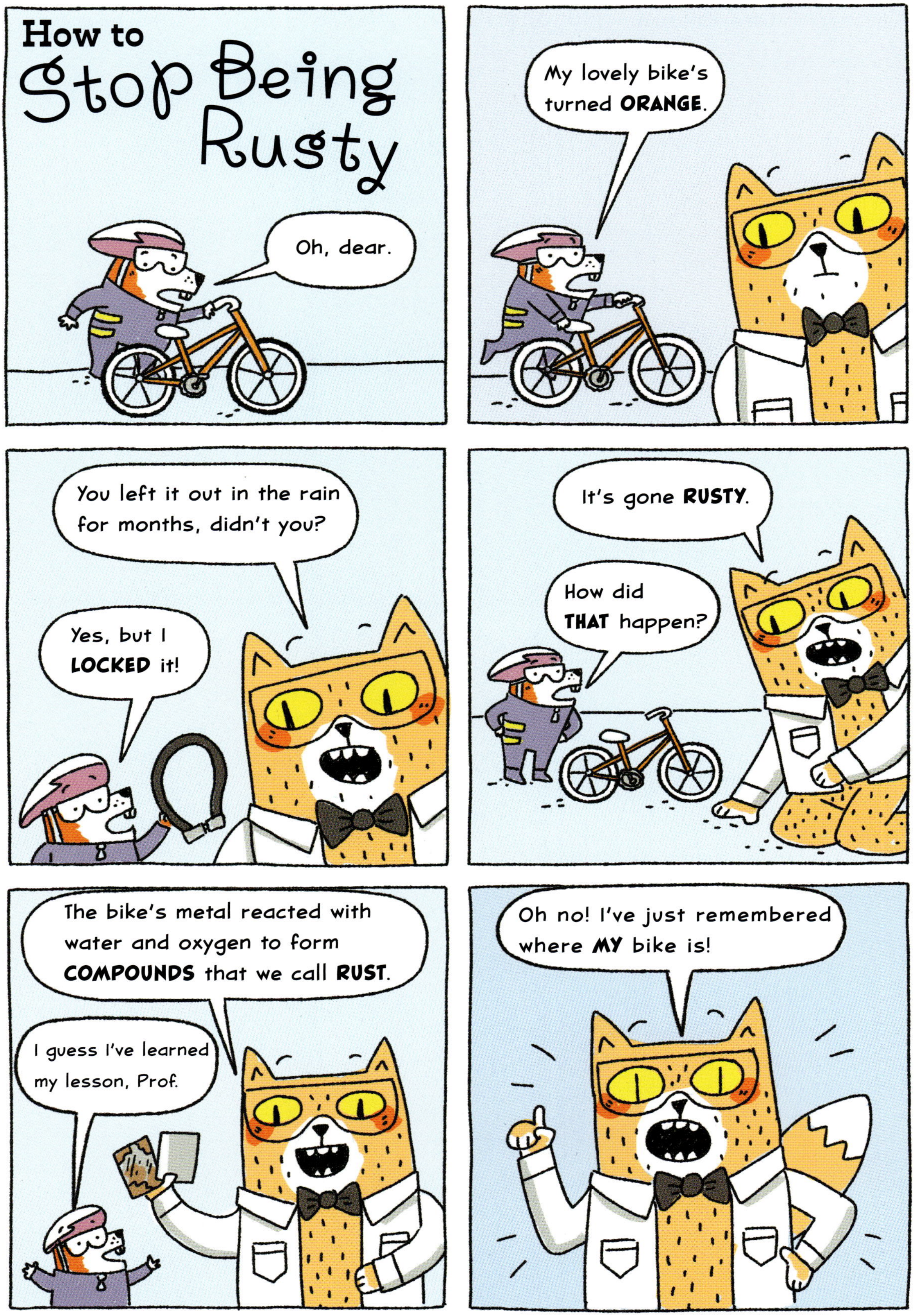
How to Stop Being Rusty
Oh, dear.
My lovely bike's turned ORANGE.
You left it out in the rain for months, didn't you?
Yes, but I LOCKED it!
It's gone RUSTY.
How did THAT happen?
The bike's metal reacted with water and oxygen to form COMPOUNDS that we call RUST.
I guess I've learned my lesson, Prof.
Oh no! I've just remembered where MY bike is!

Rust is the result of a chemical reaction called **corrosion**.

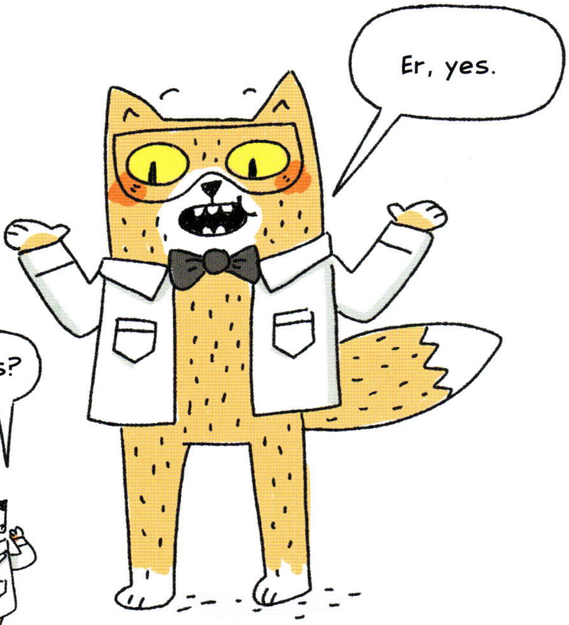
Er, yes.

When the metal **iron** comes in contact with **oxygen** and **water**, the iron atoms lose **electrons** to form **positively charged ions**.

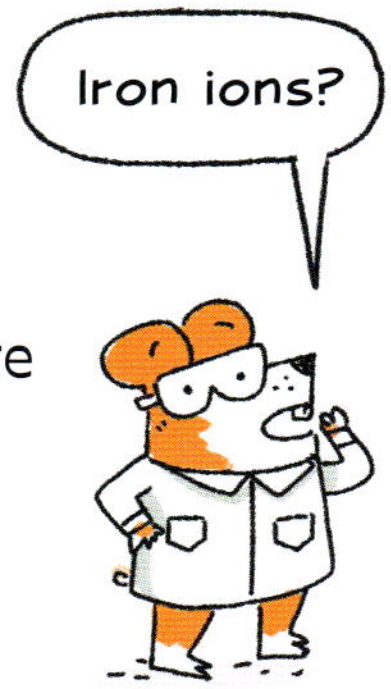
Iron ions?

Oxygen reacts with water to form **negatively charged ions**. The positive and negative ions are attracted to each other and form the compounds **iron oxide** and **iron hydroxide**, or rust.

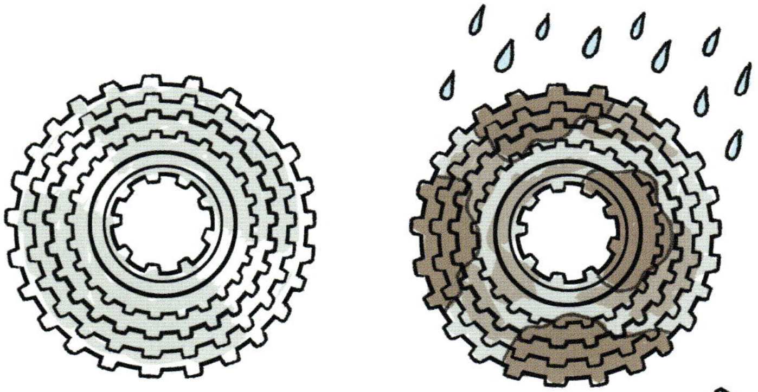

Over time, the rusty layers flake away, and the metal can turn into a pile of rusted remains.

When exposed to the weather, **copper** turns green with **verdigris**, which is why you often see statues (like the copper-plated Statue of Liberty) looking green.

Some metals, such as **gold** and **platinum**, can resist corrosion and stay shiny for centuries.

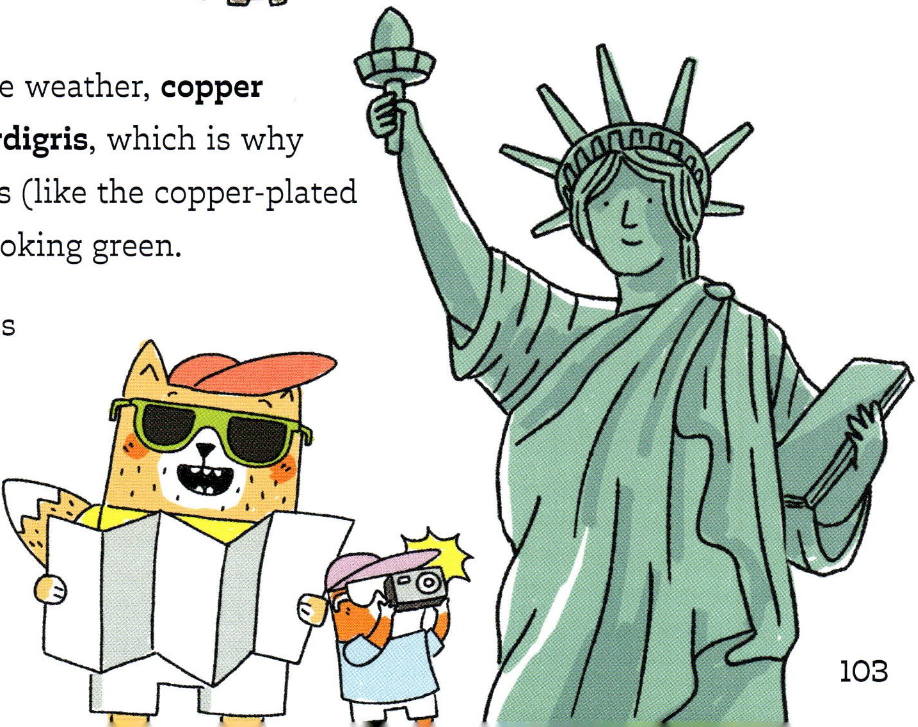

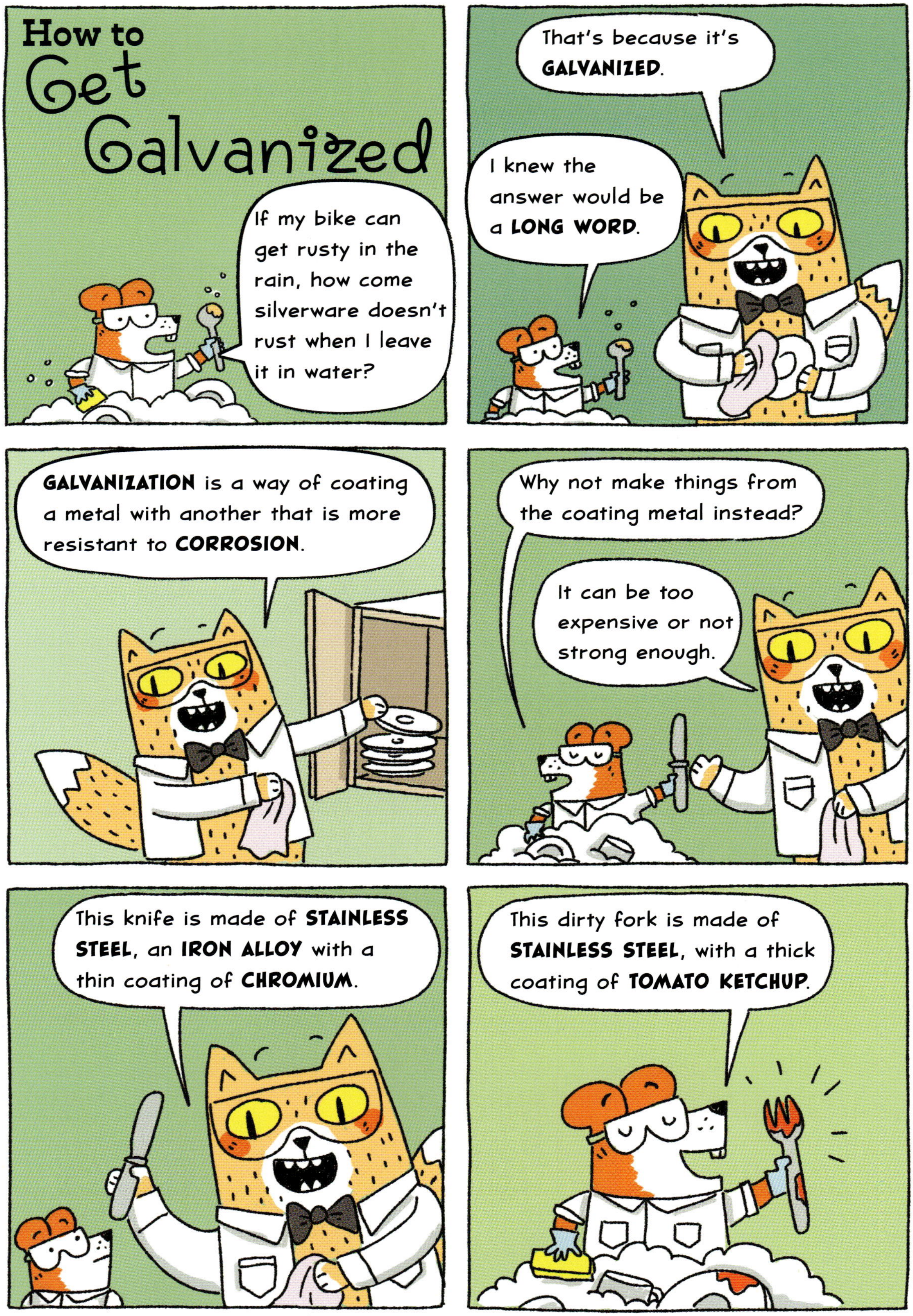
How to Get Galvanized
If my bike can get rusty in the rain, how come silverware doesn't rust when I leave it in water?
That's because it's GALVANIZED.
I knew the answer would be a LONG WORD.
GALVANIZATION is a way of coating a metal with another that is more resistant to CORROSION.
Why not make things from the coating metal instead?
It can be too expensive or not strong enough.
This knife is made of STAINLESS STEEL, an IRON ALLOY with a thin coating of CHROMIUM.
This dirty fork is made of STAINLESS STEEL, with a thick coating of TOMATO KETCHUP.

No sign of RUST!

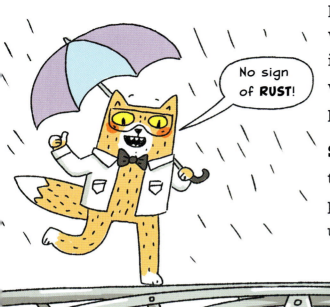

One way to stop metal corrosion is to paint the metal, so that oxygen and water can't reach it and react with it. Another method is **galvanization**, which coats the metal with a protective metal, such as **zinc**.

Stainless steel is an iron **alloy** with the metal **chromium** added for rust protection. Stainless steel is often used for silverware or building bridges.

Battery
Cathode
Zinc (Zn) Anode
Metal
Zinc (Zn) plating
Electrolyte

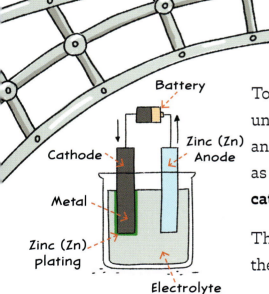

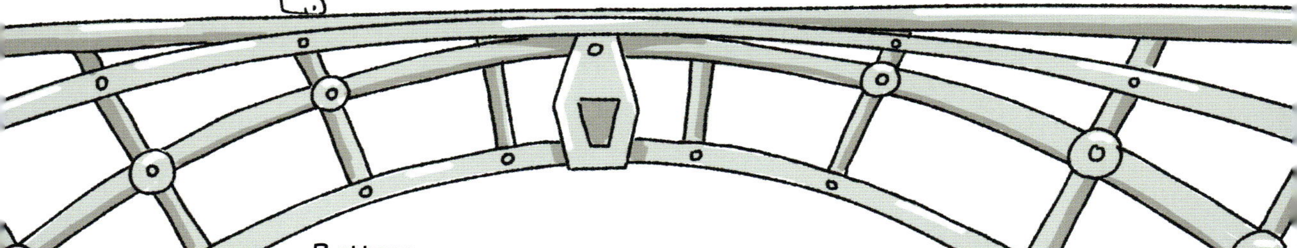

To galvanize a metal it has to undergo **electroplating**. The metal and the metal for plating are arranged as **electrodes**. The metal to be plated is the **cathode**, and the plating metal is the **anode**.

The electrodes are placed in an **electrolyte**, then an electric current is passed through it.

The current causes the anode's zinc atoms to lose electrons and become **positively charged ions**. These travel through the electrolyte to the cathode, where they gain electrons and become **zinc atoms** again. The result is a metal coated with zinc.

Clang clang!
Do you like my new ZINC COAT?

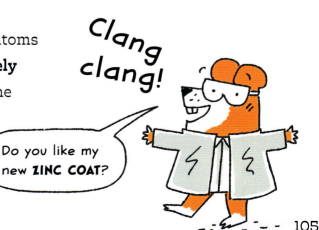

How to Turn Objects into Gold
Wow! I've been reading the story of KING MIDAS who turned everything to GOLD!
We can do that.
Then we'll be RICH!
Not exactly. First, we have to BUY the gold, then do some ELECTROPLATING.
Oh.
It's working!
The electric current has turned the gold into IONS in the ELECTROLYTE.
They bonded with our cheap metal to form a GOLD LAYER 0.005 mm (0.0002 in) thick!
Here you go, King Midas.
A GOLD-PLATED BALL BEARING?!
That's ALL the gold I could afford.

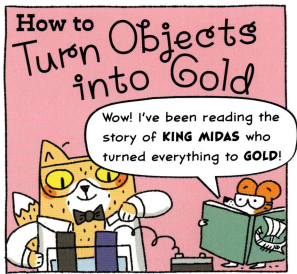

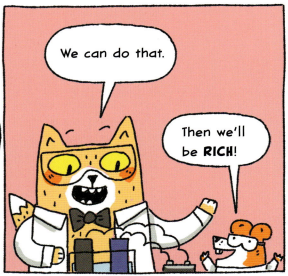

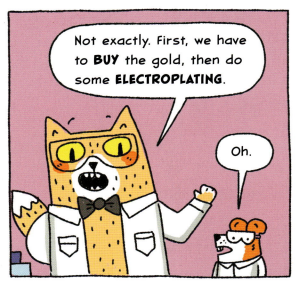

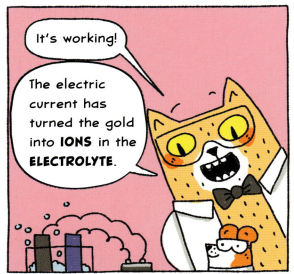

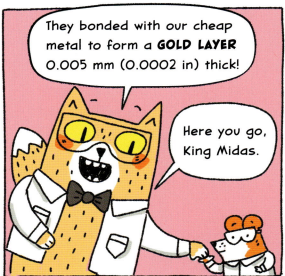

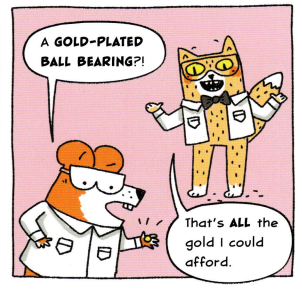

Chemical World

(Earth and Atmospheric Science, Plastics, Greenhouse Effect, Pollution)

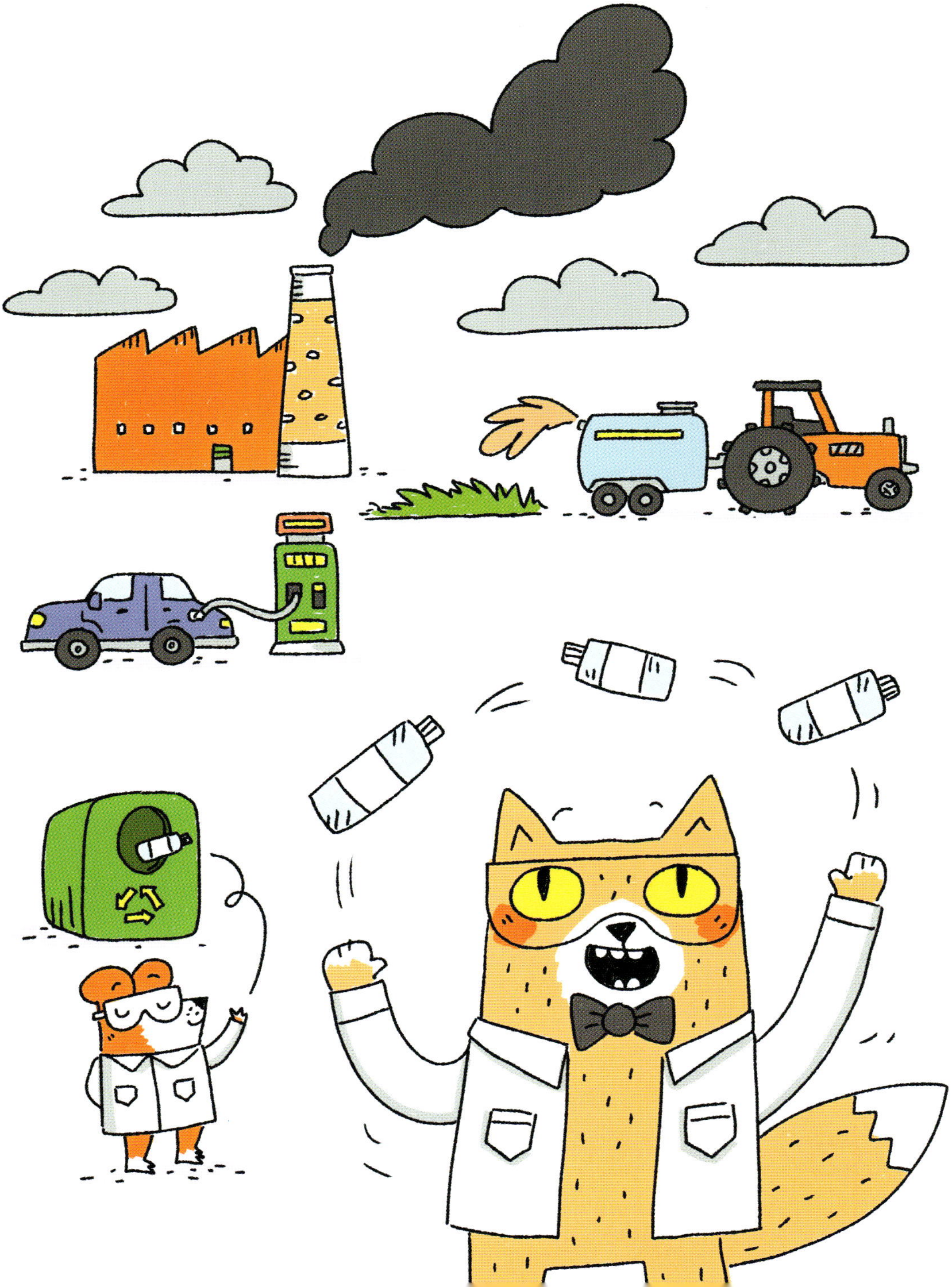

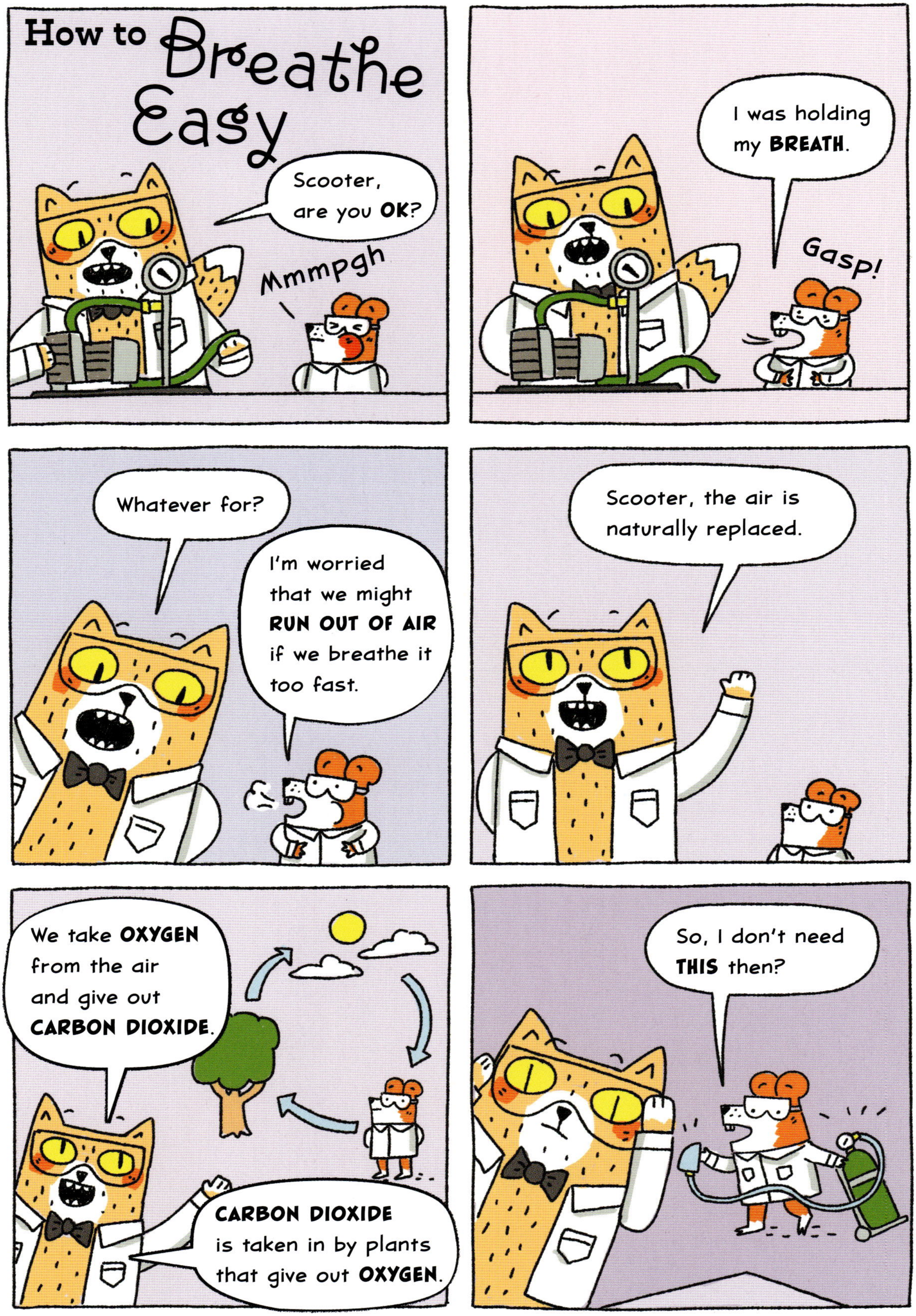
How to Breathe Easy
Scooter, are you OK?
Mmmpgh
I was holding my BREATH.
Gasp!
Whatever for?
I'm worried that we might RUN OUT OF AIR if we breathe it too fast.
Scooter, the air is naturally replaced.
We take OXYGEN from the air and give out CARBON DIOXIDE.
CARBON DIOXIDE is taken in by plants that give out OXYGEN.
So, I don't need THIS then?

The air that we breathe is made up of various gases. **Nitrogen**, a nonreactive gas, makes up 78% of it. As part of the compound **ammonia**, it helps plants grow.

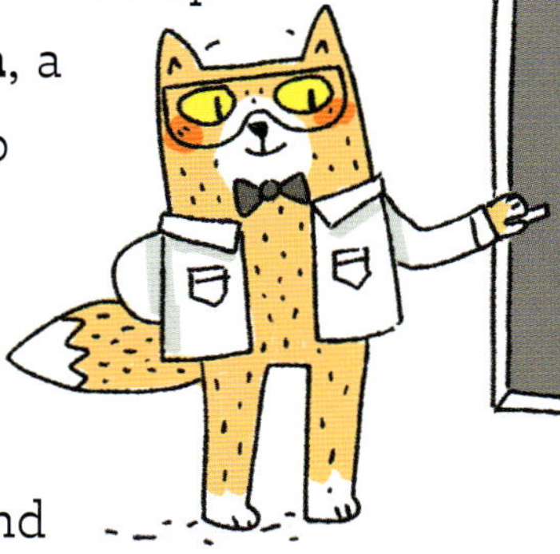

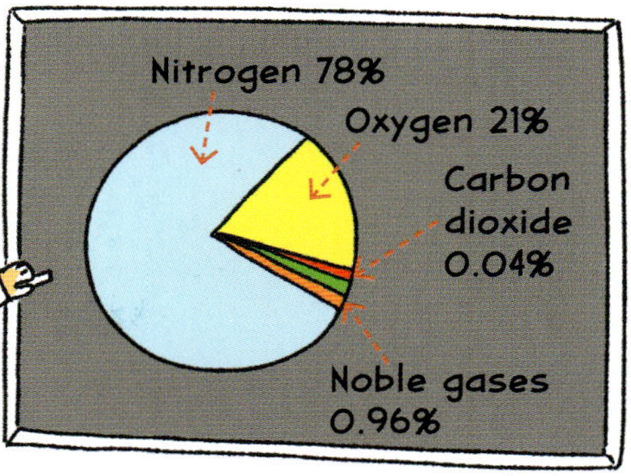
Nitrogen 78%
Oxygen 21%
Carbon dioxide 0.04%
Noble gases 0.96%

Oxygen, which humans and other animals take in when they breathe, makes up 21%. Oxygen helps us to take energy from food.

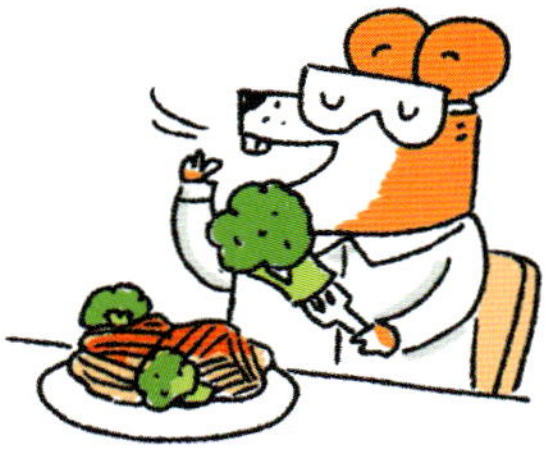

The other 1% of the air is made up of **carbon dioxide**—which humans breathe out and plants take in—along with water vapor, and small amounts of **noble gases**. Noble gases are colorless gases that do not react easily with other chemicals.

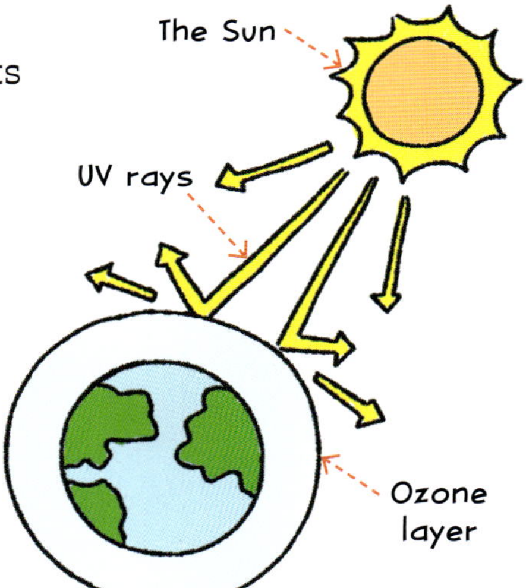
The Sun
UV rays
Ozone layer

Far above us, a layer of **ozone** (a form of oxygen) protects us from harmful **ultraviolet** rays from the Sun.

Gases such as carbon dioxide trap the Sun's heat, keeping the planet warm.

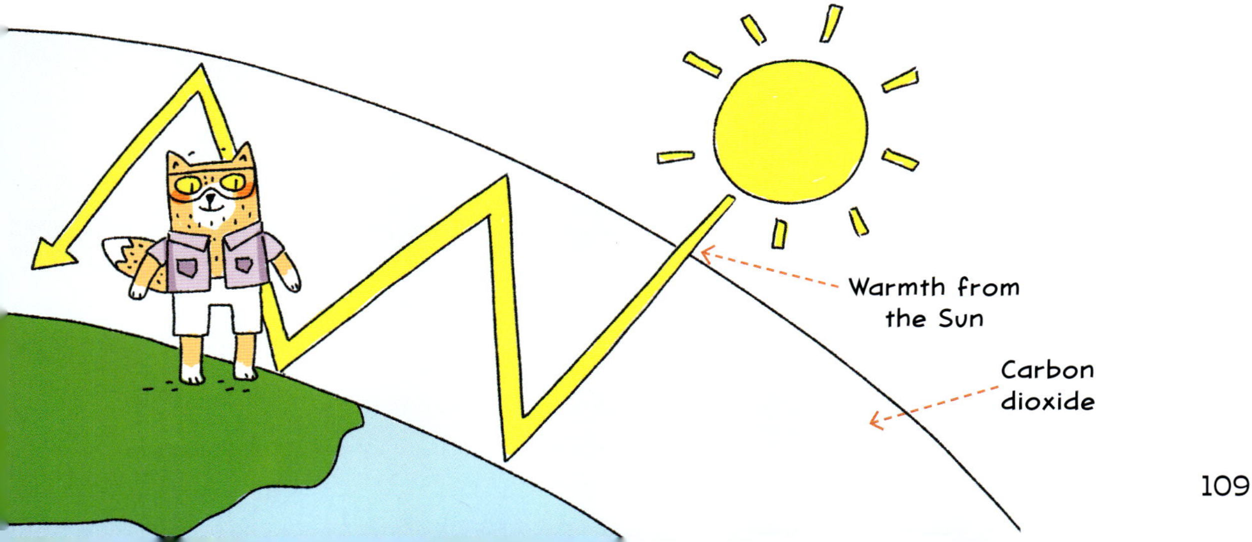
Warmth from the Sun
Carbon dioxide

How to Fry an Egg
Happy birthday, Scooter!
It's NOT my birthday.
Well, I got you a PRESENT!
YAY!
It's, um, a FRYING PAN.
The old one was covered in burned food.
This pan has a nonstick coating made of a POLYMER.
The polymer is made from chains of CARBON and FLUORINE atoms that do not bond with food molecules.
So, it will be easier for me to CLEAN ...
I also got some EGGS.
Do you want me to FRY you some eggs?
You read my MIND!

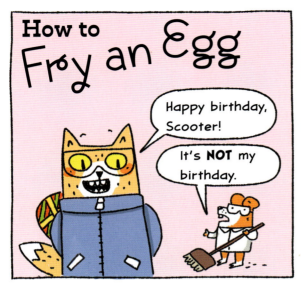

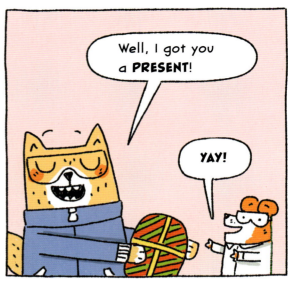

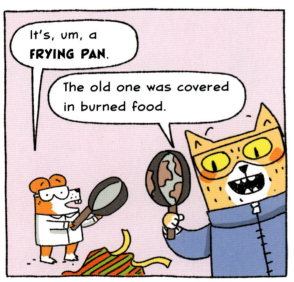

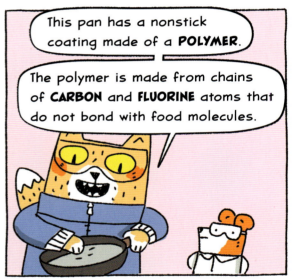

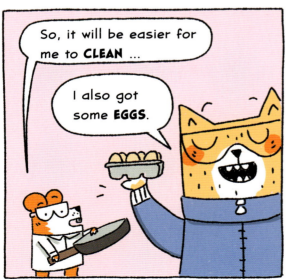

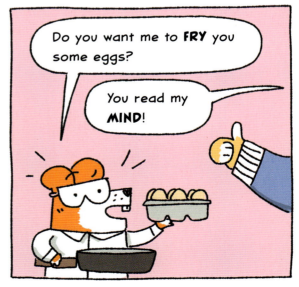

Most substances are made up of small **molecules**, but there are some with long chains of small, repeating building blocks. These are called **polymers**.

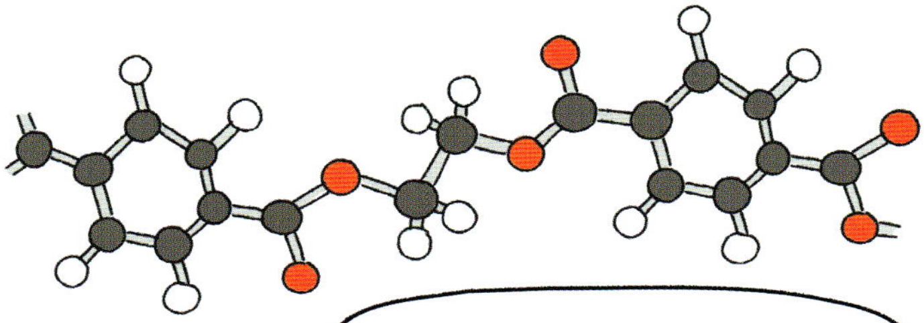

Polymer

Polymers may have thousands or millions of atoms in each molecule. Some polymers are artificial. These include nylon, and plastic.

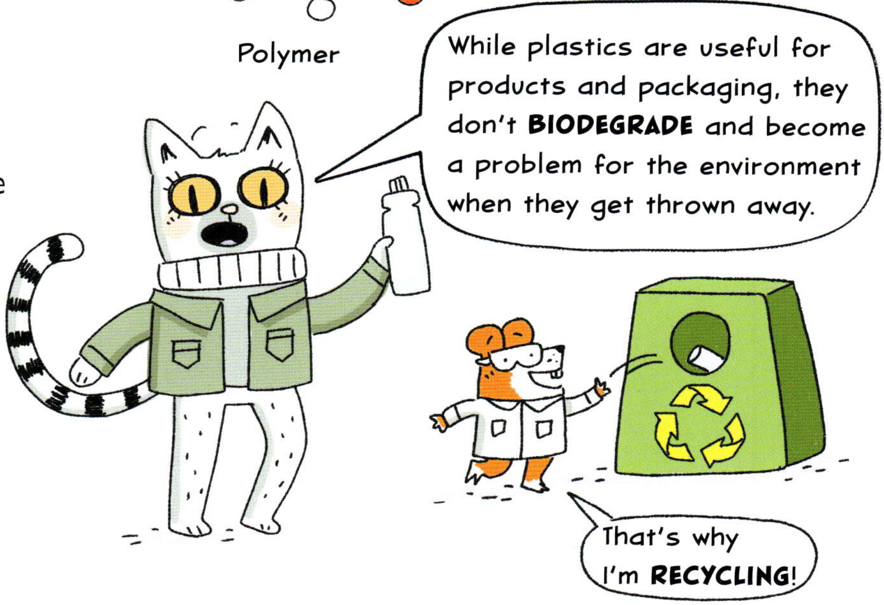

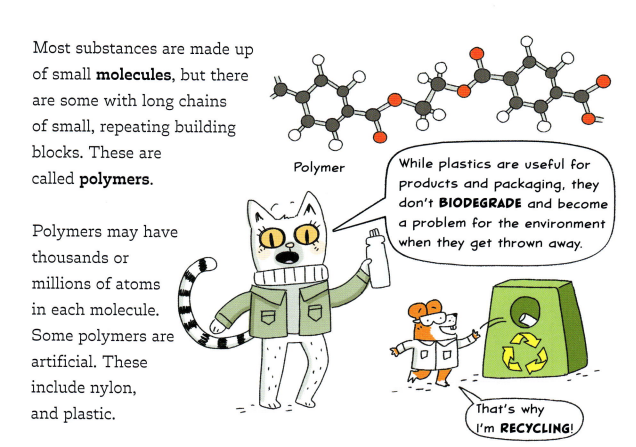

While plastics are useful for products and packaging, they don't **BIODEGRADE** and become a problem for the environment when they get thrown away.
That's why I'm **RECYCLING**!

Plastic is made from **crude oil** (unrefined petroleum). Plastic is useful because it can be molded into any shape when hot before it cools into a solid. Some plastics are made to be hard and some stretchy.

NATURAL POLYMERS

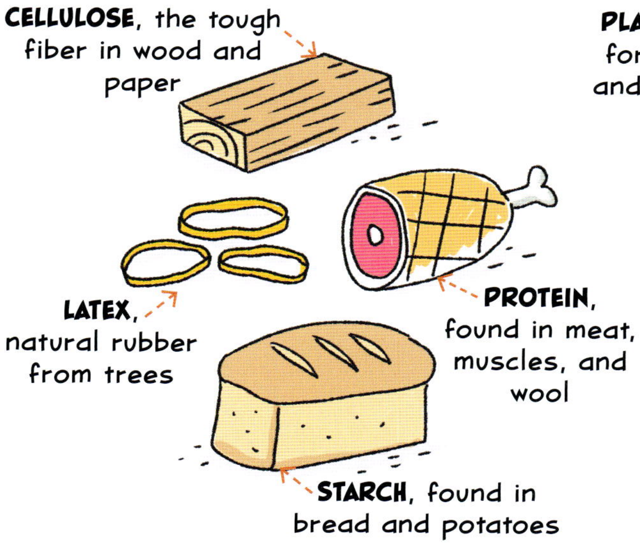

CELLULOSE, the tough fiber in wood and paper
LATEX, natural rubber from trees
PROTEIN, found in meat, muscles, and wool
STARCH, found in bread and potatoes

ARTIFICIAL POLYMERS

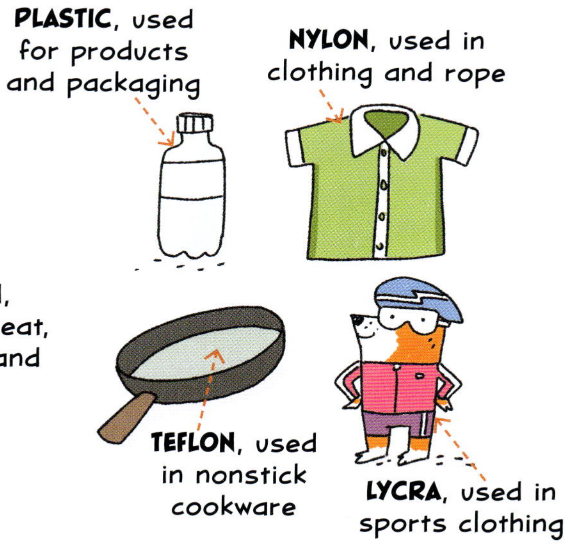

PLASTIC, used for products and packaging
NYLON, used in clothing and rope
TEFLON, used in nonstick cookware
LYCRA, used in sports clothing

Fossil Fuels

Oil, coal, and gas are **FOSSIL FUELS**.
You mean they're made of **DINOSAURS**?
No, they are made from fossilized plants and plankton.

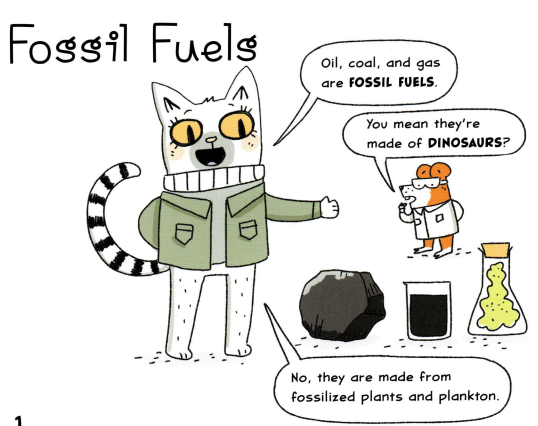

1

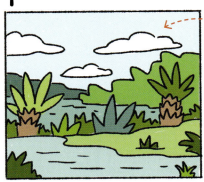

Coal is the remains of swamp forests from over 300 million years ago, long before dinosaurs ruled the Earth.

2

The plants decayed and were buried under layers of sediment (rocks and minerals deposited by wind and rain).

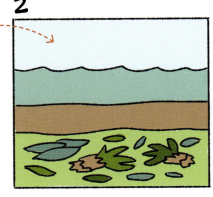

3

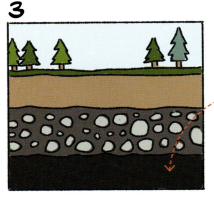

Over millions of years, the plant matter was compressed until it hardened into a rock mostly made up of the element carbon. Coal is extracted by mining on the surface or underground.

They decomposed under sand and silt, weighed down by the water above.

Oil and **gas** began in the prehistoric oceans where tiny aquatic organisms died and sank to the seabed.

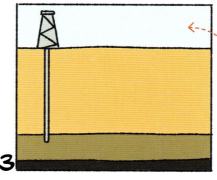

Over millions of years, the plant matter was compressed and heated until it turned into oil and gas.

Oil and gas are drilled for. Oil is refined for used as fuel and as an ingredient in plastics. Gas is usually found as **methane** above underground oil reserves.

A major problem with fossil fuels is that when they are burned, their stored carbon is released into the atmosphere, adding **carbon dioxide**, a **greenhouse gas**. This traps the heat of the Sun and contributes to **global warming**.

Fossil fuels took millions of years to form and are **NONRENEWABLE**.

What does **THAT** mean?

They will *eventually* run out, so we need to find new sources of energy.

113

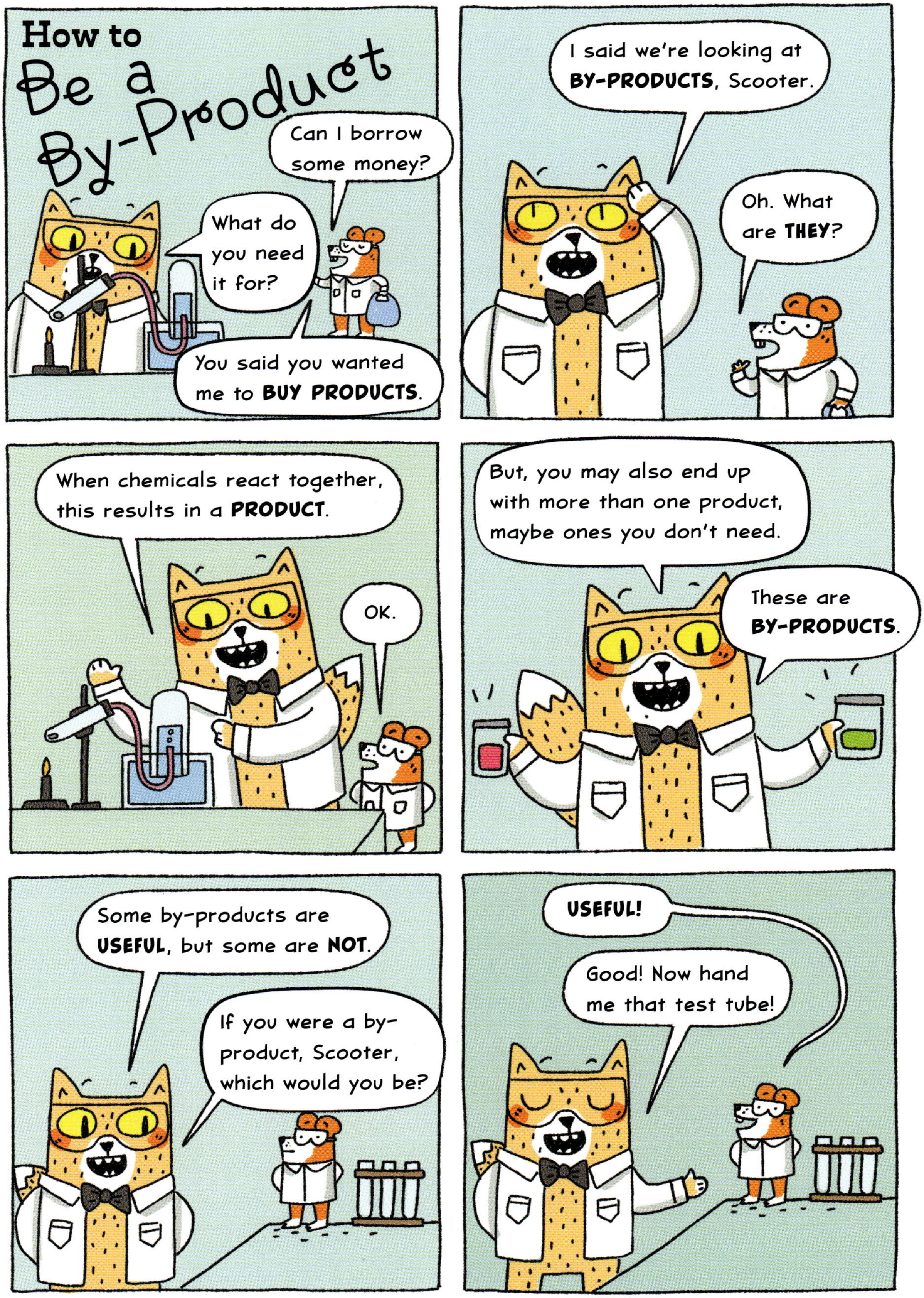
How to Be a By-Product
Can I borrow some money?
What do you need it for?
You said you wanted me to BUY PRODUCTS.
I said we're looking at BY-PRODUCTS, Scooter.
Oh. What are THEY?
When chemicals react together, this results in a PRODUCT.
OK.
But, you may also end up with more than one product, maybe ones you don't need.
These are BY-PRODUCTS.
Some by-products are USEFUL, but some are NOT.
If you were a by-product, Scooter, which would you be?
USEFUL!
Good! Now hand me that test tube!

Many processes create different by-products. Here are some examples.

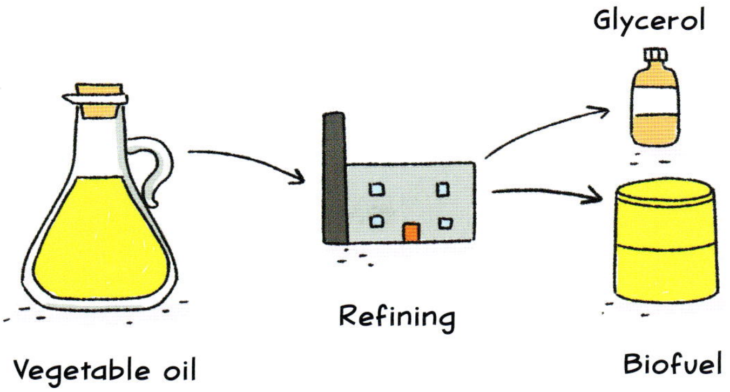
Glycerol
Refining
Vegetable oil
Biofuel

When vegetable oil is turned into biofuel for cars, a by-product called **glycerol** is produced. This can be used to treat burns or for sweetening food!

When wool is cleaned with chemicals in a factory, it produces a by-product called **lanolin**. This is used in many beauty products.

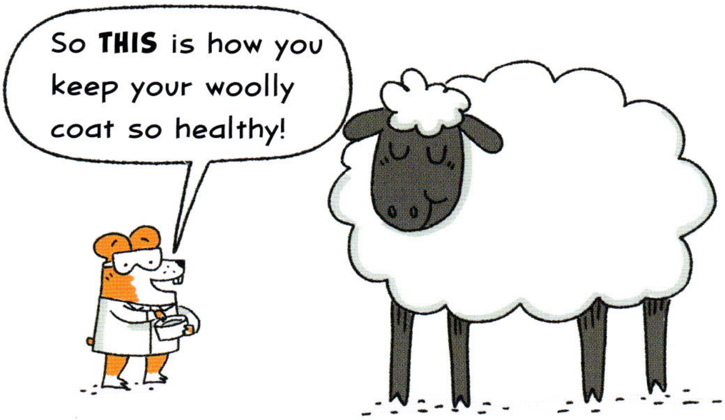
So THIS is how you keep your woolly coat so healthy!

Not all by-products are helpful, though. Some are considered waste.

Burning fossil fuels in power plants releases unwanted **carbon dioxide** into the air. This by-product pollutes the atmosphere.

Dangerous chemical waste needs to be treated to be made less harmful before being safely disposed of.

Other polluting by-products include **dioxins**. These toxic chemicals are produced when we make paper or pesticides, or burn waste. They are harmful to the environment.

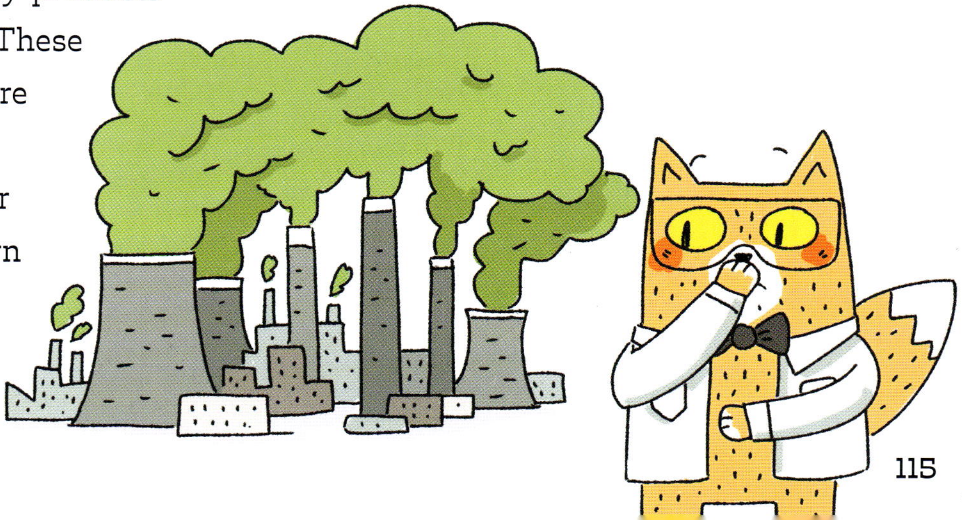

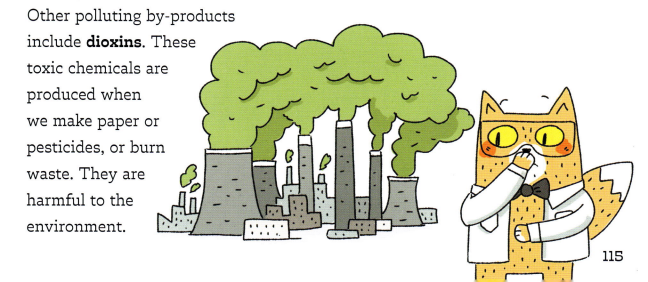

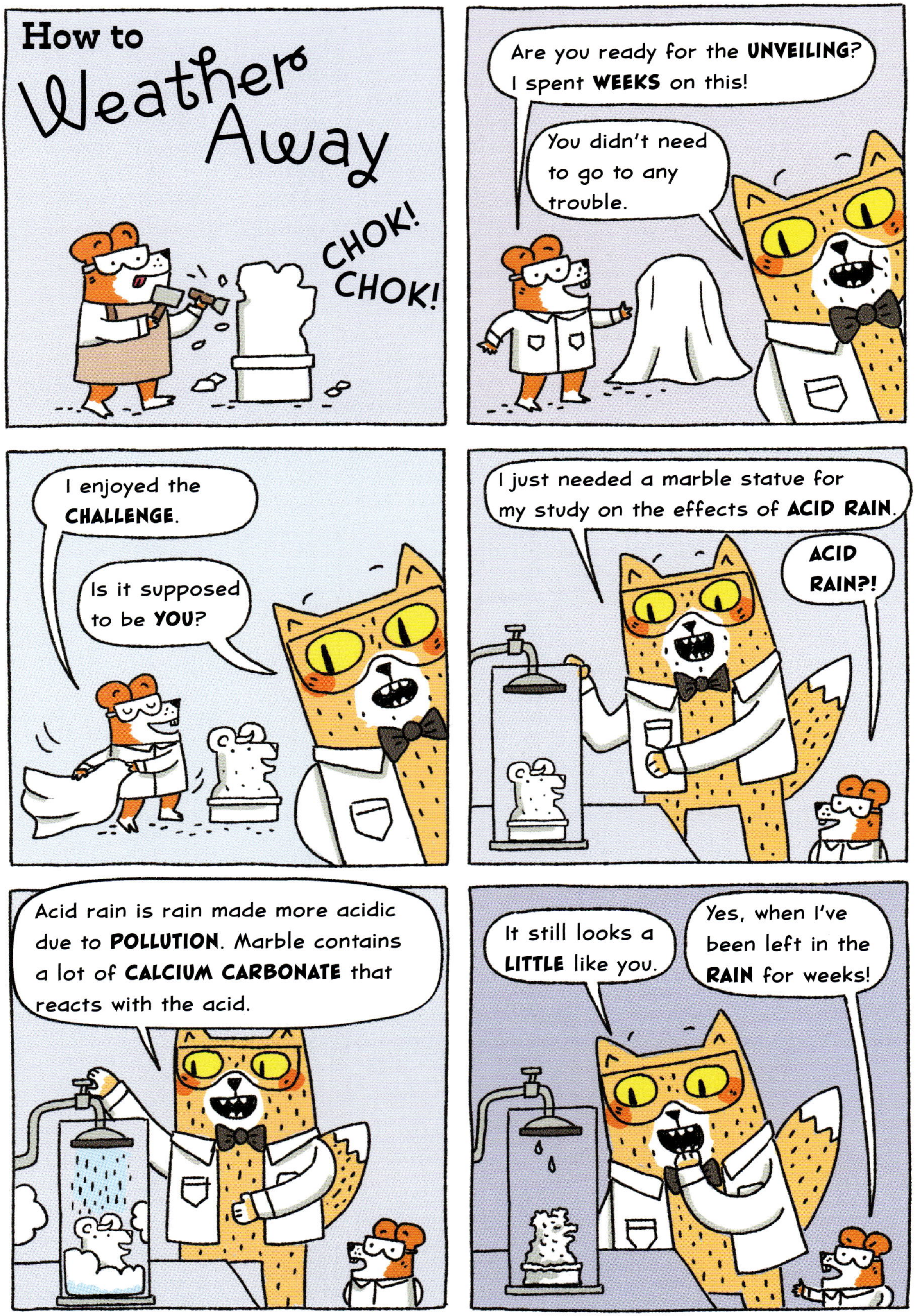
How to Weather Away
CHOK! CHOK!
Are you ready for the UNVEILING? I spent WEEKS on this!
You didn't need to go to any trouble.
I enjoyed the CHALLENGE.
Is it supposed to be YOU?
I just needed a marble statue for my study on the effects of ACID RAIN.
ACID RAIN?!
Acid rain is rain made more acidic due to POLLUTION. Marble contains a lot of CALCIUM CARBONATE that reacts with the acid.
It still looks a LITTLE like you.
Yes, when I've been left in the RAIN for weeks!

Rainwater is naturally acidic. **Carbonic acid** forms when **carbon dioxide** (CO_2) from the air dissolves in water.

The gases **sulfur dioxide** (SO_2) and **nitrogen oxide** (NO_2), released from power plants and vehicles that burn **fossil fuels**, also dissolve in rainwater, making it even more acidic.

Carbonic acid is used to make soda drinks.
Burp!

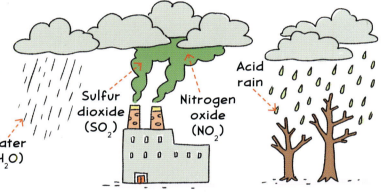

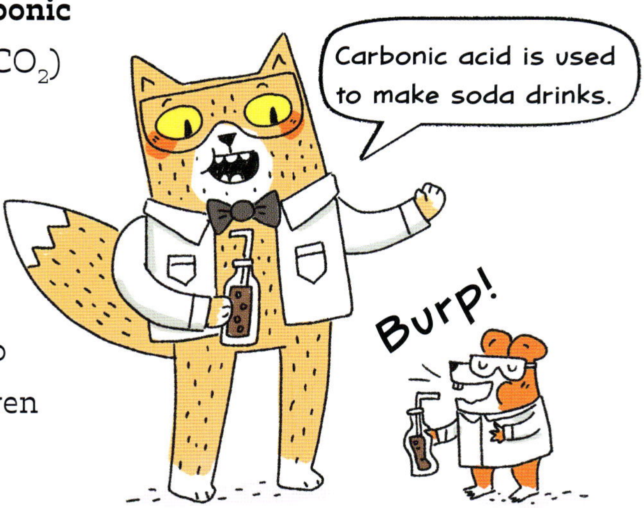

Acid rain can cause damage to nature and buildings. Trees may die, and the water in lakes can become too acidic for fish.

Water (H_2O)
Sulfur dioxide (SO_2)
Nitrogen oxide (NO_2)
Acid rain

Sulfur dioxide and nitrogen oxide react with water to make sulfuric and nitric acid.

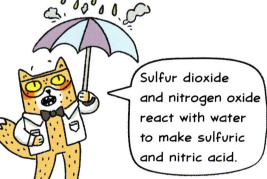

Buildings and statues made from limestone and marble suffer due to acid rain. These stones contain **calcium carbonate**, which reacts with the acids and dissolves. This can be seen in statues that have had detail worn away.

To reduce acid rain, factories must reduce their use of fossil fuels and limit pollution.

I wonder who **THIS** guy is?

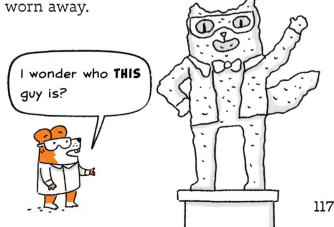

How to Feed Your Plants
Hi, Dr. Ringtail. I wonder if you can help me ...
OH, MY! What did you do to this poor plant?! It needs some TLC.
Is that a CHEMICAL?
It means TENDER LOVING CARE, Scooter, but some NPK may help, too!
NPK?
NITROGEN (N), PHOSPHORUS (P), and POTASSIUM (K). These chemicals provide food for plants.
In a small pot, plants soon use up any goodness in the soil.
I use a liquid fertilizer to give my plants these nutrients.
TFTT.
That means: "Thanks For The Tip."
HTH!
Happy To Help!

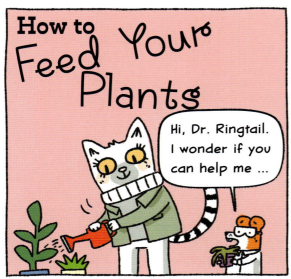

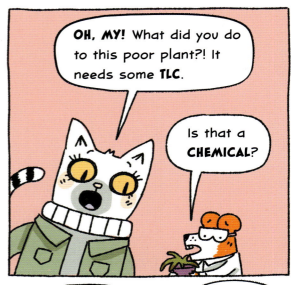

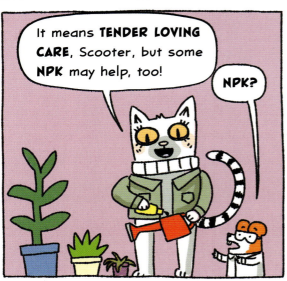

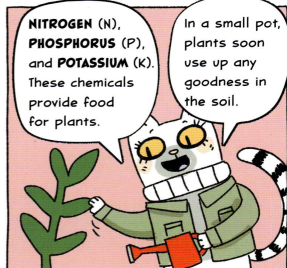

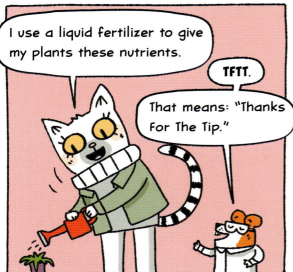

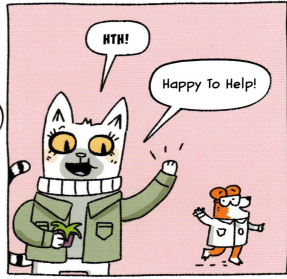

Plants benefit from the elements **nitrogen** (N), **phosphorus** (P), and **potassium** (K).

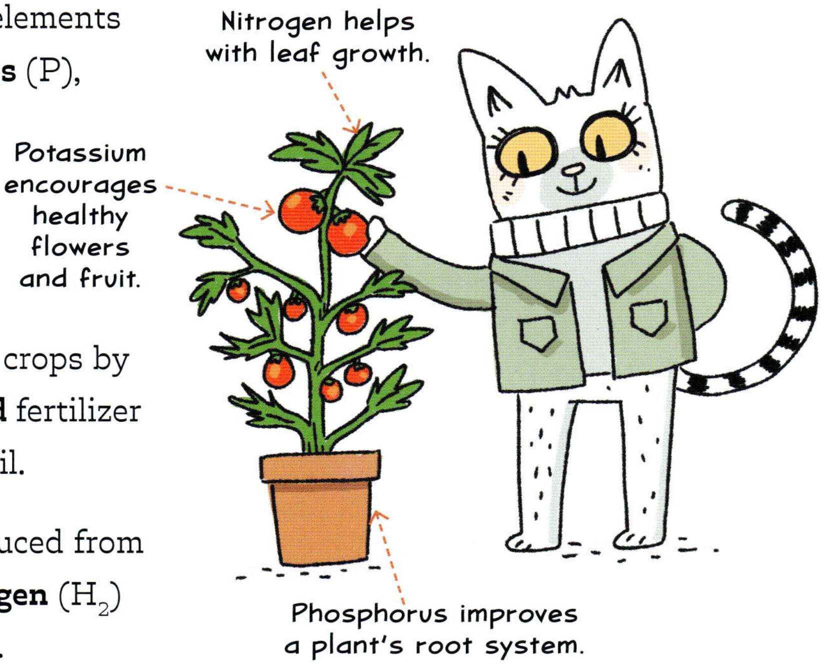
Nitrogen helps with leaf growth.
Potassium encourages healthy flowers and fruit.
Phosphorus improves a plant's root system.

Many farmers feed their crops by using an **ammonia-based** fertilizer to add nitrogen to the soil.

Ammonia (NH_3) is produced from **nitrogen** (N_2) and **hydrogen** (H_2) using the **Haber process**.

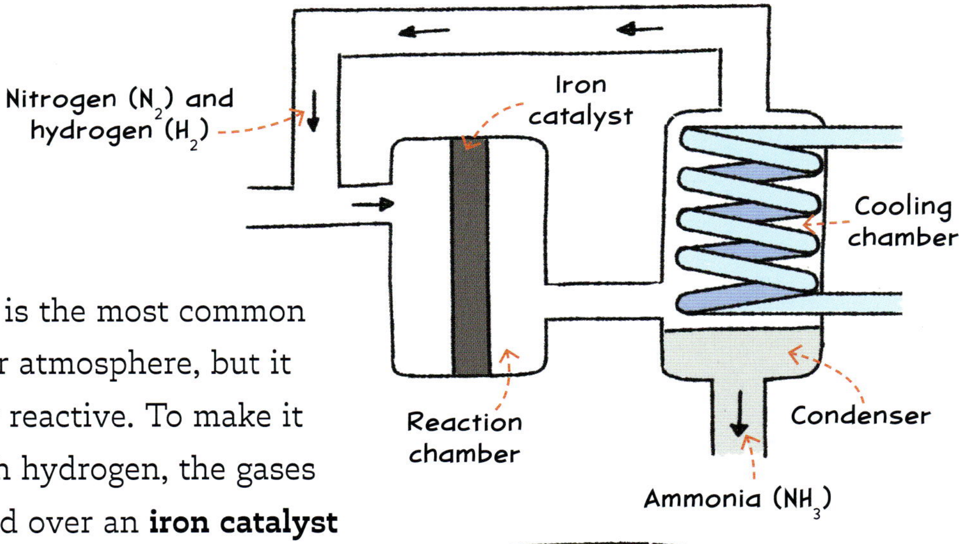
Nitrogen (N_2) and hydrogen (H_2)
Iron catalyst
Cooling chamber
Reaction chamber
Condenser
Ammonia (NH_3)

Nitrogen is the most common gas in our atmosphere, but it isn't very reactive. To make it react with hydrogen, the gases are passed over an **iron catalyst** and put under very high temperatures and pressures.

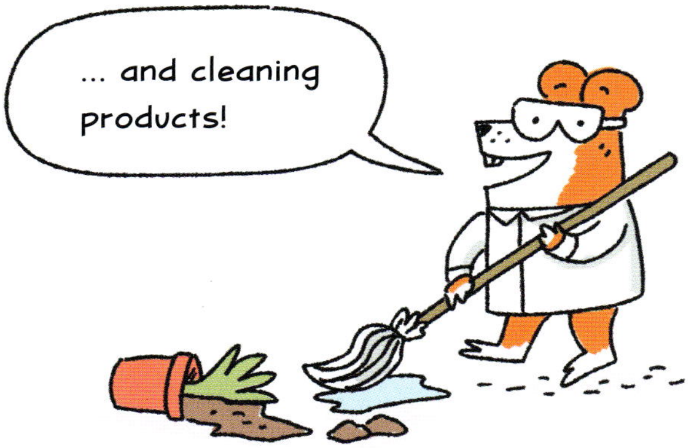
... and cleaning products!

The reaction produces ammonia gas, which is then cooled to make liquid ammonia. Ammonia is used for fertilizers, dyes, phamaceuticals, and more.

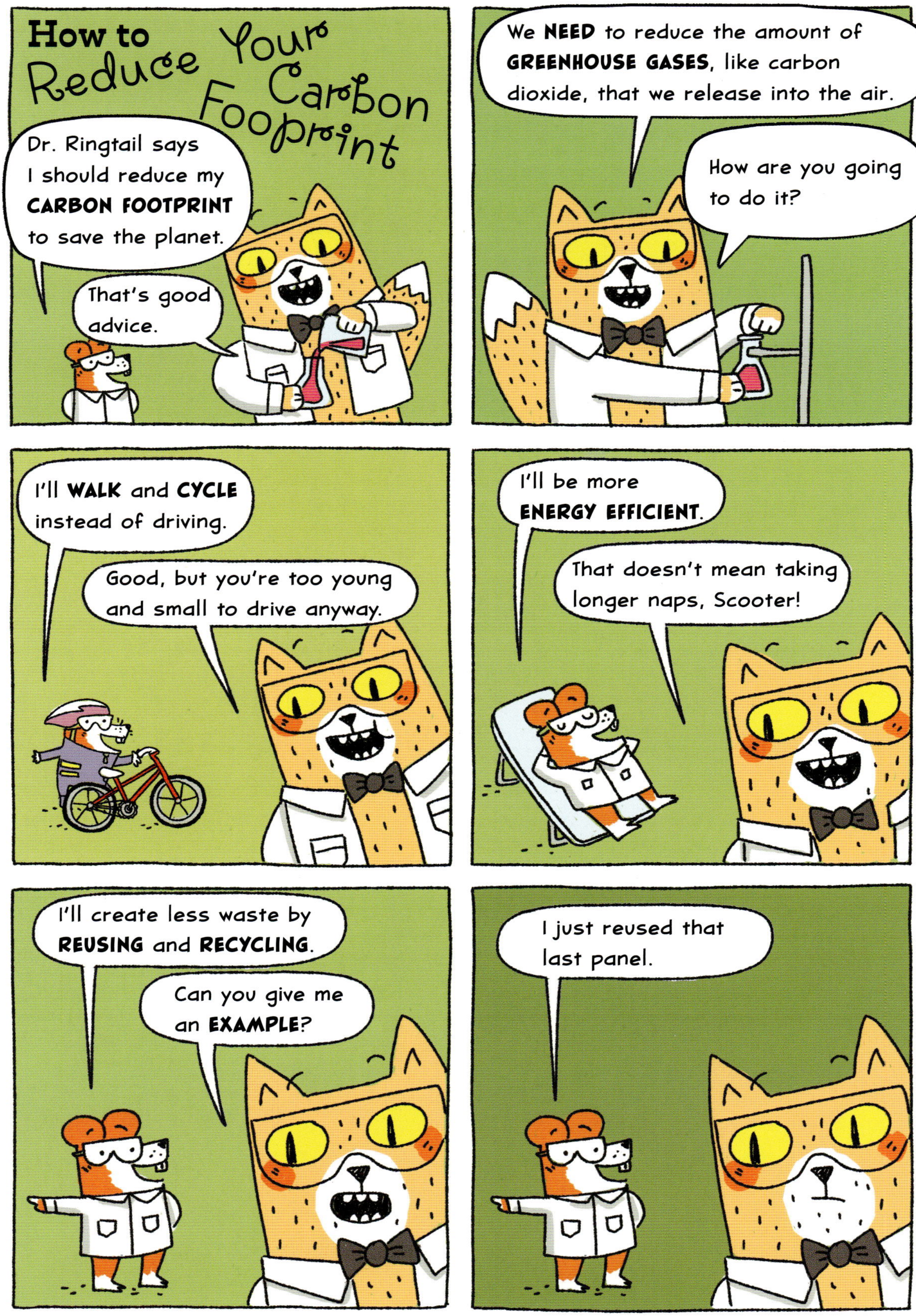
How to Reduce Your Carbon Foo[?]print
Dr. Ringtail says I should reduce my CARBON FOOTPRINT to save the planet.
That's good advice.
We NEED to reduce the amount of GREENHOUSE GASES, like carbon dioxide, that we release into the air.
How are you going to do it?
I'll WALK and CYCLE instead of driving.
Good, but you're too young and small to drive anyway.
I'll be more ENERGY EFFICIENT.
That doesn't mean taking longer naps, Scooter!
I'll create less waste by REUSING and RECYCLING.
Can you give me an EXAMPLE?
I just reused that last panel.

Your **carbon footprint** is a measure of how much carbon dioxide and other **greenhouse gases** you add to the environment through your activity. Driving a car, taking flights, and producing waste all add to your footprint. Planting trees, using less electricity, recycling, and walking and cycling instead of driving can reduce it.

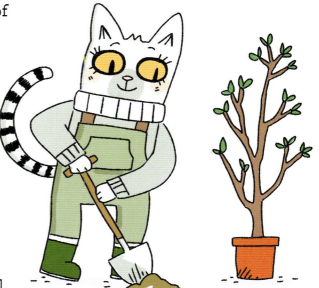

Carbon (C) is an element found in all plants and animals, the air, oceans, and the earth itself. The cycle it follows affects us all.

1. Plants take in carbon dioxide (CO_2) during **PHOTOSYNTHESIS**. Using the Sun's energy, plants convert CO_2 into sugars and other nutrients to feed on.

6. Fuels are burned for heat and energy. This **COMBUSTION** frees some carbon as CO_2.

Carbon dioxide (CO_2)
Photosynthesis
Respiration
Factory emission
Decay
Fossil fuels

2. Many plants are eaten by animals. The carbon in the plants is released through dung and into the air through respiration, breathing in **OXYGEN**, and breathing out CO_2.

5. Some CO_2 dissolves in the oceans.

3. When plants die, they return carbon to the soil. Worms, bacteria, and fungi feed on dung and dead plants and produce CO_2.

4. The **FOSSIL FUELS** coal, oil, and gas, are stores of carbon underground.

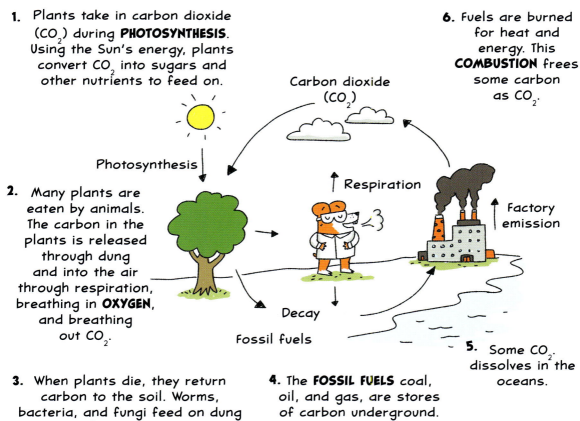

How to Heat Up a Planet
What am I STANDING in?
Don't worry about that. Just point the detector to your right.
Woorr! It's SMELLY!
PUMP!
What does the detector say?
I can confirm the presence of METHANE.
As I thought. Cattle are a major source of the GREENHOUSE GAS, methane.
GREENHOUSE GAS?
Greenhouse gases stop some of the Sun's heat reflecting from the Earth and returning to space.
They include WATER VAPOR ...
... CARBON DIOXIDE (CO_2), released by burning fossil fuels and cement production ...
... NITROUS OXIDE (N_2O), released through fertilizer use and burning fossil fuels ...

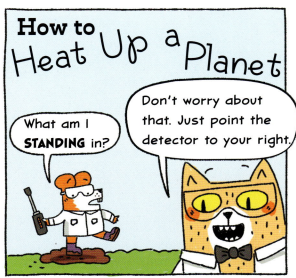

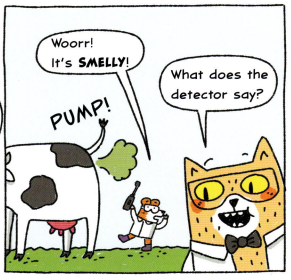

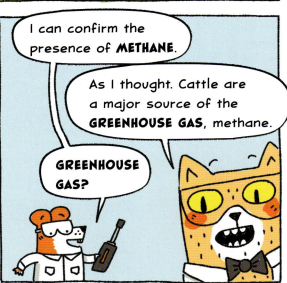

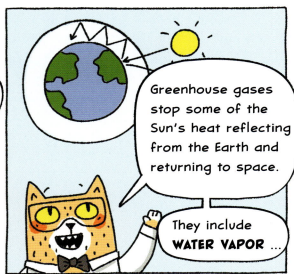

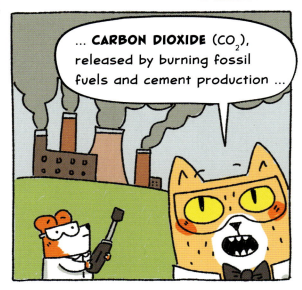

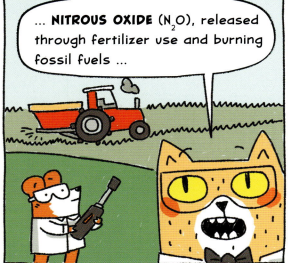

... and **METHANE** (CH_4), released through waste decomposition, fossil fuel production ...
... and animal burps and farts!
Correct!
These gases absorb energy from **INFRARED (THERMAL) RADIATION** and keep our planet warm enough for life.
So greenhouse gases are **GOOD** then?
Well, burning fossil fuels and agriculture have increased the amount of these gases in the air.
This has resulted in **GLOBAL WARMING**, a rise in average temperatures across the planet.
I like it **WARM**.
How about more **DESERTS** and **DROUGHT**?
Global warming also means more **CHANGEABLE WEATHER PATTERNS**.
WHOA!
And ice melting at the poles ...
Where's that **POLAR BEAR** going to live?
Exactly.
Scooter, we **CAN'T** take that polar bear back to live with us!
Awww.

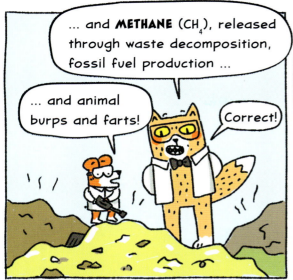

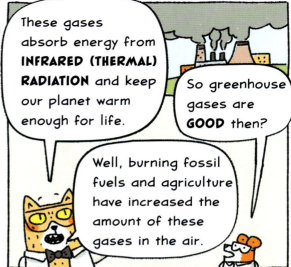

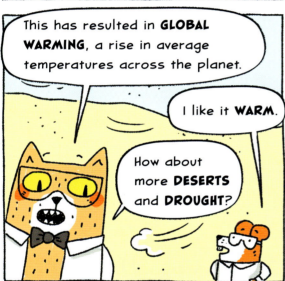

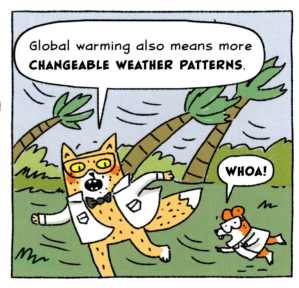

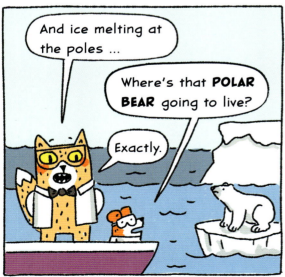

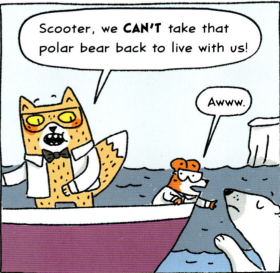

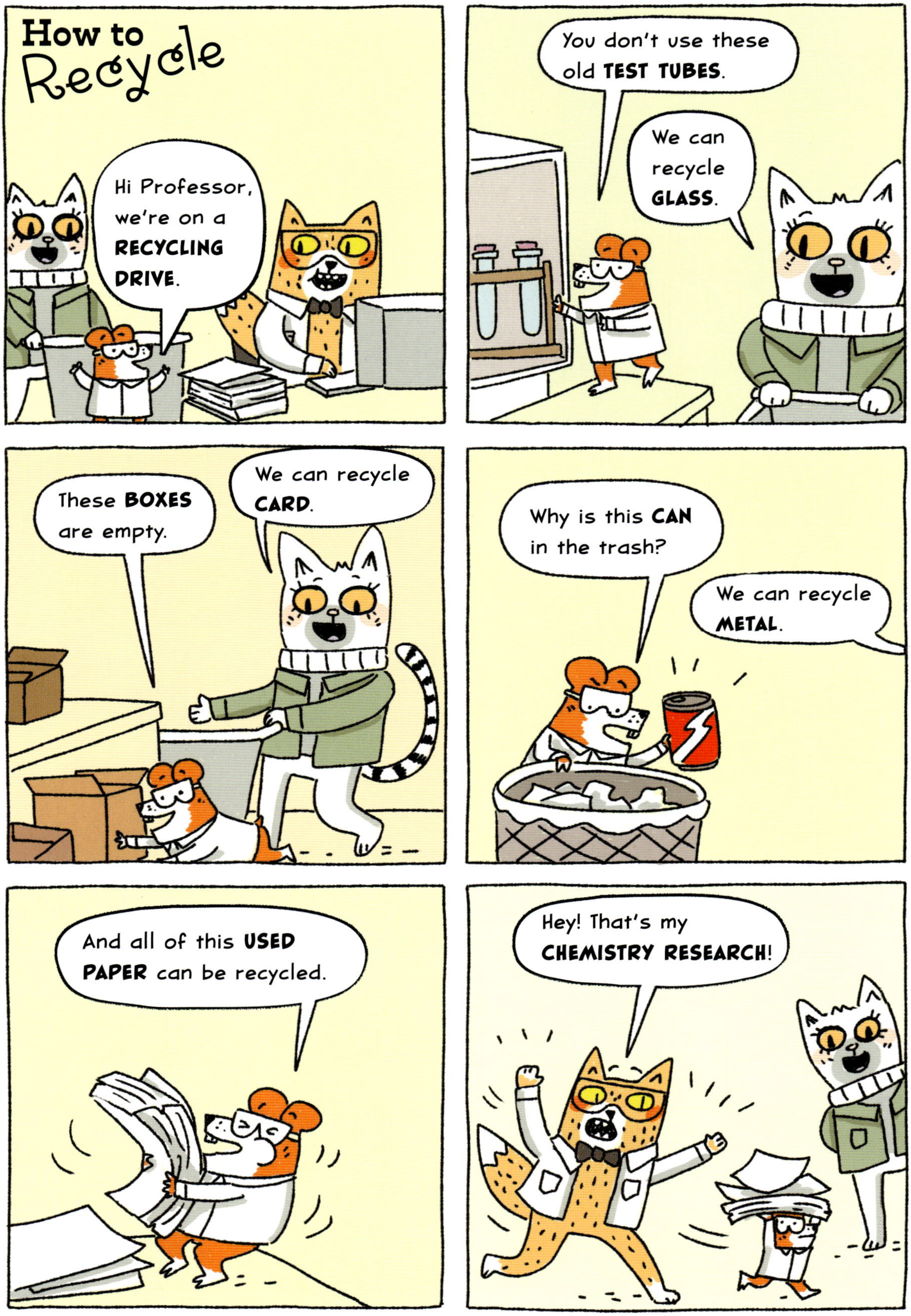
How to Recycle
Hi Professor, we're on a RECYCLING DRIVE.
You don't use these old TEST TUBES.
We can recycle GLASS.
These BOXES are empty.
We can recycle CARD.
Why is this CAN in the trash?
We can recycle METAL.
And all of this USED PAPER can be recycled.
Hey! That's my CHEMISTRY RESEARCH!

Much of our waste ends up as **landfill**. This can take years to chemically break down. It is better for the planet for us to **reuse** products and **recycle** the materials we no longer need.

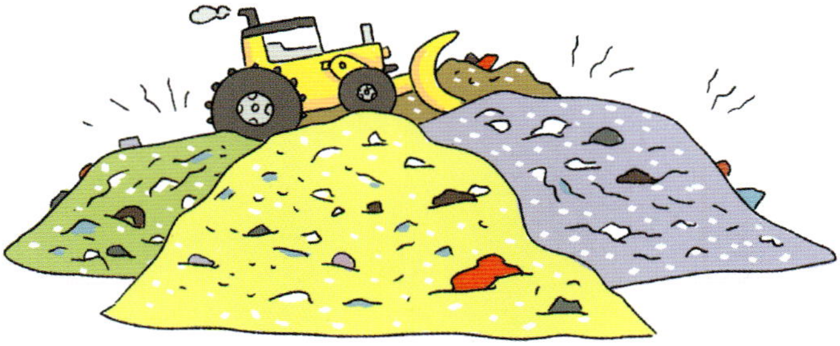

Metal

Recycling metals uses a lot less energy than that needed to dig them out of the ground. Recycling metal usually just means melting them down and casting them into a new shape.

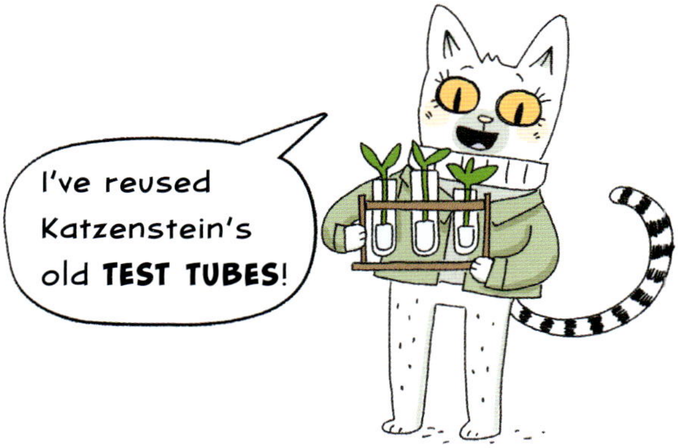
I've reused Katzenstein's old **TEST TUBES**!

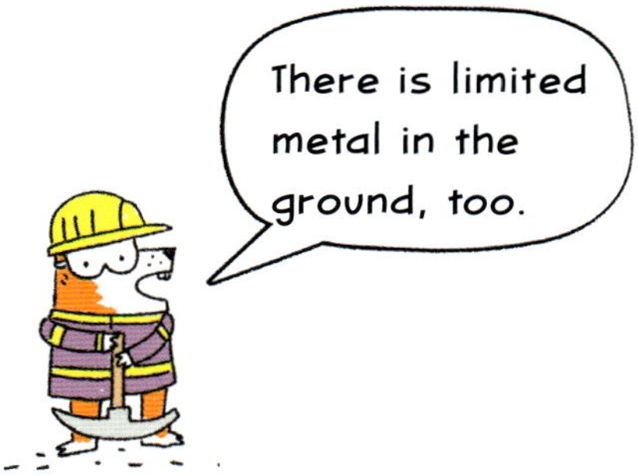
There is limited metal in the ground, too.

Glass

Glass is mostly made from **silica** (silicon dioxide). It can be reused or separated by color before being crushed, melted, and reshaped.

Plastics

Plastic is made from **hydrocarbons**. Plastics have to be sorted into chemical type, then cleaned, shredded into plastic chips for reshaping, or used as fibers for carpets or clothing.

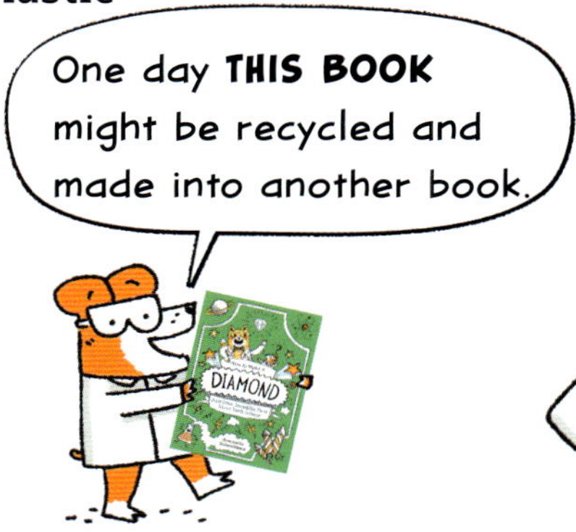
One day **THIS BOOK** might be recycled and made into another book.
DIAMOND

Paper

Paper, from wood pulp, is mixed with water and other chemicals to break it down, before it is pulped, bleached, and turned into recycled paper.

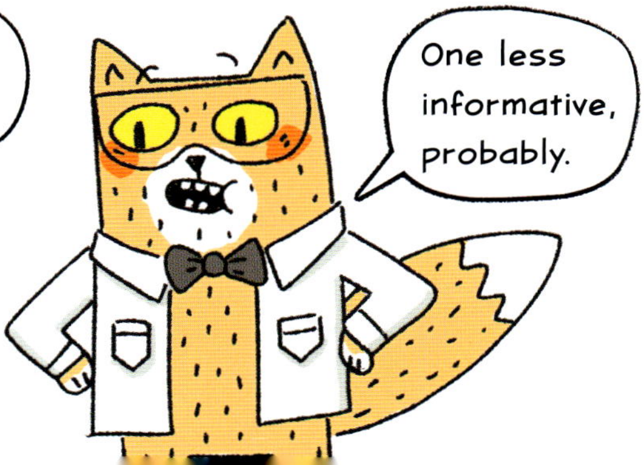
One less informative, probably.

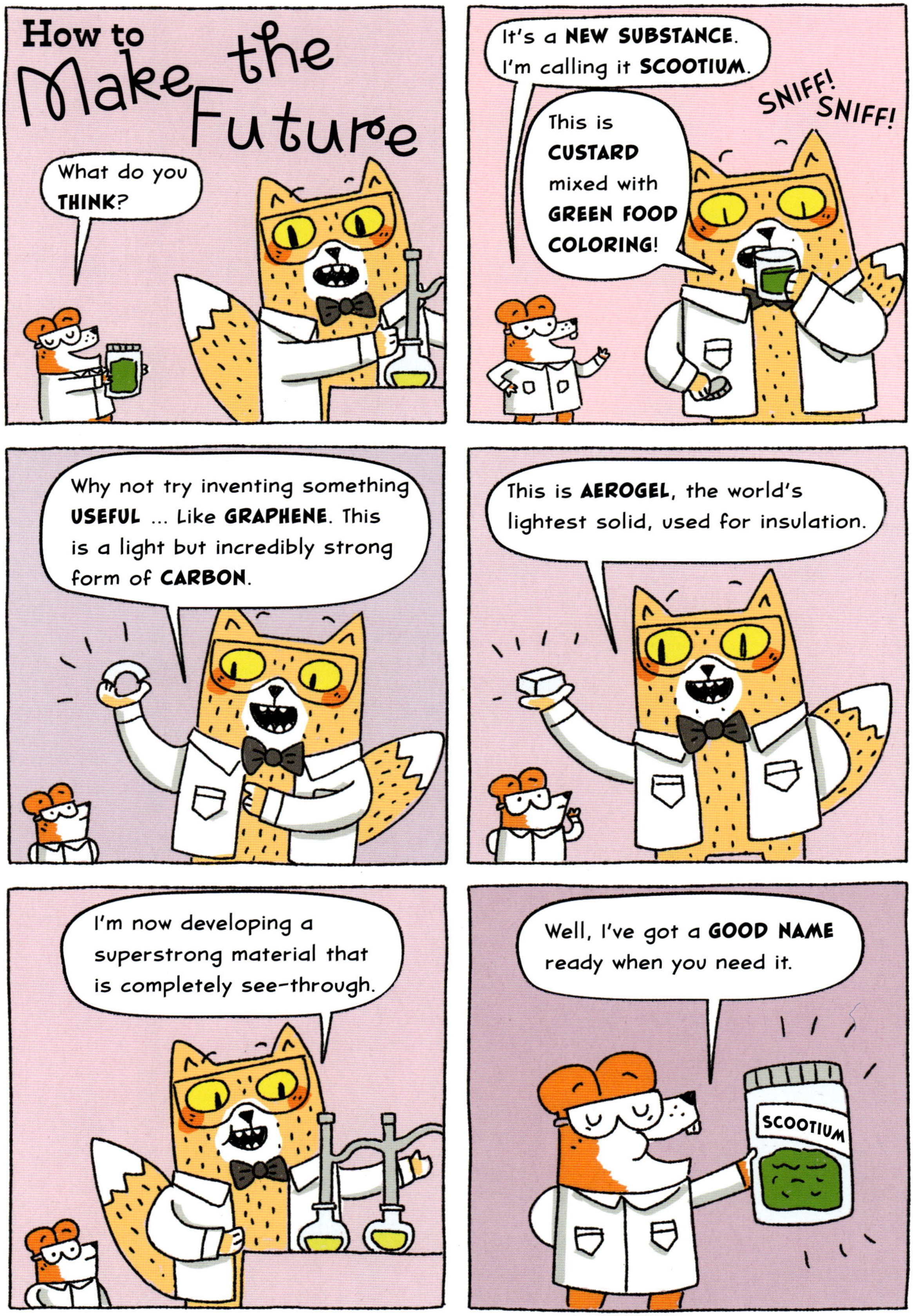
How to Make the Future
What do you THINK?
It's a NEW SUBSTANCE. I'm calling it SCOOTIUM.
This is CUSTARD mixed with GREEN FOOD COLORING!
SNIFF! SNIFF!
Why not try inventing something USEFUL ... Like GRAPHENE. This is a light but incredibly strong form of CARBON.
This is AEROGEL, the world's lightest solid, used for insulation.
I'm now developing a superstrong material that is completely see-through.
Well, I've got a GOOD NAME ready when you need it.
SCOOTIUM

Scientists are improving and inventing materials that are lighter, stronger, or better for the environment.

Some artificial materials are **composites** that use the properties of more than one substance. **Concrete** is a composite of stones and cement. **Reinforced concrete** is concrete with steel. Other composites include **plywood**, used for furniture, and **carbon fiber**, a strong, lightweight material used in racing-bike frames.

New materials include:

Graphene, made from layers of graphite. It is light, flexible, and stronger than steel. Sheets of graphene are just one atom thick!

Aerogel, a light insulator made by replacing the material's liquid with air.

Kevlar, a very tough plastic, which is woven into clothing as protection.

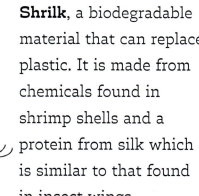

Shrilk, a biodegradable material that can replace plastic. It is made from chemicals found in shrimp shells and a protein from silk which is similar to that found in insect wings.

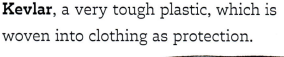

Maybe **YOU** will invent the next wonder material!

Index

Acid 37, 63, 75, 90–91, 93, 96-97, 99, 117
Acid rain 116–117
Alkali 12, 75, 93, 95
Alloy 30–31, 33, 105
Ammonia 25, 69, 93, 109, 119
Atom 8-9, 11, 13, 16–19, 21, 23, 26-27, 31, 40–41, 43, 45, 65, 91, 105
Atomic mass 17, 19
Atomic number 11–12, 65
Base 91–93, 96–97
Boiling point 45–46, 59
Buoyancy 37, 85, 88
Calcium 10, 19, 73, 93, 99–101, 116–117
Carbon 11, 15, 17, 26-27, 29, 31, 101, 110, 120–121, 127
Carbon dioxide 15, 66, 92, 108–109, 113, 115, 117, 120–122
Catalyst 68–69, 119
Chromatography 57
Combustion 70–71, 75, 115, 121
Composite 127
Compound 14–15, 23, 25, 49, 73, 91, 101–102
Concentration 51–53, 67, 91
Condensation 47, 59
Conductivity 33, 37
Copper 31, 33, 73, 103
Corrosion 102–104
Covalent bond 25, 27
Decay 28–29, 65
Density 33, 37, 57, 60, 62, 83, 85, 88
Deposition 47
Diamond 26–27, 38–39
Diffusion 51
Dilution 53
Dissolve 34, 37, 54–55
Distillation 58–59
Electrode 78, 81, 105
Electrolysis 81
Electrolyte 78, 81, 105–106
Electron 9, 11, 13, 20–21, 23, 25, 65, 72, 78–79, 105
Electroplating 105–106
Element 9-13, 17, 19, 23, 29, 49, 63
Endothermic reaction 76–77
Energy shell 12–13, 21, 23, 25
Evaporation 59
Exothermic reaction 74–75, 77, 79
Filtration 56
Fossil fuels 112–113, 117, 121
Galvanization 104–05
Gold 33, 103, 106
Graphite 26–27
Greenhouse gas 113, 120–123
Helium 9, 11–12, 17, 41, 60
Hydrogen 9, 11–12, 14–15, 19, 25, 49, 63, 69–71, 81, 85, 90–91, 97, 119
Ion 23, 81, 90–91, 93, 97, 103, 105–106
Ionic bond 23, 25
Inhibitor 69
Iron 30–31, 33, 69, 103–105
Isotope 28–29
Mass number 11, 29
Melting point 33–34, 37, 45
Methane 113, 122–123, 125
Mixture 49, 53–54
Mohs scale 39
Mole 16–19
Molecule 15, 17, 19, 25, 34, 40–41, 55, 74, 83, 85, 111
Neutralization 93, 115
Neutron 9, 11, 21, 28–29, 63
Nitrogen 25, 69, 109, 117–119
Noble gas 13, 109
Nucleus 9, 21, 65
Oxygen 11, 14–15, 19, 41, 45, 49, 66, 70, 73, 80–81, 101, 103, 105, 108–109, 121
Periodic Table 12–13, 33
pH scale 96–97
Plastic 111, 125, 127
Polymer 110–111
Potassium 10, 93, 118–119
Product 66, 69, 114
Proton 9, 11, 21, 28–29, 65
Radioactivity 12, 28–29, 64–65
Reactant 66–67, 69
Redox reaction 72-73, 115
Salt 15, 22-23, 34, 49, 58-59, 88, 93, 99
Silicon 15, 125
Sodium 15, 23, 45, 73, 92–94
Solubility 55
Solute 49, 53
Solution 49, 53–55
Solvent 49, 53–55
Steel 30–31, 38–39, 104–105, 127
Sulfur 63, 117
Transition metal 12, 32–33
Water 14–15, 19, 34, 46–49, 51, 55–57, 80–85, 88, 91, 93, 95, 97–99, 102–103, 105
Zinc 31, 33, 105